Life

UPPER INTERMEDIATE
STUDENT'S BOOK

Paul Dummett

John Hughes

Helen Stephenson

Contents Split Edition A

Listening	Reading	Critical thinking	Speaking	Writing
three people talking about important relationships in their lives a radio extract about animal friendships	an article about changing attitudes in China an article about immigrant families in New York	identifying the main aspect	your friends the generation gap family influences	text type: an informal email (1) writing skill: greetings and endings
a conversation about different accounts of Ayrton Senna's life an interview with a film critic	a true story about dangerous animals an article about the brothers Grimm	close reading	the film of the book a famous writer or filmmaker narrow escapes storytelling	text type: a story writing skill: using descriptive words
three people making predictions about the future a presentation about overpopulation	an article about augmented reality an article about appropriate technology	balancing arguments	global problems overpopulation information age predictions technological solutions	text type: short email requests writing skill: being polite
a conversation about two people who do artistic things in their free time an extract from a radio programme about what's on in Melbourne an artist's opinion about what art is	an article about unusual street art an article about the origins of rap	analysing contrasts	participation in the arts an art competition music and values	text type: an online review writing skill: personalising your writing
three speakers talking about different types of development someone talking about redevelopment in their city an interview with a journalist talking about social development in southern India	an article about urban development in Dubai an article about a hydropower dam project in Laos	fact or opinion	changes in your town a happy society sensitive development evaluating a development project	text type: an opinion essay writing skill: linking words
someone describing their stay at an ice hotel an interview about volunteer vacations	a blog about holidays at home an extract from a travel magazine about historical hotels	claims and justifications	local knowledge planning a staycation opinions about travel ideas for an unusual hotel	text type: a letter of complaint writing skill: formal language

Contents Split Edition B

Listening	Reading	Critical thinking	Speaking	Writing
an ecologist describing how we can avoid wasting natural resources four people talking about saving water	an article about Ecuador's plan to protect resources an article about Madagascar's unique ecology	emotive language	how we use water conservation wishes	text type: a letter to the press writing skill: giving vivid examples
a radio news report about the parents of Chinese university freshmen television news report of four good news stories	an article about an iconic image an article about the power of the press	different perspectives	the ethics of taking photographs good news stories reputations	text type: minutes from a meeting writing skill: impersonal language
a description of a mahout's job two friends discussing an astronaut's extraordinary career an interview about Emerging Explorers	an article about an extraordinary career an article about a woman who was king	weighing the evidence	a career path personal qualities women at work	text type: an online profile writing skill: writing in note form
an anthropologist's explanation of the quote 'manners maketh man' an extract from a radio programme about a tribe with an unusual diet	an article about the *tiger mother* approach to parenting an article about body language	sources	typical behaviour food and eating habits customs in your country wedding traditions	text type: an informal email (2) writing skill: elision in informal writing
a psychologist describing a situation in which you have to use your intuition a talk by a psychologist on memory	an article about an ethnobotanist an article about a parrot	reinforcing ideas	acquiring knowledge memory tests why you forgot types of learner	text type: an email about a misunderstanding writing skill: linking contrasting ideas
extract from a radio programme with an economist giving definitions of poverty and wealth an interview with the author of *The Servant Economy*	an article about Norway's riches an article about an alternative economic model	signposts to key information	the economy in your country getting things done gift giving and exchange	text type: a report writing skill: sub-headings and bullet points

Video in Split Editions A and B

Life around the world

Unit 1 Immigration
The history of immigration in the United States.

Unit 2 History of film
A history of film, from its early beginnings in the 19th century to the Hollywood blockbusters of today.

Unit 3 Augmented reality
Learn about a system that allows the user to see 3-dimensional images of everyday locations.

Unit 5 Aquarium on Wheels

A special aquarium that gives its student teachers lessons in life.

Unit 4 Urban art

Discover the world of graffiti and innovative music.

USA

Ecuador

Paraguay

Unit 10 Eating insects

Discover why eating insects could be good for you, and why one man is on a mission to change our tastes.

Unit 7 Galapagos energy

Find out about the impact of humans and tourism on the Galapagos Islands.

Unit 11 Paraguay shaman

Find out why it's essential to record plants from the rain forests of Paraguay before they disappear.

Japan

Egypt

East Timor

Unit 9 Queen of Egypt

The history of the most famous Egyptian queen – Cleopatra.

Unit 6 East Timor

The slow process of creating a new tourist destination.

Unit 8 Mount Fuji

Find out what Mount Fuji means to the Japanese.

Unit 12 Japan

Learn more about the history and traditions of Japan.

Split Editions A and B

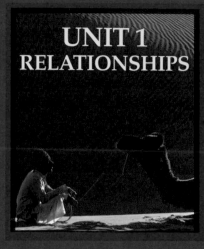

UNIT 1
RELATIONSHIPS

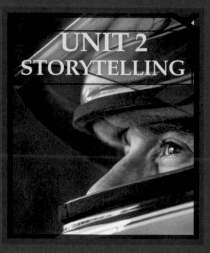

UNIT 2
STORYTELLING

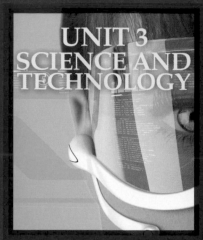

UNIT 3
SCIENCE AND TECHNOLOGY

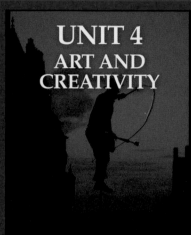

UNIT 4
ART AND CREATIVITY

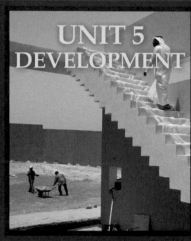

UNIT 5
DEVELOPMENT

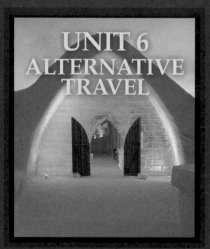

UNIT 6
ALTERNATIVE TRAVEL

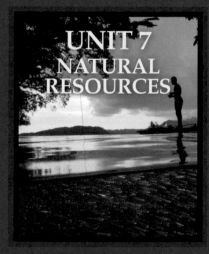

UNIT 7
NATURAL RESOURCES

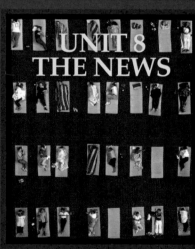

UNIT 8
THE NEWS

UNIT 9
TALENTED PEOPLE

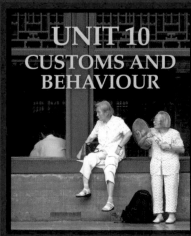

UNIT 10
CUSTOMS AND BEHAVIOUR

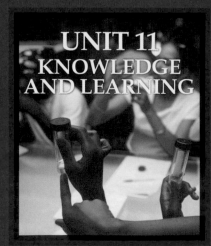

UNIT 11
KNOWLEDGE AND LEARNING

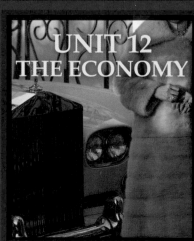

UNIT 12
THE ECONOMY

Unit 7 Natural resources

This photo taken half above, half under water shows a fisherman on an Indonesian coral island.
Photograph by David Doubilet

FEATURES

1 Work in pairs. Look at the photo. How many natural resources can you identify?

air   animals   fossil fuels (e.g. coal, oil, gas)   minerals
plants + fruits   soil   sunlight   trees   water   wind

2 Match the words (1–5) to their definitions (a–e). Then discuss which words apply to the natural resources in Exercise 1.

1	abundant	a	nature can replace what is used
2	exhaustible	b	in plentiful supply
3	inexhaustible	c	can be used up
4	renewable	d	difficult to find
5	scarce	e	will never be used up

3 🔊 **2.1** You are going to listen to an ecologist describe the three 'R's approach to saving natural resources. Discuss what these three words beginning with 'R' could be. Then listen and check.

4 🔊 **2.1** Listen again. What examples does she give for each of the three 'R's? Do you do any of these things yourself?

TALK ABOUT   ▶ CONSERVATION   ▶ WISHES   ▶ STRONG FEELINGS   ▶ CLIMATE CHANGE

WRITE   ▶ A LETTER TO THE PRESS

7a Water conservation

Speaking

1 Work in pairs. Why do people talk about the need to save water when over 70 per cent of the Earth's surface is covered by water? Read the article and see if your answer was similar.

So what if people waste a lot of water – we've got enough, haven't we? Well, we may have a lot of sea water, but we are using fresh water faster than nature can replace it. So instead we are forced to recycle waste water, cleaning it and then piping it into people's homes. That process requires a lot of energy – running a tap for five minutes uses the same energy as burning a 60 watt light bulb for fourteen hours – and a lot of money. Also, when underground natural water reservoirs (or aquifers) get low on water, they can become contaminated with high concentrations of natural minerals like arsenic, or man-made chemicals from the ground. To prevent this, we need to keep these reservoirs well-stocked. So conserve water and you will save money and the planet.

A six minute shower	55 litres
A hamburger	2500 litres*
A serving of goat meat	42 litres
A 50g bar of chocolate	1410 litres
A serving of chicken	580 litres*
A cup of coffee	135 litres
Flushing the toilet	8 litres
500 sheets of paper	22,500 litres
A slice of bread	40 litres
½ kilo of clean wool	85,000 litres

* in the case of the farm animals only a few litres were drunk by the animals or used in processing; the majority of the water went into the grain they were fed during their lives

2 Look at the facts about the water needed for various everyday things. Answer the questions.

1 Are you surprised by any of the facts? Why?
2 Can you draw any conclusions from them about the best ways to save water?

Listening

3 🔊 2.2 Listen to four people from different countries (the United Kingdom, United Arab Emirates, the United States and Mexico) talking about water. What does each say about:

1 their own attitude to water use?
2 what they think will happen if water is not conserved?

4 🔊 2.2 Listen again and answer the questions.

Speaker 1
1 How does Liam describe Manchester?
2 What does he do when he brushes his teeth?
Speaker 2
3 What is the problem with desalinating water?
4 What is Gemal researching?
Speaker 3
5 How has the Colorado Delta changed in the last 100 years?
6 What is the river water used for?
Speaker 4
7 What practical water saving measures does Carmen take in the home?
8 What does she suggest about other people's attitudes to water use?

5 Are any of the situations the speakers described similar to that of your country?

Grammar **mixed conditional sentences**

6 Work in pairs. Look at the *if* sentences (1–6). Answer the questions (a–c).

a Which sentences describe present situations and present consequences?
b Which describe past situations and past consequences?
c Which are a mixture of the two?

1 If we had known the facts, we would not have wasted so much water in the past.
Example:
We didn't know the facts, so we wasted a lot of water in the past.

2 If I had been brought up in Saharan Africa, I would be a lot more conscious of water conservation.
3 If we all used less water, the water companies wouldn't have to use so much energy treating water.
4 If desalination methods didn't exist, this country would not have been able to develop in the way it has.
5 If you had visited the area around the old delta in Mexico 100 years ago, you would be shocked to see it now.
6 If more people thought and acted like me, things would not have come to this point.

► MIXED CONDITIONAL SENTENCES

First conditional (for present or future situations)
If + present simple, ... *will* + infinitive (without *to*) ...

Second conditional
If + past simple, ... *would* + infinitive (without *to*) ...

Third conditional
If + past perfect, ... *would have* + past participle

Mixed second and third conditional
If + past simple, ... *would have* + past participle

Mixed third and second conditional
If + past perfect, ... *would* + infinitive (without *to*) ...

For further information and practice, see page 83.

7 Look at the grammar box. Then make conditional sentences based on the information in these situations.

1 We bought a cheap dishwasher that wasn't very efficient. As a result, we use a lot more water than we need to.
2 I don't use the dishwasher much, because no one told me that you use more water washing dishes by hand.
3 You wasted a lot of water in the past because you washed your car by hand instead of using a car wash.
4 Automatic carwashes are really expensive. As a result, I haven't used them very often.
5 Our water use is way above the average because we built a big swimming pool in the garden. So much of the water just evaporates away!
6 We water the garden when the temperature is cool, so that the water doesn't just evaporate away.
7 The United States has a shortage of water because they have tried to cultivate areas with a desert climate.
8 We changed our habits after we saw a shocking TV programme about how much water is wasted.

8 Pronunciation contractions in conditionals

🎧 **2.3** Listen to the contracted forms in these sentences and repeat.

1 If we hadn't built desalination plants, we'd still be fetching water from the well.
2 If you'd visited this area twenty years ago, you'd've seen a very different river.
3 If they don't act now, maybe it'll be too late.
4 If people'd been more careful, things wouldn't've come to this point.
5 If there's no rain, the river'll dry up.

9 Look at these facts about the use of natural resources around the world. Then make hypotheses based on them. Use one of the conditional forms in the grammar box.

1 The Aral Sea in central Asia (a huge freshwater lake) is now one-tenth of the size it was in the 1960s because water has been used by farmers to irrigate their fields.
2 As a desert town, Las Vegas has to import a lot of water. But a lot of it goes on watering green spaces, particularly the 60 golf courses that have been built around the city.
3 Sixteen million tourists visit Greece each year, causing shortages of water on many of its islands.
4 In the 1970s Britain found a lot of gas in the North Sea. But rather than use it carefully, they used it immediately. Now more than 50 per cent of Britain's gas is imported.

The Aral Sea

Vocabulary and speaking

10 Work in pairs. Match each verb in A with as many nouns in B as you can. Then tell each other if you do any of these actions or support others who do.

A conserve   consume   preserve   protect
run out of   save   spend   waste

B animals   food   forests   land   money
energy   petrol   time   water

11 Think about how your country has saved or wasted resources and write conditional sentences about them. Then mingle with the other students and tell each other your ideas. Choose the best idea and tell the class.

7b The minister for no oil

The
Minister
FOR NO OIL

*One thing you do not expect an oil minister to do is
to block the development of his own country's oil fields …*

One thing you do not expect an oil minister to do is to block the development of his own country's oil fields. But that is exactly what Alberto Acosta did when he was appointed Ecuador's Oil Minister in 2007.

For a relatively poor country whose main income is from oil exports, this proposal seemed like madness. But if Ecuador is not rich by economic standards, in terms of biodiversity, it is one of the richest places on Earth. When scientists studied trees in the Yasuni National Park in Ecuador's unspoiled rain forest, they found over 650 different species of tree in just one hectare – more than the total number in all of the US and Canada combined.

Mr Acosta said he would rather the oil companies did not destroy these natural riches. His innovative idea was to leave the oil reserves beneath Yasuni Park untouched, in return for compensation of half their value. The oil is worth more than $7 billion, so Ecuador asked the international community to pay $3.6 billion not to extract it.

But the plan has met with problems, both from within Ecuador and from outside. The state oil company, Petroecuador, opposes the scheme and many suspect that President Correa now wishes he had never supported it. At the same time only a few countries have shown interest, with only Germany promising $800 million over thirteen years.

Ecuador is not the only country trying to get richer nations to pay for not exploiting their forests. Both Nigeria and Guatemala are hoping they will be able to make similar deals. A spokesperson for local environmental groups explained, 'This is a fantastic initiative. If only people in developed countries appreciated that these forests absorb a lot of the CO_2 that their industries produce. I just wish they would take a longer-term view of this problem. If we don't do something to protect biodiversity and prevent climate change, we will all be losers – with consequences I'd rather not even think about.'

Vocabulary oil

1 How many of these expressions do you know? Which is shown in the photo above?

> oil field   oil refinery   oil reserves   oil rig
> oil slick   oil tanker   oil well

> ▶ **WORDBUILDING collocations related to one word**
>
> There are some nouns that have many words that collocate with them.
> *oil well, oil tanker, oil field*

> For further information and practice, see Workbook page 103.

2 Work in pairs. Discuss the questions.

1 How much is a litre of petrol in your country?
2 Are people more careful these days about how they conserve oil or petrol?

Reading

3 Look at the sentences (a–c). Then read the article and choose the sentence that best summarises Acosta's idea.

a for Ecuador to use money from oil exports to protect its forests
b for Ecuador to be paid not to extract its oil
c for Ecuador to keep the oil underground until it really needs the money

4 Answer the questions.

1 Why did Acosta's proposal seem like madness?
2 In what way was the price Acosta asked other countries to pay a fair one?
3 What has been the reaction of the international community to the plan?
4 What has been the reaction of local environmental groups?

5 Complete these statements using words from the article. Use one word per space.

1 Ecuador's riches are in its ....
2 In Yasuni park, Ecuador has oil .... worth $7 billion.
3 The main opposition to the plan in Ecuador comes from ....
4 There are other countries who would like to be paid not to .... their natural resources.
5 People in the developed world don't .... the part played by the forests in preventing climate change.
6 People need to think about what will happen in the .... - ....

6 Work in pairs. What do you think of Acosta's idea? Is it helpful for Ecuador? Is it unrealistic?

Grammar *wish, would rather* and *if only*

> ### ▶ WISH, WOULD RATHER and IF ONLY
>
> **Wish about a present situation**
> *wish* + noun/pronoun + past simple
>
> **Wish about a past situation**
> *wish* + noun/pronoun + past perfect
>
> **Wish for someone to do something about a present situation**
> *wish* + noun/pronoun + *would*
> NB subject of *wish* and noun/pronoun cannot be the same
>
> **Strong wishes about a present or past situation**
> Use *if only* in place of *I wish*
>
> **Stating what you would prefer to do**
> *would rather* + infinitive
>
> **Stating what you would prefer someone else to do**
> *would rather* + object + past simple
>
> For further information and practice, see page 84.

7 Look at the grammar box. Look at these sentences from the article. Then choose the option that describes the actual situation.

1 Mr Acosta said he would rather the oil companies did not destroy these natural riches.
The oil companies *destroy / don't destroy* these natural riches.
2 President Correa now wishes he had never supported it.
President Correa *supported / didn't support* it.
3 If only people in developed countries appreciated that these forests absorb a lot of the CO_2 that their industries produce.
People in developed countries *appreciate / don't appreciate* that these forests absorb a lot of the CO_2 that their industries produce.
4 I just wish they would take a longer-term view of this problem.
They *will / won't* take a longer-term view of this problem.

8 Choose the correct form to complete the sentences below.

1 I wish people *stopped / would stop* complaining about the price of petrol these days.
2 I wish they *didn't cut down / hadn't cut down* those trees in the park to make a playground.
3 Would you rather *walk / walked* or would you prefer we *go / went* in the car?
4 Most oil companies wish they *had / would have* the freedom to extract oil from wherever they wanted.
5 If only we *didn't have / wouldn't have* to rely on our cars so much, but that's the problem with living in the countryside.
6 If only I *could speak / would speak* better Spanish. Then I might try to get a job in Ecuador.
7 Sophie wishes that she *had taken / would take* a job with BP when she had the chance. She'd much rather *work / worked* for them than her present company.
8 I wish people *woke up / would wake up* to the problems of climate change.

Speaking

9 Look at these situations and make two sentences for each one with *wish, if only* or *would rather*. Then read your sentences to your partner.

1 Your car is old and uses a lot of petrol. You don't have enough money to buy a new one.
2 You would like to travel more, but the company you work for only gives you three weeks holiday a year.
3 Your journey to work takes you one hour by train each day. As a result you never get home before seven in the evening. You never have time to do any exercise, which you would love to do.

TALK ABOUT ▶ CONSERVATION ▶ WISHES ▶ STRONG FEELINGS ▶ CLIMATE CHANGE
WRITE ▶ A LETTER TO THE PRESS

7c A world of its own

Reading

1 Work in pairs. Look at the facts on page 15 about the island of Madagascar for two minutes and then cover the page. Get your partner to ask you three questions about these facts. Then get them to cover their books and ask them three other questions.

2 Read the article. Answer the questions.

1 Which of Madagascar's natural resources is the author most worried about?
2 How is this resource collected and where does it go from there?
3 What examples of sustainable ways of making money from these natural resources are mentioned?

3 Choose the correct option (a–c) to complete the sentences.

1 Madagascar has unusual ....
   a trees
   b animals
   c plants and animals
2 The Madagascan people are ....
   a very poor
   b very anxious
   c very practical
3 Cultivating crops meant ....
   a clearing the forest carefully
   b setting fire to forest
   c getting government permission
4 Former President Marc Ravalomanana was
   ....
   a more ecologically-minded
   b an inexperienced politician
   c popular with the military
5 The new government passed a law allowing people to ....
   a cut down hardwood trees
   b export hardwood to China
   c sell wood from fallen hardwood trees
6 For many Madagascans cutting down hardwood trees is ....
   a an easy way to make money
   b necessary to make furniture
   c against their beliefs
7 Other types of tree are cut down to
   ....
   a build boats for Madagascans
   b make medicines
   c transport the hardwoods
8 The forest offers locals other ways to make money, such as ....
   a developing new medicines
   b taking tourists on guided walks
   c exporting flowers

Critical thinking emotive language

4 Often, when writers feel very strongly about an issue, they will use strong or emotive language to try to make the reader have similar feelings. Find the key words in bold in sentences 1–6 in the article. Then find the emotive words or phrases that convey:

1 how individual **Madagascar** is (para 1)
2 how hard the lives of the local **people** are (para 2 and 5)
3 how strongly **ecologists** feel about the situation (para 3)
4 how inconsiderate the **loggers** are (para 4)
5 how impressive and special these hardwood **trees** are (para 4)
6 how **hope**less the situation is (para 7)

5 Do you think that by using such language, the writer helps his argument? Or would it be better to give a more balanced argument? What facts or information would you include to do this?

Vocabulary strong feelings

6 Replace the words in bold with words from the article to make these sentences more emotive.

1 A lot of efforts are being made to preserve this **individual** place. (para 1)
2 You could tell that she was **anxious** to get the job. (para 2)
3 Everyone **disapproves of** this use of force by the government against its own people. (para 3)
4 A number of oil companies now want to **take** oil **from** the Arctic. (para 4)
5 It is a beautiful view, with the **tall and elegant** mountains in the background (para 4)
6 Archaeology is much more **physical and tiring** work than most people think. (para 5)
7 With no prospect of a job, the future for many young people looks **hopeless**. (para 7)
8 All environmentalists seem **very interested in** climate change. (para 7)

7 Work in pairs. Think of a place that is very special and should be protected (e.g. a local green space, a traditional community). Write a short description of it (100–150 words) using emotive language. Then read your description to the class. Vote on which description is the most persuasive.

Madagascar is an island – the world's fourth largest, at over 225,000 square miles – but an island nevertheless. Although all islands have their own unique ecosystems, nature has blessed Madagascar with exceptional riches. Roughly 90 per cent of its flora and fauna is found nowhere else on the planet. The spectacle of its carrot-shaped baobab trees and ghostly lemurs make even the most well-travelled visitors wide-eyed with amazement and delight.

But its rare beauty hides the desperate situation of its people. The typical Madagascan lives on about a dollar a day, even though you would not guess this from the attitude of the Malagasy, the island's main ethnic group, who are a cheerful and optimistic race.

A world of its own

Since the first humans arrived in Madagascar some 2,300 years ago, loggers and developers have destroyed nearly 90 per cent of the island's original forest habitat, harvesting it for timber or burning it down to create room for crops and, more recently, cattle.

Considering that Madagascar's population is growing by three per cent a year, this tension between rich land and poor residents is increasing day by day. Alarmed ecologists have named Madagascar a biodiversity hot spot, deploring the practice of slash-and-burn agriculture. In 2002 the global environmental community rejoiced when green-friendly Marc Ravalomanana was elected president. But only seven years later, in the spring of 2009, the military replaced Ravalomanana with a former radio disc jockey who seemed to have little interest in protecting the environment.

Needing money, the new government reversed a ban on the export of precious hardwoods, making it legal to sell wood from trees which had already been cut down or had fallen during the cyclones that regularly hit the island. Yet in reality they did little to control the loggers who continued to rob the forests of new wood. The main targets of this environmental crime are the rosewood tree and the ebony tree. The wood from these majestic trees is in high demand: in China it is used to make exotic imperial-style furniture for the new middle class; in Europe and America it is a valued material in the manufacture of expensive musical instruments.

The locals are caught in a trap. Poverty and the high value of rosewood – at $3,000 per cubic metre it is ten times as valuable as oak – have driven them to cut down trees that are traditionally believed to be sacred. It is dangerous and back-breaking work. Using hand axes, in a few hours they bring down a tree that has stood tall for many centuries. Then they cut the trees into two-metre logs and drag these several kilometres to the nearest river.

The rare hardwood trees are not the only casualties. In order to transport the heavy rosewood logs downriver, rafts must be built from other wood. For each raft the loggers cut down four or five lighter trees from near the riverside, causing the earth to erode and silt up the rivers. At the same time animals' natural habitat has been disturbed, putting their survival at risk.

In this bleak landscape what can bring hope? One man's work may offer a possible route out of the darkness. Olivier Behra who first came to Madagascar from France in 1987 believes that the only solution is to give local people economic alternatives. Almost single-handedly, he has stopped deforestation in the Vohimana forest by encouraging the locals instead to collect medicinal plants, which they never imagined had any monetary value, and sell them overseas to companies like Chanel. The village lemur hunter has been retrained to act as a guide for tourists obsessed with lemurs. The same tourists also pay to visit the wild orchid conservatory that Behra has set up. Can small-scale and sensitive initiatives like this compete with the rosewood mafia of Madagascar? Only time will tell.

MADAGASCAR IN NUMBERS

4TH LARGEST island in the world after Greenland, New Guinea and Borneo

90% of its flora and fauna is found nowhere else on Earth

Number 1 producer of vanilla in the world

22 MILLION: population of Madagascar

70 different species of lemur live only on Madagascar

18 different ethnic groups of Asian and African origin

300 YEARS: the time it takes a rosewood tree to reach maturity

24,560 TONNES of ebony and rosewood exported in 2009, much of it illegally

TALK ABOUT ▶ CONSERVATION ▶ WISHES ▶ STRONG FEELINGS ▶ CLIMATE CHANGE

WRITE ▶ A LETTER TO THE PRESS

7d The climate change debate

Real life making your point

1 Work in pairs. What causes climate change? Is it man-made or a natural phenomenon? Use the expressions below to help you.

CO₂ emissions	natural weather cycle
fossil fuels	the greenhouse effect
global warming	

(Note: CO₂ should be CO_2 emissions; natural weather cycle, fossil fuels, the greenhouse effect, global warming)

2 ⊚ **2.4** Listen to four people discussing climate change and indicate whether each thinks it is man-made ☑ or not ☒.

Speaker 1: Erika ☐   Speaker 3: Jane ☐
Speaker 2: Andy ☐   Speaker 4: Ralph ☐

3 ⊚ **2.4** Listen again. Complete the expressions in the box (1–6) that the speakers use to make their points.

> ▶ **MAKING YOUR POINT**
>
> **Giving examples**
> Take … , for example …
> Let me give you an example …
> Imagine ¹ .... hair …
>
> **Stressing a point**
> The point is that …
> I, for one, ² .... in how I pollute …
> Look, there's no doubt that ³ .... …
> To be honest with you, …
>
> **Rejecting an argument**
> I don't accept that.
> I used to believe ⁴ .... , but …
> Yeah, but that's not the point.
> I (don't) believe it simply because ⁵ ....
>
> **Challenging the question itself**
> The whole starting point for this debate is wrong.
> We're approaching this debate all wrong by saying
> ⁶ .... problem.

4 ⊚ **2.4** Discuss which of the techniques (a–e) each speaker used to make their point. Then listen and check.

a humour
b challenging the question itself
c speaking clearly and slowly
d illustrating with examples/stories
e anticipating counter-arguments

5 Which technique did you find most effective? Which technique do you prefer yourself? Tell your partner.

6 Pronunication sentence stress

a ⊚ **2.5** When making their point, each speaker uses word stress to emphasise the important words. Listen to this example.

I don't know and I'm not sure **anyone** knows for sure. (2 words)

b ⊚ **2.6** Underline the words which you think are most stressed. Then listen and check.

1 We don't know that we're causing it, but some people say we might be. (2 words)
2 … scraping ice off the inside of my windows rather than the outside. (2 words)
3 Regional temperatures may be lower, but average global temperatures carry on rising. (2 words)
4 Because it's not just an environmental problem. It's an economic problem, a social problem, even an ethical problem. (4 words)

7 Work in pairs. Choose one of the solutions to climate change given below. Work out arguments in favour of this solution. Think about the techniques you will use to make your point and the examples you could give. Then get together with another pair who have chosen a different solution and have a debate.

The solution to climate change is:
• forcing people to use less energy by increasing the price of fuel
• paying poor countries to protect their forests
• finding a technological solution to cool the Earth (e.g. putting millions of tiny mirrors in space to reflect the sun's rays)
• trying to get all countries to sign an international agreement to limit CO_2 emissions

TALK ABOUT ▶ CONSERVATION ▶ WISHES ▶ STRONG FEELINGS ▶ CLIMATE CHANGE
WRITE ▶ A LETTER TO THE PRESS

7e Waste of energy

Writing a letter to the press

1 Do you ever read the letters page of newspapers, local or national? Do you enjoy reading these? Have you ever written a letter to the press yourself?

2 Read the letter. Answer the questions.

1 Who wrote the letter?
2 Why did they write it?
3 Do you find it persuasive? Why? / Why not?

Financial News   **Published: 20 Mar 2012**

From Mr V. Dupeyrat.

Sir, James Anderson (Travel section, 15 March) writes about the waste of energy in hotels: overheated rooms, lights that are left on all night, towels that are used once and then sent to be washed. He is right, but why stop with hotels? Would it not be better to mention all the other mindless waste that characterises modern life?

In the morning I walk down the high street past shops whose doors are wide open, blowing hot air into the street. At night I walk home past fully-lit office buildings, when the workers have already left; past enormous flashing screens where advertisers try to go one better than their competitors. At the supermarket I take my frozen vegetables from a cooling cabinet that is completely open. My children leave their computers on when they go out and their phone chargers plugged in with no phone on the other end (though of course they should know better than that).

All this waste illustrates two simple facts. Firstly, that energy is too cheap and we had better increase its price substantially to make people more energy-conscious. Secondly, that no one really considers the public interest anymore.

Just as it is in the public interest that there are speed limits on our roads – though some people may not like it – so we would all be better off if we were forced by our governments to conserve energy.

V. Tupey

V. Dupeyrat
Head of Energy services
DEF energy, London

---

3 Work in pairs. How is the letter organised? Match the functions (a–d) to each paragraph. Discuss whether these elements could be organised differently.

a Examples that illustrate the problem
b A recommendation or call to action
c The reason for writing
d A summary of the problem

4 Word focus *better*

Underline all the phrases using the word *better*. Then match each one with one of the definitions (a–e) below. Compare your answers with your partner.

a not be so stupid
b in an improved (often economic) situation
c more useful or desirable
d improve on the effort of another
e really ought to

5 Writing skills giving vivid examples

a What does the writer say about lights and towels to illustrate his argument?

b Find four more examples of illustrations of energy waste in the second paragraph.

6 Look at this list of things that annoy people about modern life. Expand three of them to explain what is annoying about it, as in the example. Then compare with your partner.

Example:
magazines that … *are full of news about celebrities*

trains which …
mobile phones that …
TV shows about …
supermarket food that …
computer programs which …

7 Write a short letter (150 words) to the press, talking about one of the items in Exercise 6. Make sure you include the same elements as in the example letter. Then exchange letters with your partner. Do they agree with the way you feel?

8 Read your partner's letter. Use these questions to check their letter. Is it correctly organised and ending with a summary?

• Does it use enough examples?
• Is it persuasive?

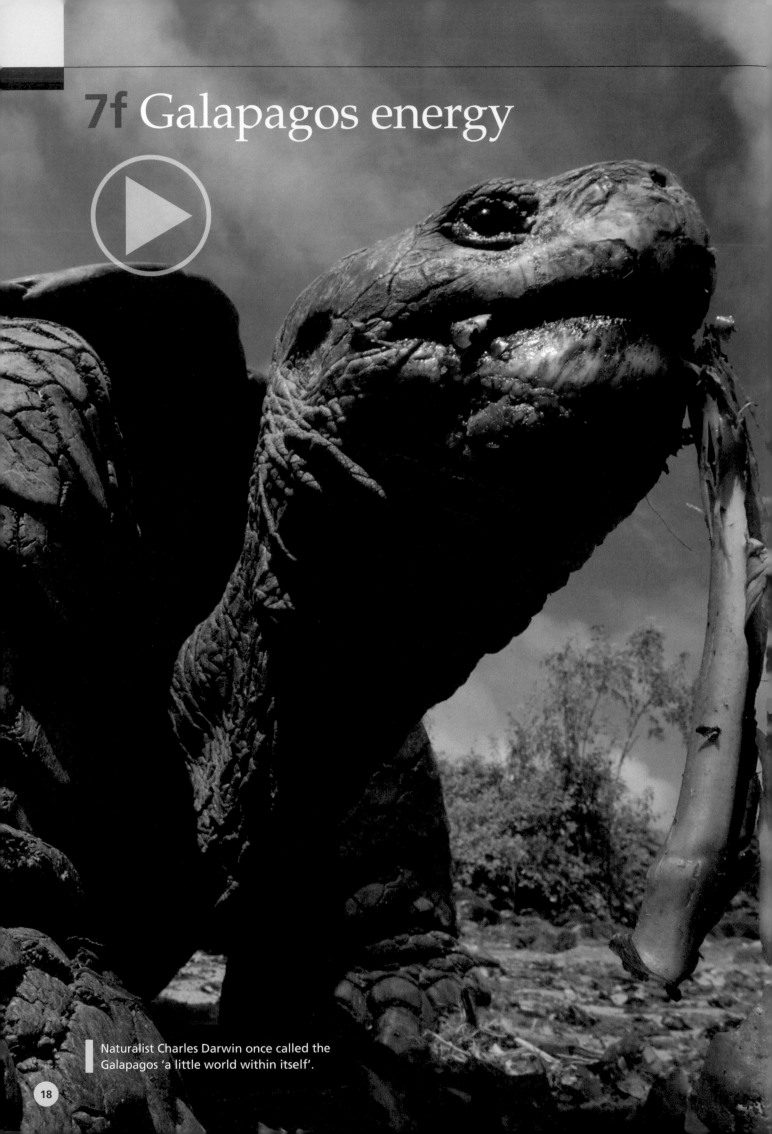

7f Galapagos energy

Naturalist Charles Darwin once called the Galapagos 'a little world within itself'.

Before you watch

1 Work in groups. Look at the photo and discuss the questions.

1 What do you know about the Galapagos Islands? Make notes about:
a their location.
b the population.
c what the islands are famous for.

2 What do you think Darwin meant when he called the Galapagos 'a little world within itself'?

2 Complete the video summary with words from the glossary below. Use the correct form where necessary.

The Galapagos Islands are home to many unique species of plants and animals. However, recently human beings have invaded this tropical ¹_____. Tourism has ²_____ and workers from the ³_____ have followed. This has created pollution from vehicle ⁴_____, the energy people use and the rubbish they produce, which harms the islands. Now, ⁵_____, corporations and the government are working to minimise human impact.

While you watch

3 Watch the video and check your answers from Exercises 1 and 2.

4 Watch the first part of the video (to 02.41) and answer the questions.

1 Why did the animals on the Galapagos evolve into unique species?

2 What do people always say about the Galapagos?

3 What do the volcanic eruptions tell scientists?

4 How long have humans been living on the islands?

5 How much has the human population of the Galapagos increased since the 1980s?

6 What is one positive aspect of tourism?

7 What happened after the recent oil spill?

5 Watch the second part of the video (02.42 to the end). Tick the things you see.

a bicycle	a bird with a blue beak
a bird with a red beak	black sandals
a blue dress	boats	a bus	a motorbike
a pink T-shirt	a recycling bin	a seal	a turtle

6 Watch the second part again and answer the questions.

1 What is the goal of the programme that international organisations and the Ecuadorian government are working on?

2 What four examples of conservation projects does the video show?
a _____
b _____
c _____
d _____

After you watch

7 Roleplay an interview with Leopoldo Bocheri More

Work in pairs.

Student A: Imagine you are going to interview Leopoldo Bocheri More. Read the information below and prepare a list of questions.

Student B: Imagine you are Leopoldo Bocheri More. A journalist is going to interview you. Look at the information below and think about what you are going to say to the journalist.

- the problems the Galapagos have
- what the government is doing
- what other help is needed

Act out the interview. Then change roles and act out the interview again.

8 Work in groups and discuss these questions.

1 Are there any natural areas in your country that have been adversely affected by human activity?
2 What can be done to protect such places?

conservationist (n) /kɒnsə'veɪʃənɪst/ a person who works to preserve nature
contaminant (n) /kən'tæmɪnənt/ something that pollutes
emissions (n) /ɪ'mɪʃənz/ smoke and gas from machines
haven (n) /'heɪvən/ a place where people or animals can escape to
leak (n) /liːk/ liquid or gas that escapes through a hole
mainland (n) /'meɪnlænd/ a large area of land that is not an island
oil spill (n) /'ɔɪl spɪl/ when oil accidentally escapes from the place it is stored
old-timer (n) /əʊld-'taɪmə/ a person or animal who has lived in a place for a long time
pristine (adj) /'prɪstiːn/ in perfect condition
relic (n) /'relɪk/ something left over from the past
revenue (n) /'revənjuː/ money earned
run aground (v) /rʌn ə'graʊnd/ hit rocks or the bottom of the sea
skyrocket (v) /'skaɪrɒkɪt/ to go up very quickly
wake-up call (n) /'weɪk ʌp kɔːl/ a warning to pay attention

Grammar

1 Work in pairs. Do you think that young people are more or less aware of the need to conserve resources than their parents' generation?

2 Read the extract from a blog discussing young people's attitude to resources. What kind of things are they aware of? And not aware of?

3 Choose the correct form of the verbs to complete the extract.

The funny thing about the younger generation is that on the one hand they seem very aware of global problems with natural resources. If you ask them about the rain forests, for example, they ¹ *will say / would say*. 'Oh, I wish people ² *stopped / would stop* cutting down the rain forests. They are destroying the planet.'
But on a personal level, they don't seem to be so aware. For example, it seems they would rather ³ *leave / left* the TV on standby than ⁴ *switch / switched* it off. If the central heating was on too high, they ⁵ *would be / would have been* more likely to open a window than turn it down! We parents are partly to blame for this. If we ⁶ *were / had been* stricter with our children when they were young, they ⁷ *would know / would have known* how to act now. I wish also that they ⁸ *had / had had* more energy-saving education when they were at school. As parents, we'd all rather schools ⁹ *teach / taught* these things because when we try our children just think we are nagging!

I CAN	
hypothesise about present and past situations using mixed second and third conditionals	☐
express wishes and preferences about the past and future with *wish*, *if only*, *would rather*	☐

Vocabulary

4 Work in pairs. Find the odd one out in each group of words. Explain why it doesn't fit.

1 conserve, waste, save, preserve
2 natural, abundant, scarce, inexhaustible
3 oil refinery, oil slick, oil rig, oil tanker
4 sunlight, minerals, air, wind
5 majestic, tall, obsessed, desperate

5 Work in small groups. Think of two natural resources that are scarce. Discuss what we can do to protect these.

I CAN	
talk about natural resources	☐
use nouns, verbs and adjectives to do with using and conserving natural resources	☐

Real life

6 Work in pairs. Which speakers (1–5) agree with this sentence and which disagree?

We should force developing countries to consume resources more carefully.

1 'Look, I can't do anything about how people in developing countries consume resources. I have enough trouble remembering to switch the light off!'
2 'The point is that the developed nations have used resources as they wanted to. So why shouldn't developing countries do the same?'
3 'Imagine a rich person in China wants to own four cars and a mansion; who am I to say he can't?'
4 'I know you'll say that it's everyone's duty, including people in developing countries, not to waste resources. But I don't accept that.'
5 'We're approaching this all wrong. It's not about what's fair; it's about what's necessary to conserve resources. We all need to be more careful.'

7 Which technique (a–e) does each speaker use to make their point?

a humour b challenging the question itself
c using emphasis d using examples/stories
e anticipating counter-arguments

8 Choose one of the techniques in Exercise 7 and make your own point about the need to conserve resources.

I CAN	
use different techniques to make my point in a debate	☐

Speaking

9 Work in small groups. Discuss the following issues.

- a regret you have about harming the environment
- a consequence of not protecting natural resources in your area
- an action to help conserve a natural resource

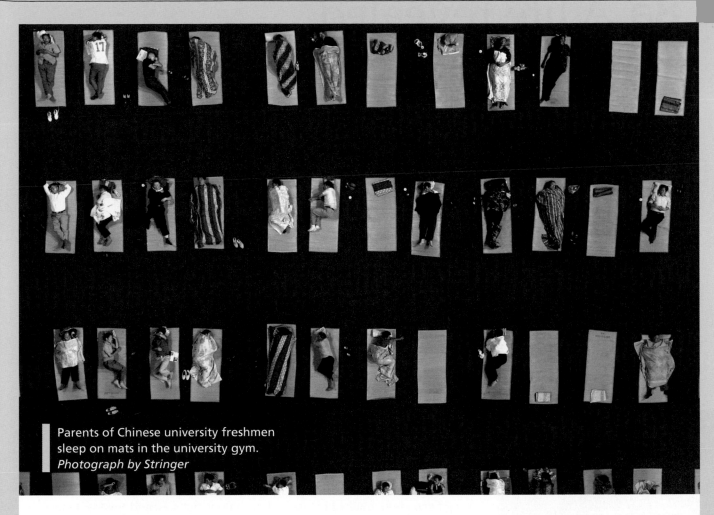

Parents of Chinese university freshmen sleep on mats in the university gym.
Photograph by Stringer

FEATURES

1 Match the two halves of each sentence to complete these English sayings about news. What sayings about news do you have in your language?

1 Good news ... ... is good news.
2 Bad news ... ... doesn't sell.
3 No news ... ... travels fast.

2 ⊚ **2.7** Work in pairs. Look at the photo and caption. Answer the questions. Then listen to a radio news report and check your answers.

1 Why did these Chinese parents stay overnight at the university?
2 Why did they sleep on the gym floor?

3 Does this story fall into the category of hard news (serious and urgent) or soft news (less serious and not urgent)? What about the following? Discuss.

- a column with celebrity gossip
- a local news story about a new housing development
- an editorial about a political scandal
- business news about interest rates
- a travel feature about Egypt
- a science news story about a cure for Alzheimer's disease

8a A life revealed

Vocabulary photography

1 Read the quotations. Find the following:

- 3 words that mean *a photograph*
- 2 words for parts of a camera
- 3 verbs that describe what a camera does with an image

2 Which is your favourite quotation? Why?

Reading

3 Work in pairs. Look at the two photos and discuss the questions. Then read the article and check your answers.

1 Have you seen either of these photos before?
2 Where are these people from?
3 How old are they?
4 What is the relationship between them?

'A picture is worth a thousand words.' - *Fred R. Barnard*

'What you have caught on film is captured forever … it remembers little things, long after you have forgotten everything.' - *Aaron Siskind*

'There is one thing the photograph must contain, the humanity of the moment.' - *Robert Frank*

'Look and think before opening the shutter. The heart and mind are the true lens of the camera.' - *Yousuf Karsh*

'I see no reason to record the obvious.' - *Edward Weston*

'A great photographer takes 100 shots and keeps just one.' - *Anon*

'Seeing and composing the beauty is what separates the snapshot from the photograph.' - *Matt Hardy*

4 Complete these sentences by finding the contrasting facts in the article.

1 Sharbat Gula let McCurry take her picture, even though …
2 The picture became world famous, even though …
3 McCurry recognised 29-year-old Gula immediately, even though …
4 Gula does not complain about her life, even though …

A LIFE REVEALED

She remembers the moment the photographer took her picture. The man was a stranger, but he asked if he could and she agreed to let him take it. She had never been photographed before and until they met a second time seventeen years later, she was not photographed again.

The photographer, Steve McCurry, remembers the moment too. It was 1984 and he was recording the lives of Afghan refugees in a camp in Pakistan. She was staring out of the school tent and he admits thinking at the time that the picture would be nothing special. Yet the 'Afghan girl', as the portrait is now known, became one of the most iconic images of our time. McCurry used her intense expression, so untypical of an average, carefree twelve-year-old girl, to warn us not to ignore the victims of war, especially its young victims.

In 2002 *National Geographic* persuaded McCurry to return to Pakistan to look for the girl. After showing her photo around the refugee camp, he found a man who had known her as a child and knew where to find her. He offered to fetch her from her home in the Tora Bora mountains and after three days returned with Sharbat Gula, a woman perhaps 29 years old. McCurry knew at once that this was her.

Time and hardship had erased her youth. Her skin was weathered. Yet her eyes still burned with the same intensity. Her brother explained the story of their lives, blaming the war for forcing them and many other Afghans out of their homeland. When Sharbat was six years old, they fled to the mountains, hiding in caves and begging people to give them food and blankets. She married when she was sixteen and now her time is occupied with bringing up her three children, cooking, cleaning and caring for them. Yet she does not complain about having a hard life. More amazingly, she is not aware of the impact that the photo of the young Sharbat with her sea-green eyes had on the world.

iconic (adj) /aɪˈkɒnˌɪk/ well-known and admired everywhere

Grammar reporting verbs

5 Look back at the article and complete these sentences using reporting verbs. Note the form that follows the reporting verb in each case.

1 She **agreed** _____ him take her picture.
2 He **admits** _____ at the time that the picture would be nothing special.
3 McCurry used her intense expression to **warn** us _____ the victims of war.
4 In 2002 *National Geographic* **persuaded** McCurry _____ to Pakistan.
5 He **offered** _____ her from her home in the Tora Bora mountains.
6 Her brother **blamed** the war _____ them out of their homeland.
7 They **begged** people _____ them food and blankets.
8 She does not **complain** _____ a hard life.

6 Work in pairs. What is being reported in Exercise 5? Discuss what the person actually said at the time. Then compare your answers with another pair.

1 She agreed to let him take her picture.
   Yes, you can take my picture.

> ▶ **REPORTING VERBS**
>
> **Verb + *to* + infinitive**
> *She agreed to let him take her picture.*
>
> **Verb + sb + *to* + infinitive**
> *National Geographic persuaded McCurry to return to Pakistan.*
>
> **Verb + *-ing***
> *He admits thinking at the time that the picture would be nothing special.*
>
> **Verb + preposition + *-ing***
> *She does not complain about having a hard life.*
>
> **Verb + someone + preposition + *-ing***
> *Her brother blamed war for forcing them out of their homeland.*
>
> For further information and practice, see page 84.

7 Look at the grammar box. Use the verb given to report each of these statements.

1 You've taken some amazing photos!
   She _____. (complimented)
2 You should think seriously about doing this professionally.
   She _____. (encouraged)
3 You are far too modest about your own talents.
   She _____. (accused)
4 Why don't you go on a proper photography course?
   She _____. (suggested)

5 I'll also introduce you to my friend, who is a wildlife photographer.
   She _____. (promised)
6 In fact, I'm sorry I haven't introduced you to him sooner.
   She _____. (apologised)
7 Also you really should enter that photo competition in *National Geographic*.
   She _____. (urge)
8 I can lend you my camera, if you don't think yours is good enough.
   She _____. (offered)

8 Complete the article about the ethics of taking photos of other people. Put the verbs in the correct form. In some cases you will also need to put a preposition before the verb.

> Photographers who take pictures without their subject's knowledge are accused [1] _____ (be) sneaky or even unethical. A photographer who takes a picture of someone in their living room at home with a telephoto lens cannot deny [2] _____ (do) wrong – they have invaded someone's privacy. Newspaper journalists are often criticised [3] _____ (do) this kind of thing – not that it stops them.
>
> But is there a difference between this kind of photojournalism and taking a picture of a stranger without them knowing? This person hasn't invited you [4] _____ (take) their picture. Perhaps they would feel uncomfortable if you asked them [5] _____ (pose) for a shot; they might even refuse [6] _____ (let) you do it.
>
> A lot of photographers insist [7] _____ (be) invisible so that the shots they get are more natural. They object [8] _____ (ask) their subject for permission first because this would spoil 'the moment'. But I disagree. I always advise photographers [9] _____ (talk) to their subjects first. In fact I strongly recommend [10] _____ (get) to know their subjects' story, because in that way the shots they get will have more meaning.

Speaking

9 Work in small groups and discuss your experiences of taking photos of other people and of being photographed by others.

1 Do you like having your photo taken? Why? / Why not?
2 What is the best way to get a good photo of someone?
3 Do you ever take photos of people you don't know? How do you approach this?
4 Have you ever felt uncomfortable about taking a photo of someone you didn't know?

TALK ABOUT ▶ THE ETHICS OF TAKING PHOTOGRAPHS ▶ GOOD NEWS STORIES ▶ REPUTATIONS ▶ WHAT YOU HEARD
WRITE ▶ MINUTES FROM A MEETING

23

8b And finally ...

Vocabulary the feel-good factor

1 News programmes often like to end with a good news story. Look at the adjectives that describe how this type of story can make people feel and match each one to a definition.

| amusing | appealing | charming | encouraging |
| inspiring | optimistic | quirky | |

1 An _____ or _____ story makes you feel hopeful.
2 An _____ story makes you smile or laugh.
3 An _____ story shows you how much people can achieve.
4 A _____ story shows you how strange people or things can be.
5 An _____ or _____ story delights or pleases you.

> ▶ **WORDBUILDING forming adjectives from verbs**
>
> We can add -ing to many verbs to form adjectives.
> *amuse* → *amusing*, *encourage* → *encouraging*
>
> For further information and practice, see Workbook page 111.

2 Work in pairs. Think of an example of a good news story you have heard recently. Tell your partner. Use one of the adjectives in Exercise 1.

> *I saw a really inspiring local news story on TV about a five-year-old boy who raised money for his sick sister by cycling round the park near ...*

Listening

3 🔊 **2.8** Listen to four good news stories from the TV news and make notes. Compare your notes with two other students and fill in any missing details.

4 🔊 **2.8** Listen again and complete these summaries.

1 People thought that the _____ , but they were wrong because _____ . As a result in the future we will see _____ .
2 Researchers believe they have found _____ . When people took _____ , the result was that _____ .
3 The world's largest _____ say they have invented _____ . But doctors say _____ .
4 Costa Rica is _____ because it has _____ . Countries like _____ on the other hand _____ .

5 Work with a student from another group and retell the stories to each other. Which story did you find the most optimistic? Quirky? Inspiring?

Grammar passive reporting verbs

6 Look at these two examples of passive reporting verbs from the listening passage and answer the questions.

It *was thought* that the large blue butterfly was extinct.
It *is estimated* that 20,000 large blue butterflies will be seen this summer.

1 What do/did people actually say or think?
2 When do/did they say or think this?

> ▶ **PASSIVE REPORTING VERBS**
>
> **Typical reporting verbs**
> *say, think, believe, report, consider, know, estimate, expect, claim*
>
> **It + is + passive reporting verb + that + sentence ...**
> *It is thought that people eat more healthily these days.* (present report of present event)
> *It is thought that people ate less healthily in the past.* (present report of past event)
> *It is thought that people will eat more healthily in the future.* (present report of future event)
>
> **It + was + passive reporting verb + that + sentence ...**
> *It was thought that the butterfly was extinct.* (report and event at same time in past)
> *It was thought that the butterfly had disappeared.* (past event before past report)
> *It was thought that the butterfly would not return.* (past report of a future event)
>
> For further information and practice, see page 85.

7 Work in pairs. Look at the grammar box. Then look at the audioscript on page 91 and underline seven more sentences with passive reporting verbs. For each one decide:

- when the reporting happened
- when the reported event happened

8 Pronunciation weak forms in verbs

a 🔊 **2.9** Look at these two sentences and underline the parts of the verbs (italicised) that you would expect to be stressed. Then listen and check. What rule can you make?

It *was said* that none of the previous studies *had given* a clear answer.
It *is believed* that 100,000 chocolate bars *have been sold* in the first week.

b Then practise saying these sentences with your partner.

1 It *was claimed* that they *had found* a cure for the common cold.
2 It *is known* that developed countries *have* a bigger ecological footprint.
3 It *was thought* that large blue butterflies *had disappeared* in the UK.
4 It *is known* that chocolate *doesn't act* as a health food.
5 In 2009 it *was estimated* that Denmark *had* the happiest citizens.

9 Transform these sentences into passive reporting sentences using *it*.

1 People report: 'Large blue butterflies are everywhere now.'
   Example:
   It is reported that large blue butterflies are everywhere now.
2 30 years ago people said: 'The large blue butterfly is a common species.'
3 People said: 'Hunters caused the butterfly to die out.'
4 In the past people thought: 'Costa Rica is a poor country.'
5 Scientists claim: 'Taking zinc helps if you have a cold.'
6 They said: 'None of the previous experiments has been conclusive.'
7 Experts claimed: 'Eating the new chocolate will improve your health.'
8 But people know: 'Eating too much chocolate is actually bad for you.'

10 Look at these other news items and facts and make sentences using the passive reporting verbs given. Tell your partner whether you think each one is true or not. Then check your answers on page 82.

1 It / believe / that chewing gum when you peel onions / prevent / you from crying.
2 It / say / Google's name originally / come / from 'Googol', meaning a number with 100 zeros.
3 It / know / that laughing regularly / increase / life expectancy by up to ten years.
4 In 2008 it / report / that air pollution in the US / fall / by 40 per cent since 1980.
5 It / claim / recently that scientists studying the Zebra fish / discover / a way for the human heart to heal itself.
6 In 2011 it / report / that a man whose house had been crushed by a huge rock in the New Zealand earthquake /sell / the rock for $10,000.

Writing and speaking

11 Work in groups of three and prepare a good news story. Choose a theme of your own or one from the list below. Then write the story together, using at least two passive reporting verbs. When you have finished, practise reading it aloud. Then each person should join a new group of three and read their stories to the other students.

- a person rescued by an animal
- the discovery of a valuable painting or antique
- a ten-year-old child that has been compared to Shakespeare
- the invention of a new clothing fabric
- a couple who are celebrating their 90th wedding anniversary
- a dentist that people actually enjoy visiting

TALK ABOUT ▸ THE ETHICS OF TAKING PHOTOGRAPHS ▸ GOOD NEWS STORIES ▸ REPUTATIONS ▸ WHAT YOU HEARD
WRITE ▸ MINUTES FROM A MEETING

25

8c From hero to zero

Reading

1 Work in pairs. Look at the headlines below, in the order they appeared in the newspapers over several months. Discuss what you think happened.

HERO BA PILOT PETER BURKILL SPEAKS: I THOUGHT WE'D DIE IN HEATHROW CRASH

'I AM NOT A HERO'
SAYS BA CRASH PILOT CAPTAIN PETER BURKILL

REAL HERO OF BA FLIGHT 38 **IS CO-PILOT JOHN COWARD**

HERO PILOT 'FORCED OUT OF BA'

FALLEN HERO: THAT DAY CHANGED MY LIFE FOREVER

OFFICIAL REPORT SAYS ICE FAULT CAUSED BA AIRPORT CRASH

2 Read the story quickly. Then check the sequence of key events with your partner. How did the story differ from your answer in Exercise 1?

3 Read the article again. Are the statements true (T) or false (F)?

1 Burkill's co-pilot was at the controls when the engines failed.
2 Some passengers were badly hurt during evacuation.
3 At the time of the accident, Burkill was a single man who liked to enjoy himself.
4 Burkill's crew read BA's internal report.
5 Burkill was praised in the AAIB report.
6 He was too loyal to BA to work for another airline.

4 Complete the sentences with words from the article.

1 Burkill went from being a hero to being a (opposite of *hero*) _villain_ . (para 1)
2 When the plane crash landed, (incredibly) _____ it stayed upright and no one was hurt. (para 2)
3 Perhaps his colleagues believed he was (no good at his job) _____ . (para 3)
4 The press portrayed Burkill as irresponsible: he (failed) _____ the people he was supposed to be responsible for. (para 4)
5 Burkill felt (completely unsupported) _____ by his colleagues and the company. (para 5)
6 After the official report was published, Burkill was (given as a prize) _____ a medal for his actions. (para 7)

Critical thinking different perspectives

5 Each participant has a different perspective and a different motivation for acting as they did after the accident. Make notes to complete the table.

People involved	Their view of Burkill's role	Motivations for their actions
Peter Burkill	*he did what any pilot would have done*	*to clear his name and keep his job*
BA staff		
BA management		
AAIB*		
the newspapers		

*Air Accidents Investigation Branch

6 Which of the people do you believe? Who do you think the newspaper's readers believed?

Word focus *word*

7 Find four expressions in the article with *word*. Match each one with the definitions below.

1 to be the one who is able to make the final point in an argument and win it
2 news or a rumour starts to circulate
3 there is no evidence other than what two people claim to be true
4 there is no news about something

8 Work in pairs. What do these other expressions with *word* mean?

1 'The new gallery is amazing. But **don't take my word for it**: go and see for yourself.'
2 'When my husband handed me the keys to a new car for my birthday, I was **lost for words**.'
3 'The hotel doesn't advertise at all. It just relies on **word of mouth** to get new customers.'
4 'I can't believe the council are closing the library. They **gave their word** that they wouldn't.'

Speaking

9 Work in groups. Discuss the media in your country.
1 How respectful are journalists towards politicians?
2 How balanced is the reporting of public scandals?
3 Are people interested in reading about the private lives of famous people?

FROM HERO TO ZERO

In January 2008, hours after saving his plane from crashing at Heathrow Airport, flight captain Peter Burkill was being praised as a hero. Only days later, when reports appeared in the press accusing him of freezing at the controls, he became a villain. How did this extraordinary transformation come about?

Peter Burkill was the pilot on flight 38 from Hong Kong and ultimately responsible for the lives of its 152 passengers. But 35 seconds from landing, two of the plane's engines failed. With the plane losing height fast, Burkill let his co-pilot John Coward take the controls while he himself adjusted the wing flaps to help the plane reach the runway. It was a risky decision, but it worked. The plane just missed some houses and landed heavily on the grass just short of the runway. After skidding for a few hundred metres, it miraculously came to a stop without turning over. The passengers escaped without serious injury. As far as Burkill was concerned, he had done what any captain would have done and the rest was luck.

However, this was not the version of events that began to circulate among BA's staff in the following days. Whether they just liked to gossip or felt Burkill was incompetent, word went around that rather than taking control of the plane, he had frozen. Worse than that, it was reported that he had failed to issue a mayday call and had not evacuated the passengers correctly.

Some newspapers, sensing a chance to sell more copies, picked up the story, claiming that John Coward was the real hero. They published details of Burkill's colourful past, painting a picture of a well-paid pilot, who had lived the life of a playboy, but – when it mattered – had let down his crew and passengers. Worse still for Burkill, it wasn't even his word against theirs. British Airways banned him from speaking about the events until the full investigation by Air Accidents Investigations Branch (AAIB) was complete.

Overnight Burkill's life changed. Before the accident, he had had everything: a great job, a beautiful home, a loving family and the respect of his colleagues. Now he felt betrayed and desperate. The stress put enormous pressure on his family. In the weeks that followed, he spent more time at home helping his wife, Maria, to look after their young children. But he became depressed. He begged the company to issue a statement to clear his name, but they refused, clearly anxious not to receive bad publicity in case the official investigation found Burkill guilty of a mistake. Even when they published their own internal report in May 2008, which cleared him of any wrongdoing, it was only read by the senior management. No word of it reached his close colleagues and rumours circulated that crew members were afraid to fly with him. He wrote to BA's chief executive asking for help, but got no reply.

The official AAIB report, the result of a completely independent enquiry, was finally published in February 2009. It concluded that ice had formed in the fuel system during the approach to Heathrow, cutting the fuel supply to the engines. The actions of the crew had saved the lives of all on board, it said, in particular Captain Burkill's split-second decision to reduce the flap setting.

The pilots and thirteen cabin crew were awarded the British Airways Safety Medal and the story of Peter Burkill the hero once again made the headlines. But the damage had been done. In August 2009, Peter Burkill took voluntary redundancy from the company he had served for 25 years. He began applying for jobs with other airlines, but he was not invited to a single interview.

So did his critics win? No. Burkill himself had the last word. BA said that he was and always had been welcome in the company and in September 2010 invited him to come back and fly Boeing 777s for them. Burkhill accepted their invitation.

Captain Peter Burkill (right) and co-pilot John Coward

mayday call (n) /ˌmeɪdeɪ ˈkɔːl/ a call for help in an emergency

runway (n) /ˈrʌnweɪ/ the part of an airport where planes land and take off

skid (v) /skɪd/ (of a car, bicycle, plane, etc.) to slide without any control

voluntary redundancy (n) /ˌvɒləntri rɪˈdʌndənsi/ to agree to leave your job in exchange for payment of money

TALK ABOUT ▶ THE ETHICS OF TAKING PHOTOGRAPHS ▶ GOOD NEWS STORIES ▶ REPUTATIONS ▶ WHAT YOU HEARD
WRITE ▶ MINUTES FROM A MEETING

8d Spreading the news

Real life reporting what you heard

1 ◐ **2.10** Listen to two neighbours discussing a traffic incident that took place in their street. Choose the picture that best illustrates what happened.

2 ◐ **2.10** Work in pairs. Discuss the questions. Then listen again and check.

1 Why didn't Phil see the incident?
2 Who did Jess learn about the incident from?
3 How could the argument between the drivers have been avoided?
4 Who was one of the drivers identified as?
5 What happened in the end?
6 What is Phil's opinion of Tara and Chris as sources of information?

3 ◐ **2.10** Look at the box. Complete the phrases Jess (J) uses to report what someone said and Phil (P) uses to say how reliable this source was. Then listen and check.

1 J: .... that it was an argument between two car drivers and .... it got quite heated.
2 J: .... both drivers got out of their cars and started shouting at each other.
3 P: I'd take what Tara says with .... She tends to .... things ....
4 J: She .... that if the police hadn't arrived, there would have been a fight.
5 J: Someone .... they had seen one of the drivers before. ...., he is a local politician.
6 P: I think I'd take .... ; he's not the type to ....
7 J: .... Chris, they took them both away.

> ▶ **REPORTING WHAT YOU HEARD**
>
> I heard that …
> Someone said that …
> They reckon that …
> According to (somebody) … ,
> It seems that …
> Apparently, …
> Supposedly, …
>
> **Expressing belief and disbelief**
> I'd take his/her word for it.
> He/She generally gets his/her facts right.
> He's not the type to spread gossip.
> Take no notice of what he/she says.
> It's been blown out of proportion.
> I'd take that with a pinch of salt.

4 Pronunciation the schwa

a ◐ **2.11** Unstressed syllables often produce the schwa sound /ə/. Listen to these examples and repeat. The stressed syllable is underlined.

/ə/ /ə/   /ə/ /ə/
app<u>a</u>rently   supp<u>o</u>sedly

b ◐ **2.12** Underline the stressed syllable and circle the schwa sound in these words. Then listen and check.

> according   generally   happened   information
> proportion   reckon   surprisingly

c Work in pairs. Practise saying the words.

5 You are going to spread news around the class. Follow these steps:

• Tell your partner two facts (one true, one false) about yourself or something you did.
• Mingle with other students in the class and tell them the facts you heard. (Speak to at least three people.)
• Return to your partner and report the facts you heard.
• Discuss which ones you think are true or not. Use the expressions in the box.
• Tell the class what you thought and see if you were right.

TALK ABOUT ▶ THE ETHICS OF TAKING PHOTOGRAPHS ▶ GOOD NEWS STORIES ▶ REPUTATIONS ▶ WHAT YOU HEARD
WRITE ▶ MINUTES FROM A MEETING

8e A residents' meeting

Writing minutes from a meeting

1 Read this report of a meeting of residents in a street where a traffic incident occurred. Answer the questions.

1 What three ideas were reported to avoid confrontations between drivers?
2 Which one did they decide was the best idea and why?

Essex Street residents' association

From: Sian Taylor

Re: Residents meeting about road rage incident

Thanks to all of you who wrote and apologised for not being able to attend on Tuesday evening. Here are the minutes from the meeting.

We met to discuss what to do about traffic in our street following the incident that took place two weeks ago. Various ideas were discussed about how we could prevent drivers from getting into these angry confrontations. One proposal was to ask the council to make Essex Street a one-way street, but most people thought that this wouldn't be good for residents. Another suggestion was to reduce the number of parking spaces to allow more places for cars to pass each other in the street. The objection to this was that it would force residents to park in neighbouring streets and just move the problem to another street.

In the end, it was agreed that the best thing would be to put some signs at each end of the road asking drivers to drive with care and consideration. Terry Miles offered to write a letter to the local council to ask if this would be possible. A draft copy of the letter will be posted here next week so that people can comment on it before it is sent.

2 Which of these elements are included in the report? In what order do they appear?

- the aim of the meeting
- what action was decided
- who said what
- who attended the meeting
- follow-up action

3 Writing skill impersonal language

a Underline the phrases that the writer uses to avoid naming people directly when reporting what was said. Why does she do this? Compare your answers with your partner and discuss.

b Rewrite the sentences from a meeting report. Use the words given to make them less personal and direct.

1 Hannah suggested that we should put speed bumps along the street.
One _____ . (suggestion)
2 Everyone thought this was a terrible idea.
It _____ . (decided / good)
3 Dan thought the speed limit should be reduced to 15mph.
Another _____ . (idea)
4 But several people said that probably no one would keep to this speed limit.
It _____ . (agreed)
5 Harry proposed having a sign with arrows giving priority to drivers from one direction.
Another _____ . (proposal)
6 Sophie argued that this would be impossible to enforce.
The _____ . (objection / difficult)

4 Read the description of a local problem. Discuss with your partner possible solutions to it. Look at the suggestions on page 81. Write a report of a meeting at which these solutions were discussed. Say which one was chosen and describe the follow-up action.

The city's university has recently bought four houses in your street to accommodate students, because they don't have enough accommodation at their main site. The students are making a lot of noise at night, playing loud music and shouting in the street. This is a problem for local residents, many of whom have young children.

5 Exchange your reports with another pair. Answer these questions. Then report your findings to them.

- Did they choose the same solution as you?
- Does their report seem too personal or direct?
- Does it follow the structure of the model in Exercise 1?
- Is any important information missing from it?

8f Mount Fuji

冨士山頂上淺間大社奧宮

Climbing Mount Fuji is a mind exercise. It's mind over matter more than anything.

Before you watch

1 Work in groups. Look at the photo and discuss the questions.

1 Where are the people in the photo?
2 Why do you think they are there?
3 What do you think the caption tells us about the people in the photo?

2 Tick the things you think you are going to see in this video.

> a bear   a bulldozer   clouds   drums
> an elephant   food vendors   a rollercoaster
> snow   sunflowers   a sunrise   umbrellas

While you watch

3 Watch the video and check your answers from Exercise 2.

4 Watch the video again and describe these things.

1 Mount Fuji

2 the 'fire and water' festivals

3 the weather when Karen Kasmauski climbs the mountain

5 Watch the first part of the video (to 02.07). Are these sentences true (T) or false (F)? Correct the false sentences.

1 Karen Kasmauski is enjoying perfect weather for her photographic shoot.
2 Karen thinks Japanese people worship Mount Fuji because it is so beautiful.
3 Mount Fuji is worshipped with fire and water festivals.
4 Karen starts her photographic shoot in the forest at the base of the mountain.
5 You can buy lots of biscuits and cakes at Mount Fuji.
6 Climbing Mount Fuji is seen mostly as something tourists have to do.

6 Watch the second part of the video (02.08 to the end). Make notes about these things. Then compare your notes with a partner.

1 How Karen feels when she gets to the top.

2 How Mount Fuji was different in the past.

3 Managing Mount Fuji.

4 What happens at the end of the climbing season.

After you watch

7 **Roleplay interviewing a *National Geographic* photographer**

Work in pairs.

Student A: Imagine you are a photographer for *National Geographic*. You are going to be interviewed by an amateur photographer. Make notes about the areas below.

Student B: Imagine you are an amateur photographer. You are going to interview a photographer for *National Geographic*. Prepare questions to ask the photographer about these areas.

- lifestyle of a photographer
- the advantages and disadvantages of the job

Act out the interview, then change roles and act out the interview again.

8 Karen Kasmauski says that climbing Mount Fuji is 'a national bonding experience'. What do you think she means? Are there any symbols of national unity in your country?

9 Work in groups and discuss these questions.

1 Are there any special places in your country where people like to go and take photographs?
2 What makes an interesting photograph for you: the place, the people or what is taking place?
3 Is there any famous place in the world you would like to go to take pictures? Why would you choose that particular place?

---

appease (v) /əˈpiːz/ keep a person or a thing calm
bento box (n) /ˈbentəʊ bɒks/ a wooden or metal box, divided into compartments, used in Japan for storing separate food dishes for a meal
bonding (n) /ˈbɒndɪŋ/ the process of becoming emotionally close to other people
bulldozer (n) /ˈbʊldəʊzə/ a large machine that moves earth
conical (adj) /ˈkɒnɪkəl/ shaped like a cone

gorgeous (adj) /ˈgɔːdʒəs/ very beautiful
pilgrimage (n) /ˈpɪlgrɪmɪdʒ/ a journey to a holy place
purification (n) /pjʊərɪfɪˈkeɪʃən/ the process of making something clean
typhoon (n) /taɪˈfuːn/ a very strong tropical storm
vending machine (n) /ˈvendɪŋ məʃiːn/ a machine that sells things, for example, drinks or food

UNIT 8 REVIEW

Grammar

1 Work in pairs. Look at the photo of a new development near Singapore's financial district. What you think the designers are trying to create?

2 Read the news article below and see if you were right.

3 Complete the article with the correct form of the verbs. Use prepositions where necessary.

Big cities are often criticised [1] _____ (be) big polluters. But it is generally considered that Singapore [2] _____ (be) an exception to this rule. For a long time the government has encouraged developers and conservationists [3] _____ (think) of ways to increase the island's green spaces. Recently green groups suggested [4] _____ (turn) the old KTM railway corridor into a nature trail. But perhaps the most striking project is *Gardens by the Bay*, a futuristic park near the city's financial centre which includes eighteen *Supertrees*. When it is complete it is said that each of the eighteen trees [5] _____ (be covered) in more that 200 varieties of plant.

The government invited various companies [6] _____ (submit) ideas for the project and this was chosen as the most exciting. A spokesman for the government complimented the designers [7] _____ (come) up with a 'truly innovative' design. The Supertrees are between 25 and 50 meters tall and mimic the function of real trees, absorbing sunlight through photovoltaic cells and collecting rainwater. The photographer who took this picture admitted [8] _____ (feel) sceptical about the project until he saw it for himself. 'It looks like something from the film *Avatar*: almost too good to be real!'

I CAN	
report speech with reporting verbs and the correct dependent verb form	☐
report what it generally said or thought with passive reporting verbs	☐

Vocabulary

4 Work in pairs. Find the odd one out in each group of words. Explain the reason for your choice.

1 film, photo, snapshot, picture
2 column, feature, scandal, editorial
3 inspiring, amusing, optimistic, encouraging
4 lens, shutter, flash, camera
5 urge, promise, encourage, persuade
6 objection, suggestion, proposal, recommendation

5 Work in pairs. Describe a news photo that had a big impact on you. What was the story behind the picture?

I CAN	
talk about photography	☐
relate good news stories	☐

Real life

6 Put each phrase into the right category: reporting what someone said (R), expressing belief (B) or expressing disbelief (D).

1 They reckon that half a million people came to the free festival.
2 I'd take that figure with a pinch of salt.
3 Apparently, a lot more people came than expected.
4 I think the number has been blown out of proportion.
5 According to official reports, around 250,000 attended.
6 It seems that the organisers were only expecting 150,000 maximum.
7 I think we can take the organiser's word for it.
8 Take no notice of what the promoters say. They just want publicity.

7 Work in small groups. Talk about an event, local or national, people have been discussing recently. Tell each other what you believe to be the real facts.

I CAN	
report what I heard	☐

Speaking

8 Work in pairs. Create a short news item about an event in your class or college. Include at least two verbs reporting what people said.

Unit 9 Talented people

A mahout (elephant driver) bathing his elephant
Photograph by Robert Harding

FEATURES

1 Work in pairs. Match the words in the box to the definitions (a–g).

> background   experience   knowledge   qualifications
> qualities   skills   talents

a   strong natural abilities
b   abilities developed by practice
c   the (generally positive) characteristics
d   certificates which show you have learnt something
e   what you've done in your life
f   what you know
g   your past in general (where you come from, where you studied, etc.)

2 Look at the photo and the caption. What qualities, skills, knowledge, qualifications and experience do you think a mahout needs to do their job well? Discuss.

3 🎵 2.13 Listen to a description of a mahout's job. Compare the description with your answers in Exercise 2.

4 Make short notes on your own background, experience, knowledge, talents, etc. Then ask each other questions.

TALK ABOUT ▶ A CAREER PATH ▶ PERSONAL QUALITIES ▶ WOMEN AT WORK ▶ SKILLS, TALENTS AND EXPERIENCE
WRITE ▶ AN ONLINE PROFILE

33

9a An ordinary man

Listening and reading

1 🎧 **2.14** Work in pairs. Look at the photo and discuss who this person is and what the occasion of the photo was. Then listen to a conversation about it and check.

2 Read the article and say in what ways Armstrong was an ordinary man and in what ways he was extraordinary.

3 Read the article again. Answer the questions.

1 Why is Armstrong called 'the ultimate professional'?
2 Who paid for his university course and what did they get in return?
3 What motivated Armstrong?
4 What do you think is meant by the phrase 'the rest is history'?
5 What did Armstrong do to avoid publicity after the Apollo 11 mission?
6 According to Armstrong, who was responsible for the success of the Apollo 11 mission?

An ORDINARY man

Neil Armstrong, the most famous of the astronauts on Apollo 11, has been called the ultimate professional. He was hired to do a job. He did the job and then he went home and kept quiet about it. In 40 years, he gave two interviews. But how can the man who first set foot on the Moon, a hero to millions of people, remain such a mystery?

People like Armstrong often develop their interests at a young age. He followed a career built on a passion for flying that he developed in his childhood in the 1930s. He learnt to fly before he had graduated from high school in Wapakoneta, Ohio. He then did a course in aerospace engineering at Purdue University in Indiana, sponsored by the United States Navy, which meant that Armstrong was obliged to serve as a naval pilot for three years. He saw action almost immediately, flying 78 missions in the war in Korea.

He left the Navy in 1952 and two years later got a job with the Lewis Flight Propulsion Laboratory where he flew experimental aircraft. He reached speeds of 6,615 kilometres an hour and altitudes of over 200,000 feet. When he decided to become an astronaut is not clear. Certainly, it was not his ambition to be famous. An extremely talented pilot, his aim was simply to push the boundaries of flight.

He was selected for a space plane pilot training programme in 1960 but shortly after news began to circulate that NASA was looking for astronauts for their Apollo programme. Incredibly excited, he applied for the job and in 1962 was accepted. The rest, as they say, is history.

When the astronauts returned from the Apollo 11 Moon landing of July 1969, Armstrong was a worldwide celebrity and could have done anything he wanted – TV shows, public speaking. Instead, he became a teacher at the University of Cincinnati and at the weekend went flying to get away from all the attention. He subsequently worked for two private avionics firms until he retired in 2002. In 40 years he only gave two interviews. Why? Certainly he felt fortunate to have had the chance to fulfil his dream, but he did not feel any more special than the thousands of people who worked on the Apollo space programme. He was just the pilot.

Vocabulary careers

4 Work in pairs. Find verbs in the article that collocate with each of these nouns. Then identify the different steps in Armstrong's career.

1 to .... a career
2 to .... a school or college
3 to .... a course
4 to .... in the navy
5 to .... an astronaut
6 to .... a firm
7 to .... , ... , ... a job

> ▶ **WORDBUILDING verb (+ preposition) + noun collocations**
>
> *follow a career*
> *graduate from a school/college*
>
> For further information and practice, see Workbook page 119.

Grammar articles: *the* or zero article?

5 Look at how *the* or zero article are used in the first paragraph of the article. Match the words in bold (1–7) with the uses of *the* and the zero article (a–g).

> Neil Armstrong, **(1) the most famous** of **(2) the astronauts** on Apollo 11, has been called the ultimate professional. He was hired to do a job. He did **(3) the job** and then he went **(4) home** and kept quiet about it. In 40 years he gave two interviews. But how can **(5) the man** who first set foot on **(6) the Moon**, a hero to **(7) millions** of people, remain such a mystery?

a to talk about an already mentioned thing
b to talk about something unique
c before a superlative adjective
d to talk about a specific thing or person
e to talk about specific things or people
f to talk about things or people in general
g before certain familiar places (e.g. work, hospital, university, school)

6 Work in pairs. Find one more example of each use in the rest of the article.

> ▶ **ARTICLES: *THE* or ZERO ARTICLE?**
>
> **definite article**
> *the* + singular/plural countable nouns, uncountable nouns = specific things
>
> **zero article**
> – + plural countable nouns, uncountable nouns = things in general
> NB We don't use *the* with most time expressions or place names. However, there are some special cases.
>
> For further information and practice, see page 86.

7 Find an example in the article of the following:

1 zero article with:
  a) a country
  b) a subject of study
  c) a month
2 *the* with:
  a) a country
  b) a professional group
  c) a period of time

8 Complete these sentences by inserting *the* where necessary.

1 While flying for .... Navy in .... Korea, Armstrong had to eject into .... sea when one of .... wings on his plane was damaged.
2 Armstrong and Aldrin only spent one day on .... surface of .... Moon.
3 Armstrong retired from .... NASA in .... 1972, but he helped with .... crash investigations in .... later years.
4 .... first investigation was in .... May 1970 following an explosion on .... Apollo 13.
5 .... other investigation involved .... space shuttle Challenger, which broke into .... pieces over .... Atlantic Ocean near .... Florida.
6 In .... nineties Armstrong stopped signing .... autographs, because .... dealers were selling them for $1,000 a time.

9 Pronunciation linking vowels

a 🔊 **2.15** Words that end with a vowel and words that begin with a vowel are linked by a 'hidden' consonant: /w/, /j/, or /r/. Listen to these phrases and say which sound links the two words. Then practise saying the sentences with your partner.

1 the‿ultimate professional
2 to do‿a job
3 a disaster‿involving
4 a teacher‿at the university
5 he‿only gave two‿interviews
6 another hero‿of our time

b Make three more phrases with either the /w/, /j/ or /r/ linking sound. Then compare your phrases with another pair.

Speaking

10 Draw a path of your own (or a parent's) career. Begin with your interests as a child. Finish with future ambitions. If it is not an obvious linear progression, show how the direction changed. Then explain the path to your partner.

Pushing the boundaries

Listening

1 🎧 **2.16** Listen to an interview about the *National Geographic* Emerging Explorers programme and answer the questions.

1 What is the aim of the programme?
2 How does *National Geographic* help those selected?
3 What sort of fields do Emerging Explorers work in?

2 🎧 **2.16** Listen again. Are the sentences true (T) or false (F)?

1 Emerging Explorers are people who are not yet fully established in their careers.
2 As well as money, Emerging Explorers get publicity for their work in the magazine.
3 Emerging Explorers generally have a scientific background.
4 Storytellers are explorers who record traditional stories from different cultures.
5 Alexandra Cousteau's grandfather filmed other Emerging Explorers.
6 Alexandra is interested in how new technology can help to spread the environmental message.

Grammar relative clauses

3 Work in pairs. Look at the relative clauses in bold from the interview (a–e). Then discuss the questions (1–4).

a Each year between eight and fifteen explorers, **whose work is really outstanding**, are selected.
b Emerging Explorers are generally people **who are at an early stage of their careers**.
c *National Geographic* awards each one of them US$10,000, **which is intended to go towards further research**.
d The magazine is a place **where other interested people can read about their work**.
e There are all these people doing important work out there in the various fields **that I have described**.

1 In which sentences is the relative pronoun the subject of the relative clause?
2 In which sentences does the relative clause explain who or what is being talked about?
3 In which sentences does the relative clause give extra information and how does the punctuation help you know this?
4 In which sentence could the relative pronoun be omitted?

▶ RELATIVE CLAUSES

Relative pronouns: *who (that)*, *which (that)*, *where*, *whose*
Subject: *She's the woman who won the award.*
Object: *That's the award which/that the woman won.*
OR *That's the award the woman won.*

Defining relative clause
This clause contains essential information for identification.
She's the woman who won an award for her photography.

Non-defining relative clause
This clause contains extra information, separated by one or two commas.
Her husband, who is also a photographer, accompanied her on the trip.

***that* or zero pronoun**
The article (that) I read about her was very interesting.

For further information and practice, see page 86.

4 Look at the grammar box. Then complete these sentences about Emerging Explorer Alexandra Cousteau by inserting the correct relative pronoun and any commas that are missing.

1 Alexandra Cousteau _____ is a conservationist believes water will be the most important issue of the 21st century.
2 Alexandra Cousteau _____ father was an oceanographer is a great advocate for environmental protection.
3 Cousteau says that the environmental movement uses communication tools _____ are old-fashioned.
4 She is currently planning an expedition _____ aim is to research different water ecosystems around the world.
5 She is currently working on a book _____ she hopes will teach people how to live on a 'Water Planet'.
6 The problem _____ she says was created by people is a problem _____ people can only solve by working together.

Grammar reduced relative clauses

5 An alternative to a relative clause is a reduced relative clause. Look at the participles in bold in these sentences from the listening passage. Which are active and which are passive?

1 We have so many different types of explorer, **chosen** from diverse fields.
2 There are all these people **doing** important work out there in the various fields.
3 That's the skill of the storytellers, **communicating** important facts about the planet.
4 She works as a conservationist, **trying** to persuade people to protect resources like water.
5 Alexandra Cousteau, **inspired** by her grandfather's success as a storyteller, is researching ways in which the environmental community can use new media.

▶ **REDUCED RELATIVE CLAUSES**

Present participle
researching
She works in Oxford, ~~where she is~~ researching biology. (active)
Past participle
researched
It's a subject ~~which is~~ researched by only a few people.
(passive)

For further information and practice, see page 86.

---

6 Look at the grammar box. Then rewrite the reduced relative clauses in Exercise 5 as relative clauses.

7 Complete the profiles of other Emerging Explorers below by inserting the missing information as a reduced relative clause where possible and if not, as a relative clause.

1 She has been called the real-life Lara Croft by the *New York Times*.
2 She cycled a distance of 700 miles.
3 They threatened to harm her.
4 He is fascinated by the truly big questions.
5 He plays music to take his mind off problems.
6 He spends his time diving into water caves deep under the ground.
7 The caves have been undisturbed for 3.5 million years.
8 Knowledge is provided by these dark and wonderful places.

8 Work in pairs. Circle the eight adjectives in the profiles that describe people's strengths and qualities.

9 Which of these people would you most like to meet? Tell your partner.

Speaking and writing

10 Think of someone you admire for the work they do. Write a short description of their achievements and qualities. In groups read your descriptions to each other and ask questions.

Kira Salak,
1 ....,
doesn't want to tell travel stories you have already heard. Independent and adaptable, she has travelled across Papua
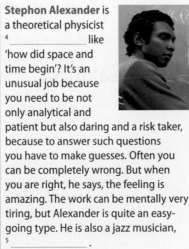
New Guinea on foot and Alaska on a bicycle, 2 .... It is not easy travelling alone as a single woman in remote and dangerous regions. In Mozambique she escaped soldiers
3 .... But she does not regret such experiences, because she says they have helped her discover her strengths.

Stephon Alexander is a theoretical physicist
4 .... like 'how did space and time begin'? It's an unusual job because you need to be not only analytical and
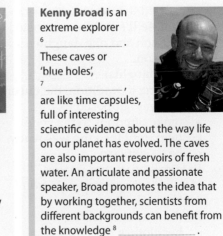
patient but also daring and a risk taker, because to answer such questions you have to make guesses. Often you can be completely wrong. But when you are right, he says, the feeling is amazing. The work can be mentally very tiring, but Alexander is quite an easy-going type. He is also a jazz musician,
5 ....

Kenny Broad is an extreme explorer
6 ....
These caves or 'blue holes',
7 ....,
are like time capsules, full of interesting scientific evidence about the way life on our planet has evolved. The caves are also important reservoirs of fresh water. An articulate and passionate speaker, Broad promotes the idea that by working together, scientists from different backgrounds can benefit from the knowledge 8 ....

TALK ABOUT ▶ A CAREER PATH ▶ **PERSONAL QUALITIES** ▶ WOMEN AT WORK ▶ SKILLS, TALENTS AND EXPERIENCE
WRITE ▶ AN ONLINE PROFILE

37

9c The king herself

Reading

1 Work in pairs. Look at the title of the article. What is strange about the words *king* and *herself* together?

2 Read the article and put these events about Hatshepsut's life in the correct chronological order.

  a Her mummy was discovered in a minor tomb.
  b The monuments she built were destroyed.
  c Thutmose III became pharaoh.
  d She ruled Egypt as king for 21 years.
  e Her mummy was identified and put in the Royal Mummy rooms.
  f She married Thutmose II.
  g She was born, the eldest daughter of Thutmose I and Queen Ahmose.

3 What were the different roles that Hatshepsut fulfilled (e.g. pharaoh)?

4 Choose the correct option (a–c) to complete the sentences.

  1 Hatshepsut's mummy was not identified at first because it:
    a was badly damaged.
    b was not in a royal tomb.
    c had another name with it.
  2 Hatshepsut was very worried that people would:
    a realise she was a woman.
    b not think she was royalty.
    c not remember her.
  3 Thutmose III did not want people to know that Hatshepsut had been:
    a king.
    b queen.
    c related to him.
  4 Thutmose II's children consisted of:
    a one son and one daughter.
    b one son.
    c one daughter.
  5 According to tradition, the queen regent was supposed to:
    a make offerings to the gods.
    b help until the king was ready.
    c be a politician.
  6 In later statues and images, Hatshepsut appears male from:
    a her body shape.
    b the way she stands.
    c her clothes.

Critical thinking weighing the evidence

5 Find evidence that supports each sentence (1–6). If the sentence is definitely true, write 100%. If there is no evidence, write 0%. Put percentages in between if it is not clear.

  1 When Hatshepsut's sarcophagus was first found in 1903, it was empty.
  2 The mummy called KV60a was Hatshepsut's body.
  3 Hatshepsut wanted to produce a male heir, but failed.
  4 Hatshepsut had a greater claim to become pharaoh than Thutmose III.
  5 Hatshepsut knew she had broken with tradition and wanted her subjects' approval.
  6 The king in waiting, Thutmose III, was angry that Hatshepsut had assumed the role of king.

6 Work in pairs. Compare your scores and the evidence you found.

Word focus *long*

7 Find these six phrases (1–6) in the article with the word *long* and match each one to its definition (a–f).

  1 at long last   a soon
  2 as long as   b over a long period of time
  3 long for   c after much waiting
  4 long after   d provided that
  5 before long   e much, much later
  6 in the long term f desire very much

8 Complete the sentences using phrases with *long*.

  1 Hatshepsut clearly _____ people to remember her.
  2 The grand monuments she built ensured she would be remembered _____ .
  3 _____ people believed she had a divine right to be pharaoh, Hatshepsut felt safe.
  4 Hatshepsut died in 1458 BC and _____ , Thutmose III had destroyed most references to her as king.
  5 No one understood the story of Hatshepsut until experts in hieroglyphs _____ uncovered the truth.
  6 Thutmose III ruled for another 34 years, _____ Hatshepsut had died.

Speaking

9 Work in small groups. Say who you would expect to find doing these jobs: mostly men, mostly women, or an equal number of men and women. Give reasons.

cleaner	company director	doctor	florist	IT technician
lawyer	machine operator	nurse	plumber	
prime minister	secretary	senior civil servant	teacher	

10 Look at the UK statistics on page 81. Which job in Exercise 9 fits in which category? Compare and discuss your answers.

THE KING *Herself*

Today she is in the Royal Mummy Rooms at the Egyptian Museum in Cairo, reunited at long last with her family of fellow pharaohs, with a sign saying she is Hatshepsut, the king herself (1479–1458 BC).

But in 1903, when the archaeologist Howard Carter found Hatshepsut's sarcophagus in the Valley of the Kings, it was empty. Had her mummy been stolen or destroyed? The truth only came out a century later when Egyptian scientists positively identified a mummy called KV60a, discovered more than a century earlier in a minor tomb, as that of Hatshepsut. None of the treasures normally found with pharaohs' mummies were with it. It was not even in a coffin.

For Hatshepsut, a pharaoh who did not fear death as long as she was remembered, the irony is great. As one of the greatest builders in one of the greatest Egyptian dynasties, she raised numerous temples and shrines. She commissioned hundreds of statues of herself and left accounts in stone of her titles, her history, even her hopes and fears. Inscribed on an obelisk at Karnak are the words: 'Now my heart turns this way and that, as I think what the people will say. Those who see my monuments in years to come, and who shall speak of what I have done.'

But following her death, her successor and stepson Thutmose III set about erasing her memory, ordering all images of her as king to be removed from monuments and temples. At Deir el Bahri, at the temple designed to be the centre of Hatshepsut's cult, her statues were smashed and thrown into a pit. Images of her as queen were left undisturbed, but wherever she proclaimed herself king, the destruction was careful and precise. Why?

Hatshepsut was the eldest daughter of Thutmose I and Queen Ahmose. But Thutmose also had a son by another queen, and this son, Thutmose II, became pharaoh when his father died. As was common among Egyptian royalty, Thutmose II married his sister, Hatshepsut. They produced one daughter; another, less important wife, Isis, gave Thutmose II the male heir that he longed for, but Hatshepsut was unable to provide.

When Thutmose II died not long after from heart disease, his heir, Thutmose III, was still a young boy. As was the custom, Hatshepsut assumed control as the young pharaoh's queen regent. And so began one of the most intriguing periods of ancient Egyptian history.

At first, Hatshepsut acted on her stepson's behalf, respecting the convention that the queen should handle political affairs while the young king learnt the ropes. But before long, she began performing kingly functions, like making offerings to the gods. After a few years she assumed the role of 'king' of Egypt, supreme power in the land. Her stepson was relegated to second-in-command and 'the king herself' proceeded to rule for an amazing 21 years.

What caused Hatshepsut to break so radically with the traditional role of queen regent? A social or military crisis? A desire for power? A belief that she had the same right to rule as a man? No one really knows. Maybe she felt, as a direct descendant of the pharaoh Thutmose I, she had a greater claim to the divine line of pharaohs than Thutmose III. At first she made no secret of her sex – in images her body is unmistakably a woman's – but later she is depicted as a male king, with headdress and beard, standing imposingly with legs apart.

Her hieroglyph inscriptions have frequent references to 'my people' which suggest that she knew she had broken with tradition and wanted her subjects' approval. Whatever their opinion was, there is no doubting the frustration of the king in waiting, Thutmose III. After Hapshepsut's death, he took his revenge, wiping his stepmother's reign as pharaoh out of history. But in the long term it is she, the King Herself, who has achieved greater fame.

---

coffin (n) /ˈkɒfɪn/ a box in which a dead body is placed to be buried
commission (v) /kəˈmɪʃn/ to order and pay for something to be made
divine (adj) /dɪˈvaɪn/ related to god
heir (n) /eə/ a successor

9d Right for the job

Real life **describing skills, talents and experience**

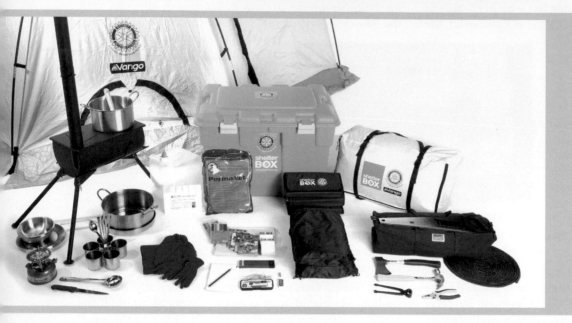

Shelterbox

is a charity which sends boxes of essential items needed in an emergency – a tent, tools, cooking utensils, a water purification kit – to places where disasters, such as earthquakes and floods, have struck. Boxes are prepared in the USA and delivered immediately by Shelterbox employees to anywhere in the world where they will help to save lives.

1 Read the description of Shelterbox. What kind of organisation is it and what service do they offer?

2 💿 **2.17** Listen to someone being interviewed for a job at Shelterbox. Answer the questions.

1 What aspect of their work is the candidate interested in?
2 What is the interviewer concerned about?

3 💿 **2.17** Look at these phrases from the interview describing the candidate's suitability for a job. Note the prepositions used in each case. Then listen to the interview again and complete each one.

> ▶ **DESCRIBING SKILLS, TALENTS AND EXPERIENCE**
>
> I'm familiar with your work because I have a friend who ¹ ....
>
> I'm very keen on the idea of ² ....
>
> I specialised in ³ ....
> I'm good at coping with ⁴ ....
> I think I would be suited to ⁵ ....
> I have quite a lot of experience of ⁶ ....
>
> I'm quite good with ⁷ ....
> I'm comfortable with all ⁸ ....
> I'm serious about wanting to ⁹ ....
> I need to become more knowledgeable about ¹⁰ ....

4 Work in pairs. Discuss if the candidate did a good job of selling himself to the interviewer.

5 **Pronunciation difficult words**

a 💿 **2.18** The spelling of a word in English is not always a clear indication of its pronunciation. How confident are you that you can pronounce these words from the interview? For very confident put a (✓), quite confident put a (?) and unconfident put a (✗). Then listen and check.

> although   business   comfortable
> environment   foreign   knowledgeable
> months   specialised   suited   world

b 💿 **2.19** Listen to eight more words and try to spell them.

6 Work in pairs.

Student A: choose one of the jobs below that interests you and think about the skills, talents and experience you have that would help you do it. Try to convince Student B why this would be a good job for you.
Student B: ask Student A questions. Then swap roles.

- a travel guide for a tour operator taking groups on walking holidays in Italy
- a sales assistant in a children's bookshop
- a fund-raiser for a charity that helps the homeless
- an assistant to a cameraman who makes films about plants and wildlife

9e Professional networking

Writing an online profile

1 Do you use any professional networking sites (e.g. Biznik, LinkedIn, Ecademy, Xing)? Why? / Why not?

2 Read the profile and summarise in no more than nine words what this person's main skills and qualities are. How effective was his profile in putting across the key points?

3 Read the tips on how to write a profile on a professional networking site. Put a tick (✓) next to each tip that has been followed, a cross (✗) next to those which have not and a question mark (?) if the tip has only been partly followed.

> Tips:
> 1 Include a personal photo and recommendations from others to show you really exist!
> 2 Give a heading and summary so that readers can get the main idea quickly.
> 3 Include your current status i.e. what you're doing now.
> 4 List all the places you have worked or studied at – someone from the same organisation or school may be looking at your profile!
> 5 Job titles may mean nothing to others so always describe what you did in each job.

4 Writing skill writing in note form

a Look at these four extracts from the profile. Which are proper sentences? Which are written in note or shortened form? Why is this?

1 responsible for new products
2 Learning is my passion.
3 published *Learning in the 21st Century*
4 Developing innovative e-learning programme for the car industry

b Insert the necessary words (pronouns, articles, auxiliary verbs) to show what the extracts in note form would look like as full sentences.

Profile

Barton McCready
Managing Director of Evercready Learning

Location: York, UK
Industry: Online learning
Current: Developing innovative e-learning programme for the car industry

Past
- Head of development, Faheys Educational – responsible for new products
- Commissioning Editor, York Books – published *Learning in the 21st Century*
- Director of Business Studies, Carston University

Education: Cardiff University

Summary
Learning is my passion. I specialise in the design and management of online learning programmes for industry, but I am also a writer, editor, blogger, educator and business consultant. My work has brought me into contact with many companies and I am now skilled at identifying and responding to the learning needs of any business sector, from cosmetics to car-making. If this experience has taught me one thing, it's that learning is the key to improvement for all of us.

---

c Convert these statements from other profiles into a shorter, more concise form by deleting the unnecessary words.

1 I worked as a personal assistant to the Marketing Director.
2 I am currently writing an article for *National Geographic* magazine.
3 I was in charge of organising corporate social events.
4 I took the official photos for the National Basketball Championships.
5 I am working for various charities.
6 I was employed by a local college to raise money for them.

5 Write your own short professional profile, similar to the one in Exercise 2. Think about the message you would most like the reader to be left with. When you have finished exchange profiles with another member of the class. Read the profile once quickly and tell each other what your main impression was.

6 Read your partner's profile again. Check the following points:

- Has the profile been laid out correctly?
- Have the tips in Exercise 3 been followed?
- Has note form been used in places to make the profile more concise?

9f Queen of Egypt

She has a reputation for beauty, power, controversy and ultimately, tragedy.

Before you watch

1 Work in pairs. Make notes about what you know about Cleopatra.

- who she was
- when and where she ruled
- important events in her life

2 You are going to watch a video about the story of Cleopatra. Write down three kinds of image you think you might see which help to tell this story.

While you watch

3 Watch the video and check your ideas from Exercises 1 and 2.

4 Watch the video again and answer the questions.

1 Why was Cleopatra forced from power by her brother?

2 How did she first meet Julius Caesar?

3 How did Cleopatra's relationship with Caesar help her?

4 Why did Octavian go to war with Antony and Cleopatra?

5 In what battle, and which year, was Mark Antony beaten?

6 How did Mark Antony die?

7 How did Cleopatra die?

5 Match the sentence beginnings (1–7) with the endings (a–g). Then watch the video again to check.

1 Julius Caesar arrived in Alexandria
2 Cleopatra's relationship with Caesar kept Rome
3 After Caesar's murder
4 Cleopatra and Antony shared
5 Mark Antony's Roman rival, Octavian,
6 Cleopatra spread numerous
7 Antony's followers carried him to Cleopatra,

a from taking direct control of Egypt.
b false rumours of her death.
c where he died in her arms.
d in pursuit of a rival Roman general.
e her position … became uncertain.
f went to war against them.
g a hunger for power.

After you watch

6 Roleplay first meeting with Caesar

Work in pairs.

Student A: Imagine you are Cleopatra. You arrive in Caesar's court hidden inside a rug. You need to charm Caesar so that he will help you become queen again. Read the information below and make notes.

Student B: Imagine you are Caesar. Cleopatra arrives in your court hidden inside a rug. Read the information below and make notes.

- how you feel (surprised, excited, curious, etc.)
- what you want from the other person
- how you can help the other person
- what you decide to do

Act out your meeting, then change roles and act out the meeting again.

7 At the end of the video, the narrator says: 'Cleopatra lives on in history through her personal story of love and tragedy.' Why do you think her story has lasted for so long? Do you think her story teaches us anything about love and power today?

8 Work in groups and discuss these questions.

1 Do you think Cleopatra was an admirable woman? Why? / Why not?
2 Are there any similar characters in the history of your country?
3 Would you like to have lived in Cleopatra's time? Why? / Why not?

---

charmed (adj) /tʃɑːmd/ fascinated by
controversy (n) /ˈkɒntrəvɜːsi/ disagreement about something
court (n) /kɔːt/ the place where a ruler lives and works
distort (v) /dɪsˈtɔːt/ change something from its normal shape
dynasty (n) /ˈdɪnəsti/ a family that rules a country for several generations
grief (n) /griːf/ great sadness
infuriate (v) /ɪnˈfjʊrieɪt/ make very angry
overjoyed (adj) /əʊvəˈdʒɔɪd/ extremely happy
pursuit (n) /pəˈsjuːt/ the act of chasing someone or something
rival (n) /ˈraɪvəl/ a person or group that competes with another
rug (n) /rʌg/ a small carpet
seize (v) /siːz/ take by force

Grammar

1 Complete this text about Emerging Explorer, Constance Adams, with *the* where necessary.

Constance Adams has had an unusual career path. She studied [1] _____ architecture at [2] _____ Yale University before working as an architect in [3] _____ Berlin and [4] _____ Japan. She then joined [5] _____ Johnson Space Centre in [6] _____ USA, where she helped design TransHab, a module for [7] _____ International Space Station. The idea of [8] _____ module was created to provide [9] _____ living quarters for [10] _____ astronauts during their stay in [11] _____ space. In [12] _____ 2005 she became a *National Geographic* Emerging Explorer.

2 Complete the text with relative pronouns in 1–5 and present and past participles in 6–10.

Adams explains that the TransHab module was intended to be a habitat for a crew of six astronauts, [1] _____ mission was to reach Mars. The team had to design a module [2] _____ would be only 4.3 metres in diameter when it was launched. But once in space, it needed to be three times that size to house the six astronauts [3] _____ lived there. So they made a structure [4] _____ could inflate and unfold in space to become a three-level 'house' [5] _____ astronauts could eat, sleep and work.

The outer shell of the module, [6] _____ (compose) of over twenty layers of different materials, had to resist the space debris [7] _____ (hit) the spaceship all the time. This debris can hit the spaceship seven times faster than a bullet, [8] _____ (cause) great damage. The outer layers were made of a kind of foam [9] _____ (use) in chairs and cushions. The inner shell was made of Kevlar, a material [10] _____ (wear) by soldiers and police for body protection.

3 Work in pairs. Discuss what was special about the size and shape of the module, and the material used.

I CAN	
use *the* and zero article	
use relative clauses and reduced relative clauses	

Vocabulary

4 Complete the sentences with these nouns and the correct form of the verbs.

background become do do experience
follow graduate knowledge qualification
quality serve skills

1 My main academic _____ is a physics degree that I got when I _____ from Sussex University.
2 I have a lot of _____ of organising things. I _____ in the army for four years.
3 I think my main _____ is that I'm very conscientious. I make sure I _____ every job properly.
4 I have good computer _____ . I _____ a course in advanced computing last year.
5 My _____ – both my parents are scientists – meant scientific research was a natural career for me to _____ .
6 My _____ of astrophysics helped me to _____ a space scientist.

5 Work in pairs. Use the nouns and verbs to describe your own skills and experience.

I CAN	
talk about my experience, skills and qualifications	
describe my career path	

Real life

6 Put the correct preposition into each space.

1 I'm familiar _____ most kinds of design software.
2 I specialised _____ mechanical engineering.
3 I think I am well suited _____ working abroad.
4 I'm good _____ people.
5 I'm good _____ persuading people.
6 I'm serious _____ following a career in the automotive industry.
7 I'm not so keen _____ sitting down all day.
8 I am quite knowledgeable _____ mechanics.

7 Work in pairs. Tell each other about a job that would be right for you and one that wouldn't.

I CAN	
describe what kind of work I am suited to	

Speaking

8 Work in small groups. Describe the work of someone you admire. Include these points:

- a description of their qualities and talents
- what they have achieved

Unit 10 Customs and behaviour

Two generations of Chinese visitors at Beijing's Forbidden City
Photograph by Nigel Swinn

FEATURES

46 Cruel to be kind

The *tiger mother* approach to raising children

48 A matter of taste

The strange eating customs of the Nochmani

50 A universal language

Understanding body language

54 Eating insects

A video about Americans with an unusual taste for insects

1 Work in pairs. Look at the photo. What is it about the behaviour of the younger tourists that surprises the older pair?

2 Look at the quotation below. Discuss what you think it means.

66 Manners maketh man 99 *William of Wykeham (1324–1404)*

3 🔊 **2.20** Listen to an anthropologist's explanation and compare your answer. Answer the questions.

1 What is the narrow view of good manners, according to the speaker?
2 What is the real meaning of the quotation and its relation to society?

4 🔊 **2.20** Complete these phrases about manners. Then listen again and check. Discuss whether you think these things are important to teach children.

1 Don't _____ with your mouth full.
2 Don't _____ when grown-ups are speaking.
3 Don't _____ or _____ at people.
4 Don't _____ or _____ gum.
5 Don't wear clothes that are _____ or _____ .
6 Be polite, _____ - _____ and show _____ to others.

10a Cruel to be kind

Reading

1 Work in pairs. Look at the photo and answer the questions.

1. What is happening in the photo?
2. How would you describe the mother's attitude: strict, intense, something else?
3. How strict were your parents with you when you were young? Are you happy that they were this way or not?

2 Work in small groups. Discuss which of these things you think should be a) controlled strongly by parents; b) controlled a little by parents; or c) left to the child to decide?

- watching TV
- playing computer games
- practising a musical instrument
- going out to play with friends
- doing homework
- choosing what subjects to study at high school
- choosing extracurricular activities

3 Read the article and find out who *tiger mothers* are. What are their attitudes to the first five items in Exercise 2? How do these compare to the attitudes of a typical western mother?

4 What does the writer say about the results of the *tiger mother* approach to child-rearing? Does she approve or not? Do you agree with her?

Vocabulary raising children: verbs

5 Work in pairs. Look at the pairs of verbs below and discuss the difference between them. You will find the first verb in each pair in the article.

1. *bring up* and *educate* children
2. *praise* and *reward* good behaviour
3. *rebel against* and *disobey* your parents
4. *push* and *discipline* yourself
5. *give in to* and *spoil* your children
6. *nag* and *pester* someone
7. *shame* and *punish* someone

C R U E L   T O   B E   K I N D

Is there a right way to bring up children? Some parents read guides to find an answer, many just follow their instinct. Whatever they do, a doubt always remains: could I have done a better job?

A recent contribution to the subject is Amy Chua's controversial book *Battle Hymn of the Tiger Mother*, which describes the approach to child-rearing of an ambitious Chinese parent living in the West. According to Chua, western mothers are far too soft on their children. She says they are always praising their children for every effort they make, even if the result is coming last in a race or playing a piano piece badly. These are the kind of parents who will give in to their children's demands to go out and play rather than do their homework, if they protest loud enough.

The *tiger mother* method is very different and the key is total control. *Tiger mothers* will accept nothing less than 'A' grades in every subject – failure to achieve these is just proof that they have not worked hard enough. They will encourage not with praise and reward, but by punishing and shaming. Chua told her own daughter that she would take her doll's house to a charity shop if she failed to master a difficult piano piece. She even rejected a homemade birthday card from her daughter Sophia because she had drawn it in a hurry.

But that highlights another difference, says Chua, which is directness and honesty. A *tiger mother* will not hesitate to tell their child that they are lazy, whereas western parents are always telling their children not to worry, that they will do better next time, even if they think they have been lazy.

The constant nagging of the *tiger mother*, the banning of TV and computer games seems harsh, but perhaps it works. Chua's children have not rebelled, and they don't resent their strict upbringing. They regularly get the top grades at school and are proficient at violin and piano – stereotypical symbols of success, critics would say. By contrast, children with more freedom and more laid-back parents will often lack self-discipline and will fail to push themselves to achieve more.

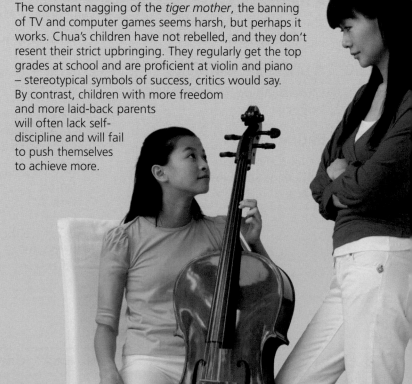

Grammar habitual actions: present tenses, *will*

> ▶ **PRESENT SIMPLE, PRESENT CONTINUOUS and *WILL* FOR REPEATED ACTIONS**
>
> **Present simple**
> *Some parents read guides to find an answer.*
>
> **Present continuous with *always***
> *She says they are always praising their children for every effort they make.*
>
> ***will***
> *These are the kind of parents who will give in to their children's demands.*
>
> For further information and practice, see page 87.

6 Work in pairs. Look at the sentences from the article in the grammar box. Which tense is used to describe:

1 typical behaviour?
2 a habit which the speaker finds annoying?
3 a simple fact or general truth?

7 Find and underline:

1 an example of *tiger mothers'* typical behaviour; an example of typical behaviour of western mothers' children.
2 a simple fact about parents and a simple fact about Chua's children.
3 another thing Chua finds annoying about western mothers.

8 Complete these comments by parents and children by underlining the correct verb forms. Sometimes there is more than one possibility. Then discuss which ones you sympathise with and which you don't.

1 My parents will *always tell / are always telling* me to practise the piano and it just makes me feel it's a chore not a pleasure.
2 In my experience, children *will do / do* as little work as they can. So you have to make them do it.
3 Children *will want / want* to be loved. It's also true that they *will perform / perform* much better in a loving and secure environment.
4 Every parent *will hope / hopes* that their children will be successful, but they *won't always admit / aren't always admitting* it to their children or even themselves.
5 You have to have a different approach with different children. Some *will respond / respond* better to gentle encouragement; others *will need / need* to be pushed and challenged.
6 I don't like parents who *will always try / are always trying* to be friends with their children. There are too many parents who *will buy / buy* their children presents and let them do what they want just to get on their good side.

9 🎵 **2.21** Read the anecdotes below by people about children in Mexico, the USA and India. Put the verb in the right form. Then listen and compare your answers.

I've seen this situation so many times in Mexico. What happens is children [1] _____ (beg) their parents for some sweets. At first the parent [2] _____ (say) no. So then the child [3] _____ (pester) and pester until the parent finally gives in – which they always do. It's against all the rules of parenting.

I teach in a school in San Francisco where we have quite a lot of ethnic Chinese and Japanese kids. By and large they [4] _____ (do) what you tell them. But the other kids [5] _____ (always / misbehave). You can tell them ten times to sit down before they do.

Where I live in India, it is common for young children to work. Kids still [6] _____ (depend) on their parents, but they have a different attitude to responsibility. Just as children in every culture [7] _____ (play) naturally, so children in India naturally [8] _____ (assume) responsibility for working and earning money.

Speaking

10 Work in pairs. Discuss the situations in Exercise 9. How familiar is each one to you? Does the behaviour seem right or wrong?

11 Think of three more examples of children's and parents' behaviour in your country: a simple fact about the way children or parents behave; an example of typical behaviour; an example of behaviour that annoys you or seems wrong.

12 Describe your examples to another pair. Are they similar to theirs?

10b A matter of taste

Listening

1 What is the strangest thing you have ever eaten? Why did you eat it? What did it taste like?

2 🔊 **2.22** Listen to an extract from a radio programme about a tribe with an unusual diet. Answer the questions.

1 Where is this tribe from?
2 What do they eat mostly?
3 How do they make sure there is enough of this food?

3 🔊 **2.22** Listen again and choose the correct word or phrase to complete the statements.

1 We live in an age where people are very _____ what they eat.
   a nervous about   b aware of
   c careless about
2 Most people need _____ in order to live.
   a red meat   b animals
   c mammals
3 In the past it was thought that the Nicobar Islands contained _____ .
   a no inhabitants   b no fresh water
   c few animals
4 The Nochmani didn't want to eat _____ .
   a sweets and cakes b meat
   c any of the food they were offered
5 Insects have a lot of _____ in them.
   a carbohydrate   b vitamins
   c protein
6 The speaker thinks we could all benefit from eating _____ .
   a less meat   b more insects
   c alternative types of food

4 What do you think of the diet of the Nochmani? Do you think what we eat is just a matter of habit? Why? / Why not? Can we learn to eat anything if we have to? Or are there some things you could never eat?

Grammar *used to, usually, be used to* and *get used to*

5 Look at these sentences from the extract (1–5). Match each verb form in bold to the meaning (a–e).

1 We **didn't use to think** so much about what we ate.
2 People **usually need** mammals in order to live.
3 The Nochmani **were not used to eating** meat.
4 If you **are used to** a certain type of food, other types may be completely indigestible.
5 If more of us could **get used to eating** unconventional foods, …

a refers to something that was strange or abnormal for someone
b refers to something that happens regularly or is generally the case
c refers to learning to cope with something difficult or unfamiliar
d refers to what someone did regularly in the past, but doesn't do anymore
e refers to something that is normal and not strange

▶ **USED TO, USUALLY, BE USED TO** and ***GET USED TO***

Past habits	Present habits
used to + infinitive	*(not) usually* + present simple
I used to eat …	*I usually eat …*
I didn't use to eat …	*I don't usually eat …*
Did you use to eat?	*Do you usually eat?*
Familiar (and unfamiliar) habits	**Habits that are becoming familiar**
be used to + noun or *-ing* form	*get used to* + noun or *-ing* form
I am used to (eating) Italian food.	*I am getting used to (eating) English food.*
I am not used to …	*I am not getting used to …*
Are you used to … ?	*Are you getting used to … ?*

For further information and practice, see page 87.

6 Look at the grammar box and then choose the right form to complete sentences 1–9 in A, B and C. Note that we use *be used to* and *get used to* for things that are not strange or difficult to do.

A In China, people ¹*do not usually finish / used not to finish* everything on their plate, because it is a sign that they have not had enough to eat. Visitors from the West find it difficult to ²*be used to / get used to* this, because they ³*usually eat / are used to eating* everything up to show that they like it. When a Chinese host sees their empty plates, he ⁴*usually assumes / is used to assuming* that they want more.

B Fifty years ago, people in the USA ⁵*got used to sitting / used to sit* down for meals with their families each evening. Families nowadays ⁶*usually eat / are used to eating* together only three times a week, because busy lives and TV get in the way. But it is believed that if more families could ⁷*be used to dining / get used to dining* together, it would strengthen family relationships.

C Eating a traditional English breakfast of eggs, bacon and sausages ⁸*used to be / was used to being* a common thing in the UK. A big breakfast was important because people ⁹*didn't use to eat / weren't used to eating* so many snacks during the day.

7 Put the verb in the most appropriate form to complete these sentences.

1 We .... (eat) out a lot, but restaurants are so expensive these days that we don't anymore.
2 I .... (have) a tuna and mayonnaise sandwich for my lunch.
3 I .... (take) sugar in my coffee, but now I have a sweetener. It took a little while to .... the taste, but now I can't tell the difference.
4 When I was staying with my friends in England, we ate at six o'clock in the evening. It was strange, because I .... (eat) much later.

8 Are any of the sentences in Exercise 7 true for you? Do you have similar experiences?

9 Pronunciation /uː/ and /juː/

a 🔊 **2.23** In the words in bold the letter *u* is pronounced /juː/. Listen to the sentences and repeat.

1 I **usually** eat a big breakfast.
2 Did you **use** to eat a big breakfast?
3 I'm not **used** to eating a lot of meat.

b Work in pairs. Practise saying the other words with the same sound.

consume   cucumber   future   human
nutritious   opportunity   produce   tuna
useful

c 🔊 **2.24** In these words there is no /j/ sound before the /uː/ sound. Practise saying them. Then listen and check. Which sounds does /uː/ follow in these words?

fruit   juice   June   rule   true

Vocabulary and speaking

10 Work in pairs. Place these four items of food into the correct category (a–d). Think of two more items for each category. Then compare your list with another pair.

breakfast cereal   chocolate bars   rice
yoghurt

a dairy products, e.g. milk
b processed food, e.g. frozen peas
c staple foods, e.g. potatoes
d snacks, e.g. crisps

11 Complete these sentences by putting in information about eating habits in your country. Go around the class and exchange your information with at least three other people. Then work with your partner. Tell each other the two most memorable statements you heard.

1 When I was growing up, a lot of families used to …
2 The main staple food is … People aren't used to eating …
3 For breakfast, people usually …
4 I think visitors find some of our eating customs strange, because they are not used to …
4 People in my country don't usually eat …
5 I think young people find it difficult to get used to …

10c A universal language

Reading

1 Work in pairs. Put the actions in the box into the correct category of body language. Then demonstrate the actions to each other. What is the meaning of each?

a handshake	standing with arms
biting your bottom lip	crossed
sitting back in your chair	waving
smiling	

posture: _____

gesture: _____

facial expression: _____

2 Read the article about body language and say which of the sentences best summarises the author's view.

a We need to learn how people from different cultures use body language.

b The differences in body language between cultures are small but important.

c There are more similarities than differences in body language between cultures.

3 According to the writer …

1 Making comparisons between cultures can be:
   a fun.   b useful.   c dangerous.

2 Standing too close to someone of another culture can:
   a cause arguments.   b cause discomfort.
   c be a serious insult.

3 A lot of the facts given in guides for travellers are:
   a very important.
   b not of much practical help.   c wrong.

4 Looking away from the speaker is a sign of:
   a sadness.   b boredom.
   c both boredom and sadness.

5 To avoid making mistakes in body language with other cultures, people need to be:
   a sensible.   b sensitive.   c both.

6 Differences in body language between people start at:
   a an individual level.
   b a cultural level.
   c an emotional level.

4 With your partner, demonstrate to each other:

• the two gestures described in paragraph 3
• the two greetings mentioned in paragraph 4
• the body language associated with boredom and anger described in paragraph 5

5 Do you agree with the writer's view about cross-cultural communication? Is your culture one that generally shows its emotions or not?

Critical thinking sources

6 The article gives a lot of information about body language and customs. But how do we know how reliable this information is? Underline the examples of different cultures' body language and customs in the article.

7 Work in pairs. Find the author's source for each example. Mark the source according to this scale: 3 = very credible source; 2 = quite credible source; 1 = incredible source and 0 = no source.

Word focus *common*

8 The word *common* has two basic meanings Look at these expressions from the article and match the meanings (1–2) with the sentences (a–d).

common (adj)
1 something usual or normal
2 something that is shared by two or more people

a It is quite common in European countries to sit with your legs crossed.
b The things that we all have in common …
c There are also common factors when people are bored.
d If we all just apply a little sensitivity and common sense, …

9 Now do the same for these expressions.

e In a negotiation, always try to find common ground between you and the other party.
f It is a common misconception that English people drink only tea, not coffee.
g Don't worry about mispronouncing my name – it's a common mistake that everyone makes.
h It's common knowledge that Chinese people use chopsticks, not knives and forks.

Speaking

10 Work in pairs. Describe the following customs in your country. Then compare your answers with another pair. How similar were they?

• The most common form of greeting
• Common gestures that visitors are not used to
• Common eating customs
• Common misconceptions foreigners have about your country

A universal language

People love to compare and contrast. In most parts of England, you buy your bus ticket on the bus. In France, you buy it at a metro station. In Australia, you can buy it from a newsagent. We all find this kind of comparison entertaining. Books on cross-cultural communication exploit our curiosity by focussing on differences between people across the world: in social behaviour, the roles they adopt in society, their attitudes to money, the significance of their body language, etc.

Proxemics, the study of different standards of personal space, is one example. How close I stand to someone when I am speaking to them depends not only on my relationship to them, but also on my culture. This is important because if the person I am with is not used to standing as near as I do when we are talking to each other, they might feel uncomfortable. Statistics tell us that the average distance at which two people stand in a social context – neighbours chatting for example – is anything between 1.2 metres and 3.5 metres. In Latin cultures (South America, Italy, etc.) and also in China this distance tends to be smaller, while in Nordic cultures (Sweden, Denmark, etc.) people usually stand further apart.

The messages sent by your posture and gestures is another case in point. For example, it is quite common in European countries to sit with your legs crossed and the top foot outstretched. But, as I know from personal experience, people in Arab countries hardly ever sit in this way – because they might show you the bottom of their shoe, which is a serious insult. It is said that in the Philippines, people often greet each other by raising their eyebrows quickly. In the USA, this is a sign of surprise.

Such information fills the pages of guides for travellers and international business people. But I would really question the usefulness of what are presented as 'essential' or 'must know' facts. Clearly it is important to know a little about eating customs, tipping and the rules concerning basic greetings – whether you should bow or shake someone's hand. But beneath the surface, we are not so different. There are many signs that are universal in the emotions that they communicate. Focussing on these similarities – the things that we all have in common – is a much more profitable route than focussing on the differences.

Smiling is the best known of these, but not the only one. Behaviourists have proven that all over the world, people show sadness in a similar way. The face 'falls': the mouth becomes downturned and the eyes begin to look glassy. The person will probably look down or away and seem distracted.

There are also common factors when people are bored. They will look at other things in a distracted way – their watches, for example. Their feet will begin to move restlessly indicating that they want to escape; they tap their fingers or scratch their heads. Anger can also be read quite easily: the facial muscles tense up, often causing people to frown; the eyes stare, fixing themselves on the target of their anger; blood rushes to the face causing it to become red. If the anger is great, the body will also tense up as if preparing itself for a physical fight.

Understanding these universal signals and reacting appropriately is the real key to cross-cultural communication. If we all apply just a little sensitivity and common sense, it is unlikely that we will cause lasting offence by making the wrong gesture or invading a stranger's personal space. Of course some cultures show their emotions more openly and others prefer to keep them more hidden. But isn't that also the case within cultures, from one individual to another?

frown (v) /fraʊn/ to lower your eyebrows, causing lines to appear on your forehead
scratch (v) /skrætʃ/ to move your fingernails backwards and forwards across your skin
stare (v) /steə/ to look intensely and for a long time at something
tap (v) /tæp/ to hit something lightly with a finger or hand

TALK ABOUT ▶ TYPICAL BEHAVIOUR ▶ FOOD AND EATING HABITS ▶ CUSTOMS IN YOUR COUNTRY ▶ WEDDING TRADITIONS
WRITE ▶ AN INFORMAL EMAIL

51

10d A pre-wedding ritual

Vocabulary weddings

1 What pre-wedding customs or events are traditional for the bride-to-be in your country?

2 Work in pairs. Look at the words related to weddings and answer the questions.

bride	groom	hen night	stag night	veil

1 Which word means a pre-wedding party for the man? And for the woman?
2 Which word means the woman on her wedding day? And the man on his?
3 Which word means a piece of fine cloth that covers the woman's face?

> ▶ **WORDBUILDING word pairs**
>
> Some words have a natural 'partner' or make a matching pair. *bride* and *groom*, *host* and *guest*
>
> For further information and practice, see Workbook page 127.

Real life describing traditions

3 🎧 **2.25** Listen to the first part of a description of a traditional pre-wedding *henna night* in eastern Turkey. Who attends the event and how is it celebrated?

4 Complete the first four phrases in the box below by writing in the details of the henna night.

> ▶ **DESCRIBING TRADITIONS**
>
> ¹ It takes place _____ .
> ² It marks the _____ .
> ³ It is an occasion for _____ .
> ⁴ It symbolises the _____ .
>
> It's traditional / customary for this to be done by ...
> Typically / As a rule / Usually the women from ...
>
> **Describing the sequence of events**
> The ceremony begins with the ...
> Then , ... / After that, ... / Next, ... / Finally, ...
>
> While this is happening / During this part, the guests ...
> After / Once the bride's head has been ...
> On the morning of the wedding, a ...

5 🎧 **2.26** Listen to the second part. Put the stages of the ceremony in the correct order by numbering each item.

a A child presents the hennaed coin to the groom.
b The bride's head is covered with a red veil.
c The guests sing separation songs.
d The bride's hands and feet are decorated with henna.
e A gold coin is put into the remaining henna.
f The henna is prepared by the daughter of another couple.

6 🎧 **2.27** Retell the events to each other using the linking words in the box to help you. Then listen again and compare your version to what you hear.

7 Pronunciation the letter *s*

a 🎧 **2.28** Listen to these words and for each one say if the letter *s* is pronounced /s/ or /z/. Note the spellings that produce each sound.

custom	dress	friends	music	suppose
symbolise	weddings			

b 🎧 **2.29** Work in pairs. Say how *s* will be pronounced in the following words. Listen and check. Think of three more words for each sound. Then compare words with another pair.

across	eastern	lose	rings	single
spends	surprise			

Speaking

8 What special events or customs take place before or after a wedding in your country? Choose one and prepare a description using the box to help you. Think about:

- the timing of the event
- the sequence of the events
- its significance
- any special symbols used

9 Working in small groups, describe these customs to each other. When each person has finished their description, ask them questions.

10e Business customs

Writing an informal email

1 Imagine you are about to go on a business trip to a country you haven't visited before. What would you want to know about the customs there before you travelled?

2 Read the first email. What is Paul asking for? What is he worried about?

3 Read Dominic's reply. Which pieces of advice should calm Paul's worries?

> Hi Dominic
>
> Good to see you briefly the other day. Forgot to tell you. I'm going out to China next week. Just wondered what to expect. I know you have experience of doing business there. Don't want to put my foot in it with any potential business partners. Could you let me know anything I should be particularly aware of?
>
> Thanks
> Paul

> Hi Paul
>
> Glad to hear you're going out to China. I think you'll enjoy it. Not Shanghai, is it? Let me know. Maybe I can fix you up with a couple of contacts. Anyway, my advice:
>
> - Take plenty of business cards – Chinese people will always give you theirs (make sure you read them carefully) and it's embarrassing if you don't have one to give in return.
> - Keep the name and address of your hotel with you when you go out. Visitors are always getting into trouble because they can't remember where they're staying.
> - The Chinese love their food and are very proud of it. They'll offer you some unusual dishes. Just be adventurous and be grateful!
>
> Good luck and speak soon
> Dominic

4 Writing skill elision in informal writing

a Look at the two emails again. Underline four phrases in the first email and four in the second email where words have been omitted to save time e.g. Good to see you briefly the other day.

b How would you write these sentences or phrases if you were writing a more formal letter? Convert the sentences and phrases by inserting the words that are missing.

Example:
It was good to see you the other day.

c Now convert these sentences into a more economical style by removing unnecessary pronouns, auxiliary verbs or the verb *be*.

1 I hope we can meet up soon.
2 It was bad luck that you didn't get the job.
3 I'll be back next Tuesday night.
4 This is my address in New York: …
5 I will look forward to hearing all about it.
6 It wasn't a bad result, was it?

5 Write a response to this email that you received in your country.

> Hi there
>
> Wondered if you could help. I'm flying over next week to meet some clients. Will have to take them out to dinner and chat to them a bit socially. Can you give me some advice about how things are done over there? Eating customs, what to talk about, etc. Sorry to ask, but very grateful for any information you can provide.
>
> Best wishes
> Sara

6 Work in pairs. Exchange emails. Read your partner's reply and answer the questions.

- Is it written in an informal style?
- Has the writer given some useful tips?
- Is the content short and to the point?
- Has the writer used some elision?

10f Eating insects

Larry Peterman is a
candy man on a mission.

Before you watch

1 Work in groups. Look at the photo and discuss the questions.

1 What do you think a candy man is?
2 How does the photo make you feel? Do you think most people would feel the same as you?
3 What do you think Larry Peterman's mission is?

2 Work in pairs. Think about the sweets you used to eat when you were a child. What can you remember about them? Describe the sweets to your partner.

3 You are going to watch a video about eating insects. Answer these questions.

1 Which countries include insects in their diets?
2 Do you think eating insects is a new habit?
3 Are insects good for you?
4 Is producing insects better for the environment than producing meat?

While you watch

4 Watch the video and check your answers from Exercise 3.

5 Watch the video again. Number the foods in the order you see them.

a banana, cream and cockroach dessert
b salt-water taffy
c lollipop with cricket
d cricket cocktail
e mealworm-covered apples
f stir fry
g caramels
h caterpillars

6 Answer the questions.

1 Where is Hotlix?

2 How long has Larry been trying to get Americans to eat insects?

3 According to Larry, why do most Americans not like eating insects?

4 How many species of insects are eaten around the world?

5 How does Larry compare insects to wine?

After you watch

7 Roleplay a meal at Larry's restaurant

Work in groups of three.

Student A: Imagine you are Larry. Prepare an interesting insect menu. Then give the menu to your customers. Explain what each dish is and answer their questions.

Student B: You don't like the idea of eating insects but are prepared to try. Ask Larry about the menu and order your meal. Also ask Larry why he is so interested in promoting insect foods.

Student C: You love the idea of eating insects. Order a meal.

Act out the conversation, then change roles and act out the conversation again. The student who is Larry should prepare a different menu.

8 At the end of the video, Larry predicts that gourmet insects will have 'snob appeal'. What do you think that means?

9 Do you think Larry will eventually win people over to eating insects. Why? / Why not?

10 Work in groups and discuss these questions.

1 Are there any unusual dishes or foods in your country?
2 What types of foods do people in your country avoid eating generally? Why?
3 Are there any foods you don't like? Why?

---

advocate (n) /'ædvəkət/ a person who supports something
brim (v) /brɪm/ be full of
bug (n) /bʌg/ insect
candy (n) /'kændi/ (American English) sweets
munch (v) /mʌntʃ/ eat
niche (n) /niːʃ/ a specialised business opportunity
revolting (adj) /rɪ'vəʊltɪŋ/ disgusting
snob (n) /snɒb/ a person who thinks he or she is better than other people
swat (v) /swɒt/ (American English) hit

Grammar

1 Work in pairs. Look at the photo. What do you know about the eating habits of the Spanish: when they eat, what they like to eat, etc.?

2 Read the extract from a travel guide. What times are Spanish meals?

3 Underline the correct forms to complete the extract.

People visiting Spain for the first time can find it difficult to ¹ *be used to / get used to* the eating customs of the Spanish. It's not so much the food itself, but the timing of the meals that visitors ² *aren't used to / don't get used to*. I ³ *was used to living / used to live* in Cadiz myself for a few years and I actually quite like the way they do things. Breakfast is a light continental affair – just a roll and some coffee usually – eaten between 8 and 9.30 a.m. The main meal of the day is lunch, which people ⁴ *are used to eating / usually eat* sometime between 1 p.m. and 3.30 p.m. Quite a few of the shops, museums and galleries ⁵ *close / will close* around this time, because the locals like to take time over lunch. They ⁶ *are always resting / will rest* for a short time afterwards, although the traditional afternoon siesta is not as common as it ⁷ *was used to being / used to be*. People eat late in the evening - rarely before 9 p.m. and at the weekend the locals often ⁸ *aren't eating / won't eat* before 11 p.m. or even midnight. This is a much lighter meal than lunch – often just a few tapas taken with a drink.

I CAN	
use *used to*, *be used to* and *get used to* correctly	☐
talk about habits and typical behaviour with present simple, present continuous and *will*	☐

Vocabulary

4 Work in pairs. Find the odd one out in each group of words and expressions. Explain the reason for your choice.

1 punish, discipline, nag, spoil
2 educate, bring up, look after, raise
3 encourage, shame, praise, reward
4 bread, cheese, rice, pasta
5 sit back, shake hands, wave, point
6 interrupt, stare, smile, chew gum
7 well-behaved, offensive, polite, courteous

5 Tell each other what postures, gestures or facial expressions you often use and in what situations.

I CAN	
talk about bringing up children	☐
talk about eating habits	☐
talk about body language	☐

Real life

6 Work in pairs. Match the two parts of the sentences to make sentences about a coming-of-age tradition.

1 It marks	a the moment when a child becomes an adult.
2 It takes place	
3 It is an occasion	b the child to stand up and give a short speech.
4 It symbolises	
5 It's customary for	c begins with the parent walking into the hall with the child.
6 Typically the ceremony	d people in the audience can also say some words.
7 Once the child has given their speech	e on the child's 16th birthday.
	f for celebration.
	g leaving childish things behind.

7 Tell your partner about a special celebration in your country and the traditions that surround it.

I CAN	
describe traditions and customs at special events	☐

Speaking

8 Work in small groups. How is children's upbringing these days different from when you were a child? Look at the example. Do you agree with this speaker?

My parents were quite strict. They used to expect us to do jobs around the house. I think children these days have it much easier, although they are always complaining that their parents expect a lot of them.

Unit 11 Knowledge and learning

Students processing their DNA at a museum learning lab
Photograph by Rajat Bansal

FEATURES

1 Work in pairs. Match each technique of acquiring knowledge or learning (1–4) to a definition (a–d). Which technique are the students using in the photo?

1 by authority   a experimenting
2 by observation   b using logic
3 by reasoning   c judging from what you see or hear
4 by trial and error   d reading or listening to an expert

2 🎵 **2.30** Sometimes we feel we know something intuitively, without having to learn it. Listen to a psychologist describing such a situation and answer the questions.

1 What situation does he describe?
2 What types of learning are needed in this situation?

3 🎵 **2.30** Listen again and complete the phrases the psychologist uses to talk about knowledge. Discuss what each one means.

1 You **have a basic** _____ of car mechanics.
2 You do a bit of research **to** _____ **out** what the best kind of car is and try **to** _____ **up** some tips from experts.
3 In other words, you _____ **the information**.
4 In the end you have to trust your instinct or _____ **feeling**.

11a Knowledge conservation

Reading

1 Work in pairs. Look at the photo in the article below of a botanist in the field. What does a botanist do?

2 Make a list of plants or plant products you use on a daily basis. Then compare your list with another pair. Which uses did your lists have in common?

Example:

cotton in my clothes

3 Read the article about Maria Fadiman and answer the questions.

   1 How is her interest in plants different from a traditional botanist?
   2 Where does she work?
   3 What two uses of plants are mentioned in the article?

4 What does the article say about:

   1 the way Fadiman collects knowledge from local people?
   2 the way that local people often pass their knowledge on?
   3 the way Fadiman passes her knowledge on to her students?

5 Do you think that Fadiman's idea of recording traditional plant knowledge is useful? Why? / Why not? What knowledge has been passed down to you by your parents or grandparents? Tell your partner.

> ▶ **WORDBUILDING idiomatic expressions**
>
> Often there are idiomatic expressions that can replace basic verbs like *think, realise,* etc.
> *It struck me that … = I realised that …*
>
> For further information and practice, see Workbook page 135.

K N O W L E D G E   C O N S E R V A T I O N

Dr Maria Fadiman is an ethnobotanist – she studies how people use plants. 'Looking at plant conservation without including people is a fantasy,' she says. 'The focus of my work is finding a balance where people use resources in a sustainable way.'

It struck Fadiman early on that this was what she wanted to do. 'I was born with a passion for conservation and a fascination with indigenous cultures,' she explains. 'Ethnobotany lets me bring it all together. On my first trip to the rain forest I met a woman who was in terrible pain because the people in her village weren't able to remember which plant would cure her. I saw traditional plant knowledge was being lost, and at that moment I knew conserving this kind of knowledge was what I wanted to do with my life.'

Visiting the Ecuadorian rain forest, Dr Fadiman was amazed at the variety of plants. 'It looked like one big, green mish-mash to me', she says. 'But the people who lived there were able to pick out the right plants for medicine and could distinguish not only the plants that were safe to eat, but also the right part of each plant.'

The problem often is that such knowledge is stored only in local people's minds and it is passed down from generation to generation. Fadiman managed to persuade inhabitants of the Ecuadorian rain forest to let her record the information in written form. 'They are excited by this idea because suddenly their knowledge is valued.'

But conservation doesn't just mean protecting indigenous plants. If bringing in non-native plants – cash crops like coffee – is beneficial to people and the environment, then that's fine too. In the Galapagos Islands, where overfishing was a real problem, environmentalists like Fadiman succeeded in getting local people to think about alternatives to fishing, such as growing coffee.

By forming close relationships with local people and joining in with their way of life, Fadiman has inspired her own students in her teaching at Florida Atlantic University. Students who couldn't easily absorb facts and statistics said they were able to engage much more easily with the subject when they heard her stories of going to the river to brush her teeth or sitting around a cooking fire.

indigenous (adj) /ɪnˈdɪdʒənəs/ native to a particular country or area
mish-mash (n) /ˈmɪʃˌmæʃ/ a confusing mixture or collection of things

Grammar *could, was able to, manage to* and *succeed in*

6 Work in pairs. Underline the sentences in the article where the following forms (1–6) are used. Then match each form to the uses (a–c). Note that some forms can have more than one use.

1 *could*
2 *was / were able to (do)*
3 *couldn't*
4 *wasn't / weren't able to*
5 *managed to (do)*
6 *succeeded in (doing)*

a to describe success in a task on a particular occasion in the past
b to describe a general ability in the past
c to describe an inability to do something in the past

> ► **COULD, WAS ABLE TO, MANAGE TO and SUCCEED IN**
>
> **could + infinitive (without to)**
> *He could tell which plants were safe and which were dangerous.*
>
> **couldn't + infinitive (without to)**
> *I couldn't remember the name of the plant.*
>
> **was / were able + to + infinitive**
> *We were able to learn a lot by talking to the local people.*
> *He wasn't able to explain how he knew it was the right plant.*
>
> **manage + to + infinitive**
> *After three hours climbing, we managed to reach the top of the mountain.*
>
> **succeed in + -ing**
> *We succeeded in finding a guide to take us into the forest.*
>
> For further information and practice, see page 88.

7 Look at the grammar box. Then complete the sentences.

1 In the past people could _____ (distinguish) plants much more than they can now.
2 Recently, a group of schoolchildren who were asked where cotton came from weren't able _____ (say) whether it was from an animal or a plant.
3 People were able _____ (use) this knowledge to find food and medicines.
4 They also managed _____ (work) out which plants were good for building and making clothes.
5 But they didn't always succeed _____ (pass) this knowledge on to the next generation.
6 So people couldn't _____ (save) some of this knowledge from being lost.

8 Underline the correct form in each of these sentences. Sometimes both forms are possible.

1 By specialising in ethnobotany, Fadiman *was able to combine / succeeded in combining* an interest in plants with her interest in people.
2 She also studied geography, which meant she *could look at / managed to look at* people and the land.
3 In Ecuador, Fadiman *could record / managed to record* data about plants that hadn't been written down before.
4 In Yucatan, Mexico, local women taught Fadiman how to weave, something that she *wasn't able to do / didn't manage to do* before.
5 On a recent trip to Ecuador, she *could visit / was able to visit* a lot of places in a short time by using a helicopter rather than buses and canoes.
6 Fadiman was impressed by how indigenous people *were able to make / succeeded in making* use of the plants around them.

Vocabulary learning

9 Work in pairs. Find pairs of words in this group with the same meaning.

> absorb   acquire   be ignorant   connect with   engage with   grasp   inspire   motivate   not know   pick up   take in   understand

10 Complete these sentences about your own learning at school using one of the forms in the grammar box. Ask and answer these questions.

1 Which teachers _____ (inspire) you at school?
2 What kind of facts _____ (absorb) most easily?
3 Which subjects _____ (engage with)?
4 _____ (pass) all your exams?
5 What knowledge _____ (acquire) that has been useful in later life?
6 Was there anything that _____ (not / grasp) that you wished you did now?

Speaking

11 🔊 2.31 Listen to someone describing her area of expertise and answer the questions.

1 What is the speaker's area of expertise?
2 How did the speaker acquire their knowledge?

12 Work in pairs. Think of a subject you know a lot about. How were you able to become knowledgeable in this area? Have you managed to record or pass on this knowledge in any way?

11b Memory

Speaking

1 Work in pairs. How good is your memory? Look at the picture below for ten seconds. Then turn your book over and write down all the objects you can remember.

2 Compare your results with another pair. What techniques did you use to remember each set?

Items left at the Vietnam Memorial, Landover, Maryland

Listening

3 What things do you commonly forget? Which failures of memory annoy you the most?

4 🔊 **2.32** Listen to the first part of a talk on memory by a psychologist and note the common failures of memory that he mentions. Were any of them the same as yours?

5 🔊 **2.33** Listen to the rest of the talk and answer the questions.

1 What is the woman 'AJ' good at remembering?
2 How does 'AJ' feel about her good memory?
3 Why are people's memories perhaps not as good as they used to be?

6 🔊 **2.34** Complete the psychologist's statements by putting in the missing words (one word per space). Then listen again and check.

1 AJ's memory is stimulated by .... in the same way that our memories can be stimulated by certain ....
2 Having a good memory should make people feel more ....
3 Our memories are selective: they remember mostly .... things and .... things.
4 We should be .... for all the things that our memories hide away.
5 Psychologists call the technology we use to store information 'our .... memory'.
6 Now medical science is trying to address the problem of .... memory.

7 Work in pairs. Discuss the questions.

1 How much do you rely on your own internal memory to remember things?
2 How much do you rely on aids, such as post-it notes, computer, diaries, etc.?
3 Do you agree with the speaker that our memories are getting worse?

Grammar future in the past

8 🎧 **2.35** Listen to the first part of the talk again and complete the first half of these sentences with the correct verb forms.

1 You _____ to make a comment at a meeting and then ...
2 You _____ to send a friend a card for their birthday, but then ...
3 You recognised someone in the street and _____ spoken to them, but ...
4 You promised you _____ post a letter for someone and two days later ...
5 You _____ to write down a great idea you had, but when you found a pen and paper, ...

9 Work in pairs. What happened next in each case? Were any of these actions completed? If not, why not?

10 Choose the right verb form to complete this description of another memory patient.

There was another interesting patient who couldn't form new memories. He could only remember events before 1960. I ¹ *was going to ask / would ask* his doctor how someone with no memory managed to cope with daily life, but she suggested I speak to him directly. So I went to interview him. Our appointment ² *was supposed to be / would be* at 2 p.m., but it made no difference to him what time it was since he lived only in the present. I ³ *would tell / would have told* him my name and why I was there, but I realised there was no point: ⁴ *it was going to mean / it would have meant* nothing to him. So I began by asking him about his past and he talked about his time as a child during the Second World War. But then the telephone rang. When he came back, I ⁵ *was about to ask / would ask* him to continue, but I realised the moment had gone. He had completely forgotten our earlier conversation. I thought he ⁶ *was about to be / would be* frustrated by this but not at all. The man was not stupid and he did not seem unhappy. If anything he seemed happier for not being burdened by memory.

> ▶ **FUTURE IN THE PAST**
>
> ***going to* and *about to***
> *I was going to call you, but I forgot.*
> *I was about to call you, but I was interrupted.*
>
> ***would* and *would have***
> *He said he would call me.*
> *I would have called you, but I didn't have your number.*
>
> ***supposed to***
> *He was supposed to call you. Did he forget?*
>
> For further information and practice, see page 89.

11 🎧 **2.36** Look at the grammar box. Transform these original plans into future in the past forms. Then listen and check your answers.

1 'I'm going to ask Sarah to come.'
   I _____ , but I asked Kate instead.
2 'She's supposed to be in Cairo this week.'
   She _____ in Cairo this week, but she's ill.
3 'I'll definitely send you the original.'
   He promised he _____ me the original, but he sent me a copy.
4 'We will be there by ten o'clock'.
   We _____ there by ten o'clock, but the train didn't get in until eleven fifteen.
5 He's about to announce that he will retire this year.
   He _____ , but now he thinks he'll stay until next year.
6 'The council will build a new shopping mall in the centre.'
   The council _____ a new shopping mall in the centre, but residents opposed the idea.

12 Pronunciation contrastive sentence stress

a 🎧 **2.36** Work in pairs. Underline the words in each sentence in Exercise 11 that highlight the contrasting facts. Listen and check. Then practise saying each sentence.

b Complete each of these sentences with a contrasting idea. Underline the words in the sentence that highlight the contrast. Then say your sentences to your partner. Ask them which words they thought were stressed.

1 I was going to order a steak, but ...
2 They were supposed to be going on holiday to Italy, but ...
3 I would have driven, but ...
4 He said he would wait for me, but ...
5 We were about to buy a new TV, but ...

Speaking

13 Work in pairs. Choose one of the three situations below. Think of a good excuse to explain why this happened. Then change pairs and explain your excuse again. At the end vote on which excuses were best.

- You were 30 minutes late for an important business meeting and didn't call to say so.
- You borrowed someone's car and were supposed to return it the following day, but they had to call you to find out where you were.
- It was a close friend's birthday two days ago. You didn't send a card or get them a present.

TALK ABOUT ▸ ACQUIRING KNOWLEDGE ▸ WHY YOU FORGOT ▸ TYPES OF LEARNER ▸ GETTING CLARIFICATION
WRITE ▸ AN EMAIL ABOUT A MISUNDERSTANDING

61

11c Who's a clever bird, then?

Reading

1 Work in pairs. Do you know a domestic animal which is particularly intelligent? How does this intelligence show itself?

2 Read the article and say how Alex the parrot's intelligence showed itself.

3 Read the article again. Are the sentences true (T), false (F) or does the article not give an answer (NA)?

1 People are right to believe that animals have thoughts and emotions.
2 Pepperberg's idea was to let Alex communicate to her how he saw the world.
3 Pepperberg didn't want people to think she had chosen Alex for his intelligence.
4 Alex showed that he could distinguish between colours and shapes but not numbers.
5 Pepperberg concluded that cognitive skills were necessary for survival in the wild.
6 Alex felt very proud of his ability to communicate in English.

4 Were you surprised by Pepperberg's experiment with Alex and its results? Why? / Why not? Tell your partner.

Critical thinking reinforcing ideas

5 Often when writers express an idea, they reinforce it to make sure the reader understands. They do this in a variety of ways:

• rephrasing or saying the same thing in other words
• giving examples
• quoting someone who also made this point

Find and underline the ideas expressed below by the author. Note how each one is reinforced.

1 How can we find out if animals can think?
2 Pepperberg's idea was to ask the parrot for his thoughts.
3 Researchers had no confidence in her idea.
4 She wanted to get inside the parrot's head.
5 Alex's cognitive abilities are not typical of all animals.
6 Alex cognitive abilities are necessary to cope with his environment.
7 Alex worked through various mental tests.
8 Alex behaved like a bored teenager.

6 Which method of reinforcing an idea did you find the most effective?

Word focus *learn*

7 Work in pairs. Find these three expressions in the article with the word *learn*. Discuss what each one means.

1 learn as you go along
2 learn by heart
3 learn the hard way

8 Look at the expressions in bold with *learn* in the sentences below and work out what each one means from its context. Which one means the same as 'learn the hard way'?

1 If Jack is interested in photography, there's an excellent four-week course at the adult college, where he can **learn some tricks of the trade**.
2 Jessica wants to design the new brochure, but she's only been here a month. I told her that you have to **learn to walk before you can run**.
3 It's **never too late to learn**. My grandfather took up the piano when he was 73.
4 I've **learnt my lesson**. I'm never going to try to build a piece of furniture again without reading the instructions first.
5 There's no point complaining about the changes in the organisation. We are all just going to have to **learn to live with it**.
6 You'd think that the government would **learn from its mistakes**, but they never do.

9 Choose two of the expressions from Exercise 8 and use them in sentences about your own learning experiences. Read your sentences to your partner, omitting the expressions with *learn*. Can your partner work out the missing expressions?

Speaking

10 Work in pairs. Do the quiz on page 81 to find out what type of learner you are. The answers are on page 82.

11 Work in small groups. Discuss how your learning style affects your language learning. What things can you do to learn more effectively? Look at the ideas below and add any others you can think of:

• watching English language films with the subtitles on
• reading stories (in English newspapers, books, magazines) and retelling them
• keeping a vocabulary book and drawing illustrations of each new word

How does a scientist find out to what extent an animal is capable of thinking? What evidence is there that it is able to acquire information about the world and act on it, learning as it goes along?

In 1977 Irene Pepperberg, a recent graduate of Harvard University, decided to investigate the thought processes of another creature by talking to it. In order to do this she would teach a one-year-old African grey parrot named Alex to reproduce the sounds of the English language. 'I thought if he learnt to communicate, I could ask him questions about how he sees the world.'

Pepperberg bought Alex in a Chicago pet store. She let the store's assistant choose him because she didn't want other scientists to say that she had deliberately chosen an especially smart bird. Given that Alex's brain was the size of a walnut, most researchers thought Pepperberg's communication study would be futile. 'Some people actually called me crazy for trying this,' she said.

With Pepperberg's patient teaching, Alex learnt how to imitate almost one hundred English words, including the names of food. He could count to six and had learnt the sounds for seven and eight. But the point was not to see if Alex could learn words by heart. Pepperberg wanted to get inside his mind and learn more about a bird's understanding of the world. She couldn't ask him what he was thinking about, but she could ask him about his knowledge of numbers, shapes and colours.

In one demonstration, Pepperberg placed Alex on a wooden perch in the middle of the room. She then held up a green key and a small green cup for him to look at.

'What's the same?' she asked.

Without hesitation, Alex's beak opened: 'Co-lour.'

'What's different?' Pepperberg asked.

'Shape,' Alex said. His voice had the sound of a cartoon character. But the words – and what can only be called the thoughts – were entirely

his. Many of Alex's cognitive skills, such as his ability to understand the concepts of 'same' and 'different', are rare in the animal world. Very few animals share these skills. But parrots, like humans, live a long time in complex societies. And like humans, these birds must keep track of the dynamics of changing relationships and environments.

'They need to be able to distinguish colours to know when a fruit is ripe or unripe,' Pepperberg explained. 'They need to categorise things – what's edible, what isn't – and to know the shapes of predators. And it helps to have a concept of numbers if you need to keep track of your flock. For a long-lived bird, you can't do all of this with instinct; cognition must be involved.'

In the demonstration, Alex then ran through various tests, distinguishing colours, shapes, sizes, and materials (wool versus wood versus metal). He did some simple arithmetic, such as counting the yellow toy blocks among a pile of mixed coloured blocks. And then, as if to offer final proof of the mind inside his bird's brain, Alex spoke up. 'Talk clearly!' he commanded, when one of the younger birds Pepperberg was also teaching mispronounced the word green. 'Talk clearly!'

Alex knew all the answers himself and was getting bored. 'He's moody,' said Pepperberg, 'so he interrupts the others, or he gives the wrong answer just to be difficult.' Pepperberg was certainly learning more about the mind of a parrot, but like the parent of a troublesome teenager, she was learning the hard way.

Who's a clever bird, then?

11d Keep learning

Real life getting clarification

1 Look at the list of short courses offered by an adult education college. Use a dictionary if you need to. Which of the courses interest you and why?

2 🎧 **2.37** Listen to a telephone conversation between someone enquiring about a course and a college receptionist. Answer the questions.

   1   What kind of course is Ahmad interested in taking?
   2   What course does Liz suggest for him instead? Why?
   3   What does Ahmad decide to do?

3 Look at the expressions used by Ahmad. Which are used for repetition (R) and which are used for explanation (E)?

> ▶ **GETTING CLARIFICATION**
>
> What do you mean by ... ?
> Can you speak up a little?
> Can you explain what ... ?
> I'm not really with you.
> Are you saying that ... ?
> Could you give me an example of ... ?
> What was ... again?
> Hang on a second. That's too much to take in all at once.
> I didn't catch ...
> Did you say ... ?

4 🎧 **2.37** Listen to the conversation again. Complete the sentences in the box that are unfinished.

5 Pronunciation linking in question forms

a 🎧 **2.38** In certain commonly used combinations – *did you, could you, what do you* – the words are strongly linked together. Listen to these examples.

> Are you saying the course is full?   Did you say Tuesday?
> Can you speak up a little?   What do you mean?
> Could you give me an example?

b Work in pairs. Practise saying these sentences.

> Can you explain what you mean?   What are you trying
> Could you repeat that?   to say?
> Did you mean September?   What do you think?

6 Work in pairs. Act out a conversation, enquiring about the course. Then change roles and repeat the conversation.

Student A: You are a prospective student. Choose one of the courses in Exercise 1 or another course you would like to do. Tell Student B your choice. Prepare questions about the course.

Student B: You are a college administrator. Prepare what you are going to say about Student A's chosen course.

ROUSHAM
ADULT EDUCATION CENTRE

COURSE TITLE	FREQUENCY	EXAM COURSE
Basic car mechanics *5 Apr, 10 wks*	1 x 2hrs	✗
Psychology of human behaviour *22 Jan, 18 wks*	1 x 2hrs	✓
Public speaking *11 Apr, 8 wks*	1 x 1.5hrs	✗
First aid *12 Apr, 4 wks*	2 x 1.5 hrs	✓
Desert and jungle survival *1 Mar, 12 wks*	1 x 1.5hrs	✓
Ikebana: Japanese flower arranging *22 Jan, 18 wks*	1 x 2hrs	✗
Art appreciation *5 Apr, 10 wks*	1 x 2hrs	✗
Screenwriting *21 Jan, 18 wks*	1 x 2hrs	✗
Surfing *12 Apr, 6 wks*	1 x 3hrs	✓
Investing in stocks and shares *11 Apr, 8 wks*	1 x 1.5hrs	✗

TALK ABOUT ▶ ACQUIRING KNOWLEDGE ▶ WHY YOU FORGOT ▶ TYPES OF LEARNER ▶ GETTING CLARIFICATION
WRITE ▶ AN EMAIL ABOUT A MISUNDERSTANDING

11e The wrong course

Writing an email about a misunderstanding

1 Work in pairs. Read the email from a student to an adult education college. Answer the questions.

1 What is the misunderstanding about the course?
a the timing   b the level   c the subject
2 How would you describe the student's feelings about the situation?
a angry   b offended   c frustrated
3 How would you describe the tone of the email?
a complaining   b reasonable   c apologetic

Dear Sir / Madam

I enrolled on your course 'car mechanics 1' in August and have attended three sessions. When I originally enquired about the course, I was told that it was suitable for people with no previous knowledge of car mechanics. But in fact everyone else on the course seems to know a lot already. So despite the fact that the lessons generally start with a basic concept, they move very quickly onto more complicated ideas.

I don't blame the teacher. On the contrary, he does his best to explain concepts to me. But I feel that I am just holding everyone else back. They know how an engine works already, whereas I have no background at all in mechanics.

I was going to leave it a couple of weeks more before saying anything, but in the last session I felt so out of my depth that I have decided to write now and ask for a refund. While I appreciate it's not really anyone's fault that this has happened, I hope you will understand how unsatisfactory the situation is for me.

I look forward to hearing from you
Yours faithfully

Karen Redman

---

2 If you were an administrator at the college, how would you react to this email?

3 Writing skill linking contrasting ideas

a Find the words or phrases in the email that link these contrasting ideas.

1 The course should be for beginners. No one else is a beginner.
2 Each lesson starts with a simple idea. It progresses quickly to difficult ideas.
3 The teacher is not at fault. He helps me as much as he can.
4 The other students know a lot. I know nothing.
5 No one is to blame for this. I still feel it is unfair.

b Match these words and phrases to the ones in the email that they could replace.

1 whilst
2 although
3 in actual fact
4 but on the other hand
5 but in reality

c Complete these sentences with appropriate linking phrases.

1 _____ the brochure says the start date is 12th September, the first real class is a week later, on the 19th.
2 The course is advertised as 'practical', _____ you learn a lot of theory as well.
3 _____ the course fee is quite high, it's a great investment because it increases your employment prospects.
4 The course isn't much fun, _____ you would expect a course in lifesaving to be serious.
5 The French conversation class focuses on everyday French, _____ in the A-level French class you cover literature and written French more.
6 Surfing is not an easy skill to learn. _____, you need to have great natural balance and a lot of perseverance.

4 Imagine you enrolled for one of the other courses on page 64. Think of a misunderstanding that occurred with the course. Write an email to the college explaining the misunderstanding and asking for a refund.

5 Exchange letters with your partner and check the following items:

- Does the email make clear what the misunderstanding was?
- Is the tone of the email reasonable?
- Has the writer used linking words and phrases correctly?
- Do you think the email will get the desired response?

TALK ABOUT ▶ ACQUIRING KNOWLEDGE ▶ WHY YOU FORGOT ▶ TYPES OF LEARNER ▶ GETTING CLARIFICATION
WRITE ▶ AN EMAIL ABOUT A MISUNDERSTANDING

65

11f Paraguay shaman

> Paraguay's renowned healers, called 'shamans', have a deep knowledge of local medicinal plants.

Before you watch

1 Work in groups. Look at the photo of the shaman, a traditional tribal healer or doctor and discuss the questions.

1 What do you know about shamans?
2 What techniques do you think they use to heal sick people?

2 You are going to watch a video about medicinal plants. Answer these questions.

1 What problem do you think faces these plants?
2 What solution to the problem might the video suggest?
3 Write down three kinds of people you're going to see in the video.

While you watch

3 Watch the video and check your answers from Exercise 2.

4 Underline the false information in these sentences. Then rewrite the sentences correctly.

1 Before going into the forest, a scientist travels to a local village by car.

2 When they arrive, Gervasio, the local shaman, is collecting plants in the forest.

3 Gervasio and the team set off to look for an insect the scientists are interested in.

4 Gervasio's wife leads the way.

5 The local people eat the root raw.

6 Later, back in the village, Gervasio shows the team a book he has written.

5 Watch the video again and answer the questions.

1 What illnesses are mentioned in the video?

2 How do traditional folk healers in Paraguay help scientists?

3 Why is it important to record shamans' knowledge urgently?

4 Why does Gervasio use chants and prayers before going into the forest?

5 Why are the scientists interested in the Suruvi root?

6 What does the scientists' book set out to do?

6 Number the extracts in the order you hear them.

a Recording and studying Paraguayan plants for possible medical cures is urgent business.
b To reach Gervasio, a group of researchers set out on a long journey through the reserve.
c Somewhere in this forest, maybe in this plant or that herb, there could be a cure for an illness.
d When he feels ready, Gervasio and his wife take the group on the search.
e The rain forests of Paraguay have been a source of medicinal cures for a long time.

After you watch

7 Roleplay interviewing a scientist

Work in pairs.

Student A: Imagine you are a *National Geographic* reporter. You are going to interview the scientist who made the documentary about Gervasio. Use the information below to prepare questions to ask the scientist.

Student B: Imagine you are the scientist who made the documentary about Gervasio. Look at the information below and think about what you are going to say to the reporter.

- the journey to the reserve
- the journey to Tekoha Ryapu
- what it feels like to work with someone like Gervasio
- the importance of Gervasio's knowledge
- what they were able to achieve on this trip
- how the book might help

Act out the interview, then change roles and act out the interview again.

8 Work in groups and discuss these questions.

1 Do you know of any modern medicines that originated from rain forest plants?
2 Do you think traditional medicines from plants are effective?
3 What do you think about other forms of traditional medicine, for example acupuncture, massage therapy, homeopathy?

chant (n) /tʃɑːnt/ a kind of rhythmical song that uses only one or two notes
deforestation (n) /diːfɒrɪsˈteɪʃən/ cutting down trees
folk healer (n) /ˈfəʊk hiːlə/ a person who uses traditional methods to cure illnesses
multiply (v) /ˈmʌltɪplaɪ/ reproduce quickly
renowned (adj) /rɪˈnaʊnd/ famous
reserve (n) /rɪˈzɜːv/ an area of land where plants or animals are officially protected

Grammar

1 Work in pairs. What do you think is the maximum number of languages someone can speak fluently? Does speaking one language help you to learn another?

2 Read the article about polyglot Ziad Fazah. Answer the questions.
1 What is a polyglot?
2 What is Fazah's regular job?
3 How many languages is he really fluent in?

When police in Brazil arrested an illegal immigrant speaking an unrecognisable language, they immediately called Ziad Fazah, the world's greatest linguist. Fazah realized quickly that the man was speaking a dialect used in Afghanistan. With Fazah's help, the man ¹*explain / was able to explain* that he had escaped Afghanistan and was seeking asylum in Brazil. At that time Fazah, originally from the Lebanon, ²*could speak / managed to speak* 54 different languages. He also ³*could get / succeeded in getting* his name into the Brazilian *Guinness World Book of Records* as the world's greatest living polyglot. Fazah used to get quite a lot of work interpreting for the police, but unfortunately they ⁴*couldn't pay / didn't manage to pay* him.

When Fazah was 17, his talents were spotted by the Lebanese government who ⁵*were going to use / would use* him as an interpreter. But soon after, he moved to Brazil with his parents. There he married a Brazilian and began giving private language lessons. Fazah ⁶*would remain / would have remained* unknown, but in 2006 his language abilities were tested on a Spanish television programme and he received international attention. It was at this point that people began to question these abilities. ⁷*Was he really able / Did he really manage* to be fluent in over 50 languages? The programme ⁸*was supposed to show / would have shown* that he could, but the evidence was not so convincing.

3 Complete the extract by underlining the correct form of the verbs.

I CAN
describe past abilities with *could, was able to, managed to* and *succeeded in* ☐
talk about past intentions and predictions with the future in the past ☐

Vocabulary

4 Work in pairs. Complete the passage about learning. The first letter of each missing word has been given for you.

There are many different ways to learn and ¹a_____ knowledge: by ²t_____ and error, from an authority, by reasoning and by ³o_____ – or in other words just watching how something works. Some things, like bringing up children, are more instinctive – you have a gut ⁴f_____ about what is the right way to do things. Some things, like playing a musical instrument, you can ⁵p_____ up as you go along. But there are other things that you need to be taught. For example, you might have a basic ⁶g_____ of mathematics, but still be completely ⁷i_____ of how differential calculus works. For this type of learning, you need an authority – a book or a teacher – that can help you to ⁸e_____ with the subject and understand it.

5 Think of two things that you know how to do (e.g. play an instrument, cook). Tell each other how you learnt to do these things.

I CAN
talk about learning and knowledge ☐

Real life

6 Work in pairs. Match 1–5 to a–e.

1 What do you mean by that?
2 Could you give me an example?
3 Can you speak up a little?
4 What was that again?
5 I'm not really with you.

a I didn't catch that.
b I don't really understand.
c For instance?
d Can you explain that?
e I can't hear you very clearly.

7 Think of something you can do, but your partner probably can't. Give your partner some instructions. As you receive the instructions ask for clarification and repetition.

I CAN
get clarification by asking someone to repeat or explain ☐

Speaking

8 Work in small groups. Read the example below. Tell each other about a similar (good or bad) learning experience you have had.

At school we had a fantastic art teacher who was able to inspire everyone, whether they had natural artistic talent or not. He had really good ideas, such as …

Unit 12 The economy

A woman in a pink mink coat next to her pink Rolls Royce, Hong Kong
Photo by Jodi Cobb

FEATURES

1 Work in pairs. Look at the photo. What does a matching luxury car and fur coat say about a person? Do rich people in your country like to show off their wealth?

2 🎧 **2.39** Listen to an economist defining poverty and wealth. Answer the questions.

1 What are the two definitions of being poor that use percentages (ten per cent and 60 per cent)?
2 How can you be rich without having a lot of money?

3 Match the word (1–7) with its synonym (a–g).

1	afford	a	poor
2	hard up	b	have enough money
3	income	c	expensive
4	loaded	d	cheap
5	pricey	e	very rich
6	reasonable	f	comfortable
7	well off	g	earnings

4 Work in small groups. How would <u>you</u> define *rich* and *poor*? What proportion of the population is rich in your country?

12a Saving for a rainy day

Reading

1 Work in pairs. What do you know about Norway: its landscape, its people, its industry? Look at the photo below for ideas.

2 Read the article. In what ways is Norway a 'rich' country?

3 Complete these summaries of each paragraph using as many words as necessary in each space. Then compare answers with another pair.

1 For a long time, Norway has had a better _____ than other countries.
2 The three reasons for Norway's success are: big oil reserves, _____ and _____ .
3 For Norwegians being rich means _____ .
4 Norway is saving money for _____ .

4 Do you think that the Norwegians are right to save their money? Why? / Why not?

Grammar focus adverbs *only, just, even*

> ▶ **FOCUS ADVERBS *ONLY, JUST, EVEN***

only
Only Luxembourg and a couple of other countries are richer.

just
Just 80 years ago, Norwegians were emigrating to the USA.

even
This isn't even a competition anymore.

For further information and practice, see page 90.

5 Work in pairs. Look at the sentences in the grammar box. Which of these statements (a–c) is true of *only, just* and *even*?

a they always come directly after the word they are emphasising
b they always come directly after the main verb
c they always come directly before the word they are emphasising

6 Find other examples of these words in the article. Do they follow the same rule?

SAVING FOR A RAINY DAY

Come on, Norway; this isn't even a competition anymore! For the last eight years, Norway has registered the highest quality of life among the world's nations. It is one of the wealthiest countries in the world – only Luxembourg and a couple of others are richer. Norwegians can also expect to get a good education, find the job they want – unemployment is only 2.5 per cent – enjoy good health and live a long life. People say the prisons are quite comfortable too!

Norway has not always been a rich country. Just 80 years ago Norwegians were emigrating to the USA in their thousands in search of a better life. The rise in oil prices in the 1970s changed all that. But Norway's success is not only the result of its huge reserves of oil. Other countries have had such riches and squandered them. It is also due to the Norwegians' natural thrift and their strong work ethic.

When you arrive in Oslo for the first time, don't expect to be met with Dubai-style skyscrapers, entrepreneurs in designer suits and rows of Ferraris and Porsches. Norway may be rich, but it is modest in its wealth. Norwegians also work hard and are always near the top in surveys of global worker productivity rates. But in today's high-tech world where work seems to follow us wherever we go, the people of Norway are redefining what wealth means. Laws just recently passed by the government emphasise the importance of family and time off, offering generous maternity and paternity leave, subsidised childcare and long holidays as well.

Also, the country is saving for the future. Every dollar earned from oil is put straight into what is now the world's biggest pension fund – worth over $200 billion. Extraordinarily, none of this money is allowed to be spent on state infrastructure projects. It is not even invested in new schools and hospitals. But at a time when most other countries are wondering how they will finance the pensions of a growing retired population, Norway is sitting pretty.

leave (n) /liːv/ time off from work
sitting pretty (v) /ˌsɪtɪŋ ˈprɪti/ in a good or comfortable situation
squander (v) /ˈskwɒndə/ waste
thrift (n) /θrɪft/ carefulness when spending money

7 Discuss the meaning of each sentence (1–8). Then match each of the sentences to the clause or sentence that follows it (a–h).

1 Only visitors think Norway is expensive.
2 Visitors only think Norway is expensive.
3 Visitors think only Norway is expensive.
4 Among the Scandinavian countries, I have visited Norway just once.
5 Among the Scandinavian countries, I have visited just Norway.
6 Even fathers are given time off to be with their new babies.
7 Fathers are even given time off to be with their new babies.
8 Fathers are given time off even to be with their new babies.

a Of course mothers are given a lot of time off too.
b I have visited the others several times.
c They are also given time off to move house and to look after elderly parents.
d … but all the Scandinavian countries are expensive.
e … but actually it's quite reasonable.
f I haven't visited the others at all.
g The residents themselves find it reasonable.
h This is in addition to the extra money the state gives them.

8 Complete these sentences by putting a focus adverb in the right place. Then compare answers with your partner. Tell them whether these facts are true of your country.

1 Many people work long hours during the week, so they see their children at weekends.
2 People with university degrees are finding it difficult to get jobs these days.
3 For most people a job is a way to make money, not something they particularly enjoy.
4 The rich represent about five per cent of the population.
5 You don't see extreme poverty. Poor people usually have food and somewhere to live.
6 The state pension gives you enough to live on, but not to live very comfortably.

Grammar focus adverbs *too, as well, also*

9 Work in pairs. Look at the position of *too* and *as well* in these sentences. Find the same sentences in the article, but with the word *also*. What do you notice about the position of *also*?

1 Norwegians can expect to get a good education too.
2 It is due to the Norwegians' natural thrift as well.
3 Norwegians work hard too.
4 The country is saving for the future too.

> **FOCUS ADVERBS *TOO, AS WELL, ALSO***

sentence + *too*	*also* + main verb
sentence + *as well*	be + *also*
Also, + sentence	auxiliary verb + *also* + main verb

For further information and practice, see page 90.

10 Look at the grammar box. Which patterns from the box can you find in the article? Underline them. Then compare your answers with your partner.

11 Rewrite the sentences twice using one of the focus adverbs given each time. Compare your answers with another pair.

1 Norwegians are happy that the country is saving for the future, but they would like to see the government increase spending on healthcare. (*as well / also*)
2 Most countries have high public borrowing and a lot of debt. Norway has neither. (*too / also*)
3 Teachers in Norway receive a good salary and if they teach 'heavy' subjects, they get extra payments. (*also / too*)
4 Artists can get a grant – not a loan – from the government of around $20,000 a year and support with childcare. (*also / as well*)
5 The prices for food and drink seem very high to outsiders and fuel is expensive. However, house prices are relatively low and so property is a good investment. (*too / also*)
6 Nurses in Norway get 42 weeks' maternity leave on full pay. They have access to the hospital kindergarten when they return to work. (*as well / also*)

Vocabulary money

12 Look at the verbs below and find the right noun in Exercise 11 to make phrases with the same meaning.

1 pay money = make a _____
2 invest money = make an _____
3 borrow more money = increase your _____
4 spend less money = reduce your _____
5 be lent money = take out a _____
6 owe money = have a _____
7 earn money = receive a _____
8 be given money (by the government) = receive a _____

Speaking

13 Work in pairs. Prepare questions to ask each other about the economy in your country or countries (the cost of living, work-life balance, government spending, government grants for certain professions, etc.). Use the items in Exercise 11 to help you get ideas.

14 Now change partners with another pair and ask and answer your questions.

12b Don't do it yourself

Vocabulary domestic help

1 Work in pairs. Which of the domestic workers listed below is the woman in the photo? Discuss what each of the other jobs involve.

> au pair   child minder
> cleaner   cook   dog walker
> gardener   handyman   maid
> nanny   personal shopper

2 Discuss these questions about the jobs in Exercise 1.

1 Have you done any of these jobs yourself?
2 Have you (or your family) employed anyone in these roles?
3 Which jobs involve the greatest skill?
4 Would you like to do any of them? Why? / Why not?

Listening

3 🎧 **2.40** Listen to the interview with the author of a book entitled *The Servant Economy*. Answer the questions.

1 How many domestic workers are there in Britain today? Who are they?
2 Does the author think the growth of the servant economy is a good thing or a bad thing?

4 🎧 **2.40** Listen again and identify:

1 which jobs from Exercise 1 the speakers mention
2 what other jobs are mentioned
3 whether many people or only the rich employ such workers

> ▶ **WORDBUILDING** *the* + adjective
>
> We can refer to a group of people using *the* + adjective. *the rich*, *the poor*
>
> For further information and practice, see Workbook page 143.

5 Work in pairs. What did the interviewer find strange about the person who hired a Christmas tree installer? Do you agree with her?

6 Complete Hilaire Belloc's quotation. Do you agree with it? Or do you think it is lazy to employ people to do all your domestic chores?

> " It is the duty of the _____ man to give _____ to the artisan. *Hilaire Belloc* "

Grammar causative *have* and *get*

7 Look at the forms in bold in sentences (a–d). Answer the questions (1–2). Then look at the transcript on page 94 and find one more example of each type of phrase.

a Thirty years ago, the idea of **getting a worker to hand wash** your car would have been unthinkable.
b Nowadays, you can **have it washed** inside and out for as little as £6.
c You don't have to be rich **to have a cleaner come** once a week.
d Another example would be **getting your windows cleaned** every few months.

1 Which phrases mean someone does a job for you?
2 Which phrases tell you who actually does the job?

> ▶ CAUSATIVE *HAVE* and *GET*
>
> ***have/get*** + something + past participle
> *I had/got the fence fixed yesterday.*
>
> ***have*** + someone + infinitive (without *to*)
> *I had the gardener fix the fence.*
>
> ***get*** + someone + *to* + infinitive
> *I got the gardener to fix the fence.*
>
> For further information and practice, see page 90.

8 Look at the grammar box. Then complete this passage about a survey into paying people to help with domestic chores.

> Nearly half of all homes in Britain get outside staff [1] _____ (do) their domestic chores for an average of six hours per week. The most common reasons that people gave for having someone [2] _____ (help) around the house were their own long working hours and to avoid arguments with their partner. A third of people said if they didn't have help, nothing would get [3] _____ (do). The most popular jobs to pay for are having the house [4] _____ (clean) regularly, getting someone [5] _____ (do) the garden and having a handyman [6] _____ (fix) things when they are broken. Some of these services do not come cheap either. People pay up to £500 per week to have a personal assistant [7] _____ (organise) their affairs or have their young baby [8] _____ (look) after.

9 Look at these things that a rich couple gets other people to do for them. Complete the sentences with causative forms. Note that you can complete the sentences in two different ways.

1 When they had a party last month, someone organised everything for them.
They _____ everything for them. (get)
2 A personal trainer takes their children to the park to play football.
They _____ to the park to play football. (have)
3 A driver picks their children up from school each day.
They _____ from school each day. (have)
4 A travel consultant chooses their holidays for them.
They _____ for them. (have)
5 A nanny looks after their children when they are on holiday.
They _____ when they are on holiday. (get)
6 Someone even packs their bags for them, I think!
They even _____ for them, I think. (get)

10 Write down one thing that you would never consider getting someone else to do and one thing you would always get someone else to do. Compare your list with your partner.

11 Pronunciation the sounds /ʃ/, /tʃ/, /ʒ/ and /dʒ/

a 🔊 **2.41** Listen carefully to how the underlined letters are pronounced in the following words. Then practise saying them with your partner.

/ʃ/	/tʃ/	/ʒ/	/dʒ/
carwa<u>sh</u>	<u>ch</u>ores	deci<u>s</u>ion	<u>ch</u>ange
<u>sh</u>elves	ri<u>ch</u>er	gara<u>g</u>e	colle<u>g</u>e
<u>sh</u>opper	wat<u>ch</u>	plea<u>s</u>ure	fri<u>dg</u>e

b 🔊 **2.42** Listen to these words. Discuss which of the four sounds above each one contains. Then practise saying them.

> agent   arrange   champagne   cheese
> choice   fashion   general   January   sugar
> television   usual

Vocabulary and speaking

12 Work in pairs. How many DIY jobs can you make by matching verbs in A with nouns in B?

A assemble clean	**B** a bed a carpet
decorate do	a picture a tap
fit fix hang	a wall some curtains
plaster put up	some shelves
tile	the bathroom
	the garden the roof

13 Look at the flat in the photo. First make a list of all the things that need to be done before you can live in it. Then decide what you will do yourself and what you will get professional help to do. Explain your plans to another pair.

TALK ABOUT ▶ THE ECONOMY IN YOUR COUNTRY ▶ GETTING THINGS DONE ▶ GIFT GIVING AND EXCHANGE ▶ NEGOTIATING
WRITE ▶ A REPORT

73

12c The gift economy

Reading

1 Look at the title of the article. How do you think a gift economy works?

2 Read the article and see if you were right. What three illustrations of the gift economy at work does the author give?

3 Read the article again. Choose the correct option (a–c).

1 The false understanding of human nature mentioned is that we are all trying to:
   a compete to get as much as we can.
   b be individuals.
   c keep from being hungry.
2 Hunter-gatherers:
   a had plenty and needed plenty.
   b had little and needed little.
   c had plenty and needed little.
3 American companies found it difficult to recruit Japanese employees because they:
   a couldn't offer good conditions.
   b couldn't offer job security.
   c didn't understand Japanese culture.
4 The message of the 4th paragraph is that Japanese employers are involved in:
   a organising employees' holidays.
   b their employees' lives.
   c the quality of employees' work.
5 According to the writer of the article, the Internet has made it easier for people to:
   a get to know each other.
   b discuss problems.
   c give and receive help.
6 The message of the last paragraph is that big organisations need to:
   a be made smaller.
   b think about the common good.
   c give more of their profits back.

4 Look at these pairs of words from the article. Which definition (a or b) matches each word?

1 gain / reward
   a profit   b compensation
2 strive / thrive
   a do well   b do your best
3 common / mutual
   a shared by two or more groups   b shared by many
4 abundance / excess
   a too much   b plenty
5 prospects / aspects
   a future possibilities   b characteristics
6 accuracy / promptness
   a being precise   b being on time

5 Work in small groups. Tell each other what kind of relationship exists between employer and employees in your country. Is it more like the American system or the Japanese relationship?

Critical thinking signposts to key information

6 There are certain phrases that act as signposts for key information (just given or about to follow). Find the following phrases in the article and then draw out the key information they refer to.

> at the heart of …   not only …   rather …
> the main …   the real …

7 Work in pairs. Compare your answers. Did you agree on what the key information was?

Word focus *hard*

8 Work in pairs. Find three expressions in the article containing the word *hard*. Discuss their meaning.

9 The sentences below contain six more expressions with the word *hard*. Work with a partner and try to guess the meaning of each one from its context. Then compare your answers with another pair.

1 I'm sorry the boss didn't like your idea and preferred mine. **No hard feelings**, I hope.
2 Fran and Chris are pretty **hard up** these days. He lost his job two weeks ago and she only works part-time.
3 **Hard luck** about the job. I'm sure you'll get other opportunities though.
4 Kate's feeling pretty **hard done by**. The college didn't accept her because her French wasn't good enough, even though she's spending a year in France before the course starts.
5 Don't **be hard on** Jake. It's not his fault he was late – his car broke down.
6 I tried to get him to sympathise with our situation because we're newly established, but he's a pretty **hard-headed** businessman.

Speaking

10 Work in groups of three. Discuss the customs of gift giving and exchange that you are familiar with. Think about:

- specific occasions (e.g. weddings, dinner parties)
- visiting people
- help and favours
- business gifts
- returning home after a trip abroad

The banking crisis of 2008 again raised concerns that our economy is based too much on individual greed. Such an economic model, critics say, comes from a false understanding of human nature. Human society is not made up of individuals pursuing private gain through competition with each other. The real essence of human nature lies in the social bonds that we make through family, friendships, professional associations and local communities. These bonds produce a sense of common purpose and shared values, in which groups of people strive for the things that are for the common good: a sound education, a pleasant environment to live in, a healthy population. It is this idea of shared social interests that is at the heart of the gift economy.

Gift economies thrived in earlier times when people lived in a world of greater abundance and when their wants were fewer. Stone Age hunter-gatherers had shelter and enough food and did not need many possessions – a few weapons for hunting and clothing to keep warm. They helped each other by sharing food and tools without any expectation of payment or immediate reward. But this is not only an idea that applies to a more primitive way of life. There are also many recent examples of the gift economy at work.

In the past, American companies operating in Japan found it difficult to attract Japanese recruits, even though, compared with Japanese employers, they offered more generous wages, shorter work hours and better promotion prospects. But these factors were traditionally not so important to Japanese employees, who did not think of their services as being 'bought'. Rather, they felt they were entering into a long-term – 'gift exchange' – relationship with their employer, which was of mutual benefit.

This relationship had many aspects. At its most basic it involved the simple exchange of physical gifts. For example, if the employee got married, the company sent a gift and even a departmental manager to represent it at the wedding.

Another company gift which is still popular among Japanese employees is the yearly company vacation. On these organised weekends co-workers share dormitories, eat together and visit the same attractions, largely at the company's expense. For their part, the main gift given by the employees to their company is their hard work and this is why each Japanese employee gives such great attention to accuracy, quality in their work and promptness in its delivery. Even the simplest tasks are carried out with extraordinary care.

Elsewhere, the Internet is facilitating the re-emergence of the gift economy. Neighbourhood groups use online networks to share tools and skills. Someone who needs a long ladder to repair their roof does not need to go out and buy one; they simply put a message up on the neighbourhood discussion board and soon a neighbour will offer theirs. They will probably even help them with the repair, because helping and giving is part of human nature. Via the Internet, knowledge and advice can be shared on almost everything, from how a nuclear reactor works to how to plan your holiday or build your own canoe.

All this is very well, but these are hard times: helping our neighbour with his roof isn't going to pay the bills, I hear you say. But in an indirect way it is. The point is that by stressing the co-operative side of human nature, the gift economy helps us all. It keeps in check the excesses of big commercial organisations that seek to exploit situations for their own gain. So the big supermarket chains must understand that it is in the common interest not to force small shopkeepers out of business. Big industrial farms must realise that they cannot go on intensively farming the land until there is nothing left in it. Other large companies should not always seek to drive the hardest bargain possible with their suppliers, but just pay them fairly. That is the real lesson of the gift economy.

The Gift Economy

TALK ABOUT ▶ THE ECONOMY IN YOUR COUNTRY ▶ GETTING THINGS DONE ▶ GIFT GIVING AND EXCHANGE ▶ NEGOTIATING
WRITE ▶ A REPORT

75

12d The bottom line

Real life negotiating

1 Read this advice about negotiating. Do you agree with it? How does it relate to your own experience?

> Herb Cohen was a famous negotiator. His advice was to 'Care, really care … but not that much.' In other words, don't become too emotionally involved. The other person will see how much you want the thing and then you will be at a disadvantage.

2 🎧 **2.43** Listen to a woman who is trying to negotiate a lease on a building for her young business with a letting agent. Answer the questions.

1 How much does each person seem to care about agreeing the lease?
2 On what point do they have trouble agreeing?
3 What does the woman suggest to get around this problem?
4 How does the negotiation end?

3 🎧 **2.43** Work in pairs. Listen again and complete the expressions in the box.

> ▶ **NEGOTIATING**
>
> To be honest, it's absolutely ¹ _____ .
> A key thing for us is how long we'd be ² _____ the lease.
> I was hoping we could ³ _____ .
> If you look at it from our point of view, we're a ⁴ _____ .
> Let's face it, fifteen years is ⁵ _____ .
>
> If your client could ⁶ _____ on that …
> I think what you have to appreciate is that our client's main concern is …
> At the end of the day, it gives them some security.
> To tell you the truth, that's why the rent ⁷ _____ .
>
> That's a bit of a sticking point.
> Is there not some way around that?
> Perhaps if we signed … , then we could pay …
> If I were in your shoes, I think I'd just ⁸ _____ .
> When all's said and done, it has to ⁹ _____ for you.

4 Work in pairs. Look at the expressions in the box and discuss which are used to:

• say what the important thing is
• be direct
• talk about an obstacle to the agreement
• ask the other person to see your side

5 How do you think each person could have done better in the negotiation? Tell your partner.

6 Pronunciation sentence stress in idiomatic phrases

a 🎧 **2.44** Listen to these phrases again and underline the one or two words that are most stressed in each phrase.

1 To be honest …
2 A key thing for us is …
3 Let's face it …
4 At the end of the day, …
5 To tell you the truth …

b 🎧 **2.45** Work in pairs. Look at these other phrases. Mark the words where you think the stress falls. Then listen and check.

1 The bottom line for us is …
2 The long and short of it is …
3 The fact of the matter is …
4 One thing that's bothering me is …
5 To be frank, …
6 Am I right in thinking that … ?

7 You are spending eight months in a foreign country and want to get a car to use while you are there. You see a second-hand one advertised in the newspaper. It seems to be exactly what you are looking for. Work in pairs and negotiate the sale of the car. Student A look at page 81; Student B look at page 82.

TALK ABOUT ▶ THE ECONOMY IN YOUR COUNTRY ▶ GETTING THINGS DONE ▶ GIFT GIVING AND EXCHANGE ▶ **NEGOTIATING**
WRITE ▶ A REPORT

12e This is what I propose

Writing a report

1 Work in pairs. Look at this quotation by the French mathematician, Blaise Pascal. Discuss what he was saying about the art of writing.

> 'I'm sorry I wrote you such a long letter; I didn't have time to write a short one.'

2 Look at these elements of a good report. Which is the one referred to by Blaise Pascal?

> clear aims   clear recommendation   conciseness
> good organisation

3 Read the report below. What is the aim of the report? What is the recommendation? Tell your partner.

Summary

I visited our potential new offices at 1 Paradise Square yesterday, 4 May, and was very impressed. They seem ideal for our needs, but the lease is for fifteen years, much longer than the six or seven we agreed at our last meeting. These are the details:

Advantages
- 200m² of flexible office space
- Low rent – only £40,000 per annum
- Central location – close to shops and train station
- Serviced – cleaning, repairs are included

Disadvantages
- Long lease – fifteen years
- Service charge quite high – £10,000 per annum

Recommendation

I propose taking these offices. We have been looking for five months and these are the best offices I have seen at a reasonable rent. If we have to leave before the end of the lease, I am confident that the remaining part of the lease can be sold to a new tenant.

4 Writing skill sub-headings and bullet points

a The writer of the report has organised it into sections using sub-headings and bullet points. What do you notice about the language after each bullet point?

b Read this first paragraph of a report on a language training course. Rewrite the report, dividing it into two sections, with subheadings. Then break the points in the second section into bullet points.

> Last month the company sent me on a two-week 'professional English' course at Falcon Business Language Training in London. I stayed with a host family in west London. Although the course did not focus on my particular job as an engineer very much, it was well organised. On the positive side, I was made to speak English all the time, both in the school and with my host family. The teachers were very professional and had a good knowledge of the business world. We were put in small groups of three to four students which meant that we got a lot of individual attention.

c Work in pairs. Compare your answers. Did you organise your reports in the same way?

5 Now write the second half of the report including any negative comments and a recommendation. When you have finished, exchange your report with your partner.

6 Read your partner's report. Check the following:

- Is the report concise and clear?
- Has it been broken down into clear sections using sub-headings and bullet points?
- Does it end with a clear recommendation?

TALK ABOUT ► THE ECONOMY IN YOUR COUNTRY ► GETTING THINGS DONE ► GIFT GIVING AND EXCHANGE ► NEGOTIATING
WRITE ► A REPORT

77

12f Japan

It is a land of dual identities.

Before you watch

1 Work in groups. Look at the photos and discuss the questions.

   1 What do the photos show? Describe each photo.
   2 What two identities do you think the caption refers to?

2 Work in pairs. Write down things you associate with Japan.

While you watch

3 Watch the video and check your ideas from Exercise 2. Which of the things that you wrote down appeared in the video?

4 Watch the first part of the video (to 02.04). What do these numbers and dates refer to?

   1 127 million
   2 4
   3 35 million
   4 1868
   5 1941
   6 1945

5 Watch the second part of the video (02.05 to the end). Answer the questions.

   1 What gave Japan political stability after the war?

   2 What has helped it become a world leader in technology, manufacturing and finance?

   3 What three things does the tea ceremony emphasise?
      a
      b
      c
   4 Who did painters like Hiroshige influence?

6 Match the sentence beginnings (1–5) with the endings (a–e).

   1 Japan is a country that harmonises the forces of what is Western and modern
   2 The bustling urban area of greater Tokyo is
   3 It looked to the West for a new, more modern
   4 Although it is a land of few natural resources, Japan has become
   5 Beyond the bullet trains and neon of Tokyo,

   a with those that are traditional Japanese.
   b political and industrial model.
   c there lies a rich cultural tradition.
   d the largest metropolitan area on Earth.
   e one of the most industrialised countries in the world.

7 Work in pairs. Describe the snow scene painting by Hiroshige.

After you watch

8 Roleplay a conversation between two different generations

Work in pairs.

Student A: Imagine you grew up in a small village in pre-war Japan. Look at the information below and think about what you are going to say to your grandchild.

- what life was like (the work you did, how you travelled around, the food you ate, etc.)
- the differences between life then and now
- the war years

Student B: Imagine you are a young Japanese business person talking to one of your grandparents. Look at the information below and think about what you are going to say to him / her.

- what life is like in the city (the work you do, how you travel to work, the food you eat, etc.)
- how you combine modern and traditional life in the city

Act out the conversation. Compare life in Japan pre- and post-war. When you have finished, change roles and act out the conversation again.

9 Work in groups and discuss the questions.

   1 How has your country changed culturally and economically in the last 100 years?
   2 Do cultural traditions always support economic innovation?
   3 Are economic advances always beneficial? Why? / Why not?

bustling (adj) /ˈbʌslɪŋ/ busy
feudal (adj) /ˈfjuːdəl/ relating to a social system where most people work and fight for more powerful people who own the land
forge (v) /fɔːdʒ/ make something in difficult conditions
glitz (n) /ɡlɪts/ the quality of being shiny and superficially attractive
neon (n) /ˈniːɒn/ a kind of bright artificial light
raid (n) /reɪd/ a quick attack
shrine (n) /ʃraɪn/ a place where people go to meditate or pray
ubiquitous (adj) /juːˈbɪkwɪtəs/ present everywhere
wrestling (n) /ˈreslɪŋ/ a sport where the contestants try to throw each other on the ground

Grammar

1 Read the article and say why Japan has had a problem of relative poverty in recent years.

2 Compete the sentences by inserting the focus adverb into the right place in each sentence.

When we picture poverty we often think of people in under-developed countries without food or shelter. [1] But the so called advanced economies of the world have their share of poverty (even). [2] Japan, for example, a few decades ago was enjoying an economic boom (just). [3] Yet by 2000 it had one of the highest rates of relative poverty among developed countries, with the USA having a higher rate (only). [4] One reason was that Japan had one of the highest rates of non-regular workers (also). This means people who are working without proper social protection. [5] An increasingly elderly population – people who were not actively working – contributed to the problem (as well). Making savings last when you live to be over 90 is a problem that people in many developed countries will face in the coming years. [6] It is beginning to be a problem already (even).

3 Put the verbs in the right form to complete this advice to people who are long-term unemployed.

1 CV. The first thing to do is to rewrite your CV and then get it _____ (check) by an expert. Make sure that it includes activities that you have done while you have been unemployed.

2 Interview. Practise your interview technique. Have a friend _____ (play) the part of the interviewer and get them _____ (ask) you tricky questions.

3 Appearance. Try to look smart when you go for a job. Get your hair _____ (cut) and make sure your clothes are suitable. Again, get a friend _____ (help) you with this.

4 Job seeking. Telephone employers and go to see them in person. Show enthusiasm and get them _____ (see) that you are keen to work. Even offer to work for a trial period without pay!

I CAN	
use focus adverbs to add emphasis	☐
talk about things that others do for me with *have* and *get*	☐

Vocabulary

4 Find a synonym or close synonym in B for each word/expression in A.

A	B
hard up	paint
hang	child-minder
decorate	earnings
borrow from the bank	reasonable
cheap	take out a loan
income	put up
nanny	poor
owe money	have a debt

5 Work in pairs. Make a list of luxuries and domestic help that you think most people can afford now and again.

I CAN	
talk about money and the economy	☐
talk about getting domestic jobs done	☐

Real life

6 Work in pairs. Put this conversation between a travel agent (TA) and customer (C) into the right order.

TA: To tell you the truth, they're not the kind of hotels you can negotiate with.

TA: So we're suggesting one week in the north of the island and one week in the south. Is this the kind of holiday you were looking for?

TA: OK. I'll give them a call and see what I can do.

TA: I understand that and if I were in your shoes, I think I'd just go for it. At the end of the day, you only get one honeymoon.

TA: What you have to appreciate is that you've chosen two top hotels which aren't cheap.

C: I was hoping we could negotiate the price.

C: I know they aren't, but the key thing for us is to have nice accommodation.

C: Perhaps if we stayed at just one of them for the full two weeks we could get a better deal.

C: Yes it is, but to be honest it's much more expensive than we expected.

7 Take the roles of travel agent and customer and finish the negotiation.

I CAN	
state my position and negotiate from it	☐

Speaking

8 Work in small groups. Do you think the idea below for a domestic service would work? Think of another idea. Then tell it to others in the class.

What about offering a cooking service where busy couples can have a meal prepared for them at home rather eating out or buying a takeaway?

UNIT 8e Exercise 4, page 29

- write to the university and ask them to speak to students about being considerate neighbours
- threaten to call the police if the students make noise after midnight
- have a friendly meeting with the students to explain your point of view
- complain to the local council and ask them to put pressure on the university to find another solution

UNIT 9c Exercise 10, page 38

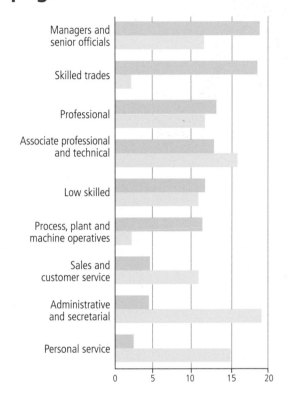

UNIT 12d Exercise 7, page 76

Student A

You want to buy this car. It is a seven-year-old VW Golf and the advertised price is £3,000. It is in good condition but has a lot of miles 'on the clock' (100,000). Obviously you would like to get it for less, if you can. The problem is you have been looking for a long time and want to get a car quickly so that you can drive to work each day.

UNIT 11c Exercise 10, page 62

Quiz

Ask each other these questions and make a note of the answers. Then look at the key on page 82 to see what type of learner you are. Discuss if you agree with this.

1 WHEN I STUDY GRAMMAR I LEARN BEST BY ...
   A reading clear rules   B writing down examples
   C putting it into practice in conversation

2 IN LESSONS, I PREFER ...
   A discussing   B looking at pictures, maps, diagrams or videos
   C doing something practical

3 I REMEMBER NEW VOCABULARY BEST WHEN IT IS ACCOMPANIED BY ...
   A a clear definition   B an image   C a demonstration

4 IF I AM DISTRACTED IN CLASS, I USUALLY ...
   A hum or sing to myself   B make little drawings in my book
   C play with a pen or pencil

5 WHEN LEARNING A NEW SKILL, I PREFER ...
   A someone to explain it to me   B someone to demonstrate it
   C just to get on with it myself

6 WHEN I'M NOT SURE HOW TO SPELL A WORD, I ...
   A say the word aloud to myself   B try to visualise it in my mind
   C write down different versions

7 I PREFER TO READ STORIES WITH LOTS OF ...
   A dialogue and conversation   B descriptive passages
   C action or adventure

8 I PROBABLY LEARN MOST WHEN I'M ...
   A listening to others speak English
   B watching an English film or documentary
   C trying to use English myself

UNIT 8b Exercise 10, page 25

1   false
2   true
3   half-true – it does increase life expectancy but
    no one can say how much
4   true
5   false – the Zebra fish can heal its own heart, but
    not humans – yet!
6   true

UNIT 11c Exercise 10, page 62

Answers to quiz

Mostly As – this means you have an auditory learning
style. In other words you remember best when you
hear things.

Mostly Bs – this means you have a visual learning
style. In other words you remember best when you
see things.

Mostly Cs – this means you have a kinaesthetic
learning style. In other words you remember best
when you do things or when things are acted out.

UNIT 12d Exercise 7, page 76
Student B

You want to sell this car. It is a seven-year-old VW
Golf and the advertised price is £3,000. It is in
good condition but has a lot of miles 'on the clock'
(100,000). You would like to get as close to the asking
price as you can. However, it has been advertised for
two months and you would like to sell it soon.

UNIT 7
Mixed conditional sentences
Form

	If-clause	Main clause
First conditional	*If* + present simple	*will* + infinitive without *to*
	*If it **rains**, the drought **will end**.*	
Second conditional	*If* + past simple	*would/could/might* + infinitive without *to*
	*If everyone **used** their own shopping bags, there **wouldn't be** so much plastic waste.*	
Third conditional	*If* + past perfect	*would/could/might* have + past participle
	*If they **had saved** more water, there **wouldn't have been** a drought.*	
Mixed second and third conditional	*If* + past simple	*would have* + past participle
	*If the policy **worked**, the government **wouldn't have needed** extra food.*	
Mixed third and second conditionals	*If* + past perfect	*would/could/might* + infinitive without *to*
	*If the water **hadn't been stored**, there **wouldn't be** a harvest this year.*	

Remember, we can use *if* in two positions:
- *If*-clause first: *If we use less water, we should be able to provide enough for the whole population.*
- Main clause first: *We should be able to provide enough water for the whole population if we use less water.*

When the *if*-clause is at the beginning of the sentence, we use a comma to separate it from the main clause.

Use
First conditional
We use the first conditional to talk about a possible future action or situation. We can also use it to talk about things that are generally true.
*If they **pollute** the water, we **won't be able** to drink it.* (It's possible that they will pollute the water in the future. Then we won't be able to drink the water.)

Second conditional
We use the second conditional to talk about unreal or imagined (hypothetical) situations in the present or future.
*If they **changed** their environmental views, perhaps they **would get** the contract.* (This is an imagined situation in the future.)
Note that when we use the past simple with *if*, it refers to the present or future. It <u>does not</u> refer to the past. We can also use *could* and *might* instead of *would* in the main clause. We use *could* or *might* to talk about events that are possible but not certain.
*If you visited the polluted region, you **could** see the contamination quite clearly.*

*Fossil fuels **might not** run out if people didn't use scarce resources.*

Third conditional
We use the third conditional to talk about situations or events in the past that did not happen and the hypothetical consequence or result of the imagined past situation.
*If they **had built** the dam, those villages **wouldn't have flooded**.* (But they didn't build the dam and the villages were flooded.)

We can use *could/might (not) have* to speculate on a possible consequence of the imagined past situation.
*If they had built the dam, those villages **might not** have flooded.* (They did build the dam, and it's possible that the villages wouldn't have been flooded but we are not certain.)

Mixed conditionals
We use mixed conditionals to talk about unreal situations when the *if* clause and the main clause don't refer to the same time.

We use mixed second and third conditionals to talk about an imagined situation in the present or future with the hypothetical past result or consequence.
*If the pro-forest organisation **didn't exist**, more of the Amazon forests **would have disappeared**.* (But the organisation does exist, and so more of the Amazon forests didn't disappear.)

We use mixed third and second conditionals to talk about an imagined situation or action in the past, with the imagined consequence in the present or future.
*If the activists **hadn't intervened**, the Amazon **would be** much smaller now.* (But the activists did intervene, so the Amazon is bigger than it would have been without their help.)

Practice
1 Complete the sentences. Use mixed conditionals.

1 Rafa went to the summit meeting, but he didn't say anything because he didn't know the correct information.
If Rafa <u>had known</u> (know) the correct information, I'm sure he <u>would have said</u> (say) something.

2 They didn't dam the river because people protested about it.
If people _____ (not protest) about it, the river _____ (be) dammed today.

3 The organisation was looking for someone who knows about the environment. Katrin doesn't know about environment, so she didn't apply for the job.
Katrin _____ (apply) for the job if she _____ (know) about the environment.

4 They need people with experience of conservation, but I haven't got any.
If I _____ (have), I _____ (join) them.

5 I worked hard on the mining project, so I felt I deserved a rest.
   If I _____ (not work) hard on the project, I _____ (be) tired.

6 You were writing reports last week. You're feeling very tired today.
   If you _____ (not write) so many reports, you _____ (not feel) so tired today.

wish, would rather and if only
Form

wish / if only + noun/pronoun + past simple
I wish I knew more about the proposal.
If only I knew more about the proposal.

wish / if only + noun/pronoun + past perfect
I wish he hadn't signed up to the agreement.
If only he hadn't signed up to the agreement.

wish / if only + noun/pronoun + would + infinitive (without to)
I wish they would approve the plan.
If only they would approve the plan.

would rather + infinitive (without to)
They would rather save the rain forest than mine for oil.

would rather + object + past simple
The company would rather you proposed a more energy efficient solution.

Note that when we use the verb *to be*, we use *was* in everyday speech; we use *were* in formal speech and writing, for example:
• Informal spoken: *I wish I was on holiday now.*
• Formal spoken/written: *I wish I were on holiday now.*

Use

We use *wish* and *if only* to talk about regrets and to describe an imaginary situation which is the opposite of the real situation.
• To express a wish about a present situation, we use *wish / if only* + past simple.
  I wish I knew the answer. (But I don't.)
• To express a wish about a past situation, we use *wish / if only* + past perfect.
  I wish I'd bought a smaller car. (But I didn't.)
• To express a wish for someone to do something differently in the present or future, we use *wish / if only* + noun/pronoun + *would* + infinitive (without *to*).
  I wish you would be more environmentally friendly.
  (You won't be more environmentally friendly, but I want you to be.)
  Notice that you can't use the same subject in both clauses with *would*. You can't say: *I wish I would be more environmentally friendly.*

We use *would rather* + infinitive (without *to*) to talk about preferences.
I don't want to spend more on petrol. I would rather use my car less.

When we use *would rather*, we can also include *than* + an alternative.
I'd rather use my car less (than spend more on petrol).
I'd rather travel by train (than by plane).

We use *would rather* + object + past simple to state what we would prefer someone else to do.
I'd rather you used energy-saving lightbulbs.
He'd rather they met every week.

Practice

2 Complete the sentence using the correct form of the verbs.

1 If only there _____were_____ (be) a way to stop people using up fossil fuels, but there isn't.
2 I wish they _____ (stop) using pesticides on crops, but they won't.
3 If only the river _____ (not flood) their village, things would be OK now.
4 I wish they _____ (understand) how to protect their environment, but they don't.
5 If only people _____ (consider) the consequences before cutting down the forest, but they didn't.
6 I wish there _____ (not be) a nuclear power station here, but there is.
7 I'd rather the government _____ (not let) them register the oil tanker, but I imagine they will.
8 I wish they _____ (leave) the town centre as it was, but they didn't.

UNIT 8
Reporting verbs
Form

Reporting verbs are followed by different verb patterns.

verb + to + infinitive
She promised to investigate the story.
Reporting verbs with this pattern include: *agree, offer, promise, refuse, threaten.*

verb + someone + to + infinitive
He asked the photographer to send the files immediately.
Reporting verbs with this pattern include: *advise, ask, convince, encourage, invite, persuade, remind, tell, urge, warn.*

verb + -ing
He admitted faking the document.
Reporting verbs with this pattern include: *advise, admit, deny, mention, propose, recommend, suggest.*

verb + preposition + -ing
He complained about working long hours.
Reporting verbs with this pattern include: *apologise (for), complain (about), insist (on), object (to).*

verb + someone + preposition + -ing
The editor blamed him for not checking his facts.

Reporting verbs with this pattern include: *accuse (+ of)*, *blame (+ for)*, *compliment (+ on)*, *congratulate (+ on)*, *criticise (+ for)*, *forgive (+ for)*, *thank (+ for)*, *warn (+ about)*.

Other common verb patterns are:
verb + someone + *that*
He **warned us that** *the journey would be difficult.*
Reporting verbs with this pattern include: *advise, persuade, tell, warn.*

verb + *that*
We **agreed that** *she was the best candidate.*
Reporting verbs with this pattern include: *admit, agree, explain, deny, know, realise, say, think, warn.*

Use

Say, tell, think and *ask* are the most common reporting verbs, but we often use other reporting verbs to report what people said. When we decide what reporting verb to use, we think about the function or the purpose of the speaker's words.
'Remember to download your photos.' = **remind**
(*He reminded me to download my photos.*)
'I'll sign up for the media course when I get back.' = **promise** (*She promised to sign up for the media course when she got back.*)

Practice

1 Report the statements using these verbs. You may need to use a preposition after the verb.

admit	apologise	complain	invite	offer
tell	thank	~~urge~~		

1 I really think you should go to the meeting.
   Kailey ___*urged me to go to the meeting.*___
2 It was me that informed the press.
   Rebecca ___
3 I'm really grateful that you read my article, thank you.
   Susanne ___
4 I really dislike having to write business reports.
   Leo ___
5 I'm sorry, but I made a mistake.
   Clara ___
6 Please come and discuss it at the newspaper office tomorrow.
   Pieter ___
7 I'll give you a lift to the press conference.
   James ___
8 Don't send that email.
   Aisha ___

Passive reporting verbs

Form

Passive reporting verbs are formed with *It + be* + past participle of reporting verb + *that* + clause.

When we report ideas in the present, we use the verb *be* in the present simple.
*It **is** said that …*
*It **is** believed that …*

For a present report of a present event, we use the present simple in the *that*-clause.
*It is said that people **are** less happy nowadays than they were 50 years ago.*

For a present report of a past event, we use the past simple in the *that*-clause.
*It is believed that they **lived** unknown to the outside world for over 200 years.*

For a present report of a future event, we use *will* + infinitive in the *that*-clause.
*It is understood that reporters **will leave** the area immediately.*

When we report ideas in the past, we use the verb *be* in the past simple.
*It **was** believed that …*
*It **was** reported that …*

For a report and event at the same time in the past, we use the past simple in the *that*-clause.
*It was claimed that the break-in **happened** that morning.*
For a report in the past of an event that happened before the report, we use the past perfect in the *that*-clause.
*It was believed that the break-in **had happened** late at night.*

For a past report of a future event, we use *would* + infinitive in the *that*-clause.
*It was understood that the survivors **would go** straight to hospital when they returned.*

Use

We use passive reporting structures to talk about events when the speaker is unknown or unimportant, or when someone wishes to remain anonymous. We can report ideas in the present or in the past.
*It **is** said that people consume on average 50 times more sugar than ten years ago.*
*It **is** believed that tickets for the championships will be available next week.*
*It **was** reported that there had been violence at the demonstration.*
*It **was** thought that there wouldn't be any money to fund the proposals.*

We use passive reporting structures with reporting verbs such as *said, thought, believed, claimed, considered, estimated, expected, known, reported, suggested* and *understood.*

Practice

2 Write sentences using the prompts.

1 Present report about a present event: report / story / not be / true
   It is reported that the story is not true.
2 Present report about a past event: understand / those people / live / there / for twenty years
   ___
3 Present report about a future event: suggest / people / travel / to Mars / next year

4 Past report about a past event: think / women / be / less intelligent

5 Past report about a distant past event: said / men / not see / the Arctic ice / then

6 Past report of a future event: not believe / newspapers / become / so powerful

UNIT 9

Articles: *the* or zero article?

Form

The definite article is *the*.
When we do not use an article, we call it *zero article*.

Use

We use *the* + singular countable noun, plural countable noun or uncountable noun:

- to refer back to the same thing or person for a second time. *I applied for a job. It was **the** perfect job for me.*
- when there is only one. *He was the youngest person to cross **the** Atlantic Ocean by boat.*
- before a superlative adjective: *That was **the** most terrifying experience I've ever had!*
- to talk about a specific thing or person. *Did you see **the** space shuttle landing earlier?*
- to talk about specific things or people. *I have a lot of admiration for **the** relief workers in Somalia.*
- to talk about professional groups. *He worked in **the** navy for many years.*
- with certain countries, place names, geographical regions, oceans and seas, deserts, mountain ranges and rivers, for example: *the USA, the UK, the Netherlands, the Philippines, the United Arab Emirates, the Eiffel Tower, the White House, the Middle East, the Antarctic, the Pacific, the Mediterranean, the Kalahari Desert, the Alps, the Himalayas, the Amazon, the Nile.*

We use zero article + plural countable and uncountable nouns:

- to talk in general about things or people. *Do you use computers in your job? I don't like potatoes.*
- before certain familiar places (*work, home, hospital, university, school,* etc.). *What time do you go to work? Are they at home?*
- before most cities, countries, continents, lakes, mountains, languages and names of people. *Have you ever been to **Beijing**? She lives in **Poland**. He worked in **India** for many years.* Other examples are: *New York, London, Australia, China, Africa, Europe, Lake Geneva, Mount Everest, English, Spanish, Japanese, Christopher Columbus.*
- before certain time expressions. *I'll meet you **next week**. He set up the company **last year**. Their anniversary is in **June**. He was born in **1953**.*

Notice that there are exceptions, for example: time expressions: *in **the** sixties, at **the** weekend, in **the** summer, in **the** 18th century.*

Practice

1 Complete the text with *the* or zero article (–).

I was listening to [1] ___the___ news at ten o'clock [2] _____ last night, when it was reported that [3] _____ President of [4] _____ USA was on [5] _____ holiday for [6] _____ two weeks. They said that he was visiting [7] _____ town where he was born. Apparently he doesn't like going to [8] _____ places where there are lots of people, preferring [9] _____ peace and quiet. [10] _____ reasons why someone in his position does this are obvious!

Relative clauses

Form

The relative pronouns *who, which, whose, where, when* and *that* introduce defining relative clauses.

- to give information about people, we use *who* or *that. He's the man **who** got the job.*
- to give information about things, we use *which* or *that. That's the network **which** is used for public access.*
- to give information about places, we use *where. This is the place **where** the information is stored.*
- to give information about possession, we use *whose. She's the person **whose** job was advertised.*

Reduced relative clauses

We can sometimes shorten relative clauses by omitting the relative pronoun and using a present or past participle.
If the verb in the relative clause is in the active, we use the present participle.
*People **who visit** the area have complained about the traffic.*
*People **visiting** the area have complained about the traffic.*

If the verb in the relative clause is in the passive, we use the past participle:
*It is a subject **which is studied** by many people.*
*It is a subject **studied** by many people.*

We can't use a reduced relative clause when the relative pronoun is the object of the relative clause.
The expedition, which I am leading, is in June.
Not: ~~The expedition leading is in June.~~

Use

We use a relative clause to give more information about a noun in the main clause of the sentence.
We use a **defining** relative clause when the extra information in the relative clause is essential for identification. The meaning in the main clause is unclear without it.
*This is the team **who filmed beneath the ice**.*
*This is the forest **where the new species was discovered**.*

We use a **non-defining** relative clause when the extra information is not essential. The meaning of the main clause is still clear. The non-defining relative clause is separated from the main clause by commas.

*Stefano Calabrio, **who is eighty-five**, still works as a mountain guide.*
*The ship Arctic Kestral, **which was built in Glasgow**, is registered in Russia.*

The relative pronoun in a relative clause can be:
- the subject of the clause. *Explorers are people who make discoveries.*
- the object of the clause (with a noun or pronoun following it). *He's the explorer who I met in Cambodia.*

We can omit the relative pronoun when it is the **object** of a **defining** relative clause.
That's the explorer (who) I met in Cambodia.
The place (that) I would like to visit is Madagascar.
We cannot omit the relative pronoun when it is the subject of a defining relative clause or in a non-defining relative clause.

We often use reduced relative clauses in announcements and reports.
Passengers ~~who are~~ travelling to Mumbai, please proceed to gate number 25.
Due to the bomb scare, all bags ~~which were~~ left unattended were removed and destroyed.
The miners, ~~who were~~ trapped underground, managed to find their way to the surface.

Practice

2 Write sentences using relative clauses. Use reduced relative clauses where possible.

1 He is an explorer. He likes travelling to remote places.
   He's an explorer who likes travelling to remote places.

2 This is the desert. The fossils were discovered here.

3 Equipment is often left on Mount Everest. It is regularly removed.

4 That is the biologist. Her papers were lost in the storm.

5 Lake Titicaca is very large. It is on the border of Bolivia and Peru.

6 GreenSpace created the prototype. The prototype was copied by a rival company.

UNIT 10

Present simple, present continuous and *will* for repeated actions

Form

Present simple
Adverbs of frequency come before the main verb with the present simple, but after the verb *be*.
*We **always have** a family celebration at Thanksgiving.*
*He's **usually** on time for his extra class.*

Present continuous with *always*
Always comes between the verb *be* and the *-ing* form of the verb.
*They're **always** criticising their children.*
*She's **always** talking about herself.*

will
*Children **will** naturally choose to play rather than study.*

Use

We use the present simple for repeated actions (often with adverbs of frequency) or to talk about a simple fact or general truth.
*He **listens** to the radio news every morning.*
*Water **freezes** at 0° Celsius.*

We use the present continuous with *always* to talk about a habit which we find annoying or which we wish to criticise.
*I try to avoid John at work. He **is always talking** about his children's achievements.*
*She's **always complaining** about how much work she has to do.*

We use *will* to talk about typical behaviour.
*The bower bird doesn't build an ordinary nest. It constructs an incredible tower. It **will** often use pieces of plastic and glass to decorate this tower.*

Practice

1 Write sentences using the prompts. Use the present simple (PS), present continuous (PC) with *always* and *will* (W).

1 (PS) Mary / read / detective novels
   Mary reads detective novels.

2 (W) Cats don't like swimming. They / do / anything to avoid getting wet

3 (PS) James / ride / his bike everywhere

4 (PC) Nicola / talk / with / her mouth full

5 (PS) Steve is hard-working. He / stay / at work until 7.00 or 8.00 in the evening

6 (W) Cats / sleep / all day / rather than go out

7 (PC) My mum / complain / about the mess / in my bedroom

8 (PS) Jack / get / to work early most days

used to, usually, be used to and *get used to*

Form

Affirmative	Negative	Interrogative
used to + infinitive I/you/he/she/it/we/they **used to** live	I/you/he/she/it/we/they **didn't use to** live	**did** I/you/he/she/it/we/they **use to** live?

usually + present simple I/you/we/they **usually play**	I/you/we/they **don't usually play**	**do** I/you/we/they **usually play?**
he/she/it **usually plays**	he/she/it **doesn't usually play**	**does** he/she/it **usually play?**

be used to + noun or -ing **I'm used to playing**	**I'm not used to playing**	**am** I **used to playing?**
you're/we're/ they're **used to playing**	you/we/they **aren't used to playing**	**are** you/we/they **used to playing?**
he's/she's/it's **used to playing**	he/she/it **isn't used to playing**	**is** he/she/it **used to playing?**

be getting used to + noun or -ing **I'm getting used to playing**	**I'm not getting used to playing**	**am** I **getting used to playing?**
you're/we're/ they're **getting used to playing**	you/we/they **aren't getting used to playing**	**are** you/we/they **getting used to playing?**
he's/she's/it's **getting used to playing**	he/she/it **isn't getting used to playing**	**is** he/she/it **getting used to playing?**

Use

We use *used to* (+ infinitive) to talk about past habits, situations and states.
*I **used to go** out to eat a lot when I lived in Paris.*
*She **didn't use to enjoy** opera when she was younger.*

We use *usually* + present simple to talk about present habits.
*We **usually have** dinner with my parents on Sundays.*
***Do** you **usually go** shopping on Friday nights?*

We use *be used to* to talk about familiar (and unfamiliar) habits and situations.
*Is he **used to using** his new laptop yet?*
*He **isn't used to** his new laptop yet.*

We use *get used to* to talk about habits that are becoming familiar.
*Sara **is getting used to working** in the shop now.*
*Sara **is getting used to** the shop now.*

Practice

2 Choose the correct option.

1 Since his illness, he _____ very healthy food.
   a (usually eats)
   b used to eat
   c is getting used to eat

2 Paul has worked for a multinational company for years, so he _____ now.
   a usually travels
   b used to travel
   c is used to travelling

3 They both _____ golf when they were boys.
   a usually play
   b used to play
   c are used to playing

4 Lizzie _____ at her new college.
   a usually studies
   b used to study
   c is getting used to studying

5 Jessica _____ to her co-director every day.
   a usually speaks
   b is used to speak
   c is getting used to speaking

6 John _____ different food since he went to Thailand last week.
   a used to
   b is used to trying
   c is getting used to trying

7 Petra's worked here for years, so she _____ early.
   a used to get up
   b is used to getting up
   c is getting used to getting up

8 My brother _____ very late on Saturday nights.
   a usually stays out
   b is used to staying out
   c is getting used to staying out

UNIT 11

could, was able to, manage to and *succeed in*

Form

Affirmative	Negative	Interrogative
could + infinitive (without *to*) I/you/he/she/it/we/ they **could do**	I/you/he/she/it/we/ they **couldn't do**	**could** I/you/he/she/ it/we/they **do?**
was/were able + *to* + infinitive I/he/she/it **was able to do** you/we/they **were able to do**	I/he/she/it **wasn't able to do** you/we/they **weren't able to do**	**was** I/he/she/it **able to do?** **were** you/we/they **able to do?**
manage + *to* + infinitive I/you/he/she/it/we/ they **managed to finish**	I/you/he/she/it/ we/they **didn't manage to finish**	**did** I/you/he/she/it/ we/they **manage to finish?**
succeed in + *-ing* I/you/he/she/it/we/ they **succeeded in making**	I/you/he/she/it/ we/they **didn't succeed in making**	**did** I/you/he/she/it/ we/they **succeed in making?**

Use

We use *could* and *was / were able to* to talk about a general ability to do something in the past.
*He **could swim** when he was three years old.*
*He **couldn't study** much last month.*

*I was the only one who **was able to understand** what he was talking about.*

We also use *was / were able to* to talk about success in a particular task or activity.

*She **was able to find** the quickest route immediately.*
*__Were__ they **able to take** their exams in the end?*

We can use both *couldn't* and *wasn't / weren't able to* to talk about not succeeding in a particular task or activity.

*They **weren't able to finish** the journey.*
*He **couldn't find** the herbal medicine he was looking for.*

We use *manage to + infinitive* and *succeed in + -ing* to talk about success (or lack of success) in a particular task or activity, but not to talk about general ability.

*He finally **managed to publish** his book after trying six different companies.*
*Did she **manage to get** that scholarship in the end?*
*After some time, Marco **succeeded in raising** enough money for his trip.*
*Unfortunately, Sue **didn't succeed in getting** the job she wanted.*

We often use expressions such as *finally* and *in the end* with *manage to* and *succeed in* to emphasise that the activity was an effort.

*I **finally** managed to pass my exams.*
__In the end__, I succeeded in becoming a doctor.

Practice

1 Look at the sentences (a and b) and choose the best option.

> (1a) Did you manage to find out about the Mexican cure for blisters?
> 1b Could you find out about the Mexican cure for blisters?
> 2a In the past people didn't succeed in accessing as much information about plants as they can today.
> 2b In the past people weren't able to access as much information about plants as they can today.
> 3a A recent survey found that most people in the UK weren't able to identify common plants.
> 3a A recent survey found that most people in the UK didn't manage to identify common plants.
> 4a The medicine didn't always succeed in treating the illness.
> 4b The medicine couldn't treat the illness.
> 5a Sally didn't manage to publish her latest article. She submitted it too late.
> 5b Sally couldn't publish her latest article. She submitted it too late.

Future in the past

Form

Affirmative	Negative	Interrogative
would + infinitive (without *to*) I said (that) I/you/he/she/it/we/they **would do**	I said (that) I/you/he/she/it/we/they **wouldn't do**	they asked if I/you/he/she/it/we/they **would do**

would have + past participle I/you/he/she/it/we/they **would have made**	I/you/he/she/it/we/they **wouldn't have made**	**would** I/you/he/she/it/we/they **have made?**
be supposed to + infinitive I/he/she/it **was supposed to finish** you/we/they **were supposed to finish**	I/he/she/it **wasn't supposed to finish** you/we/they **weren't supposed to finish**	**was** I/he/she/it **supposed to finish?** **were** you/we/they **supposed to finish?**

Use

We use *was / were going to* to talk about the future in the past:

- to talk about an intention which may or may not have been fulfilled. *I'm sorry, Mike. I **was going to phone** you, but then I was too busy.*
- to talk about a plan or arrangement which then changed. *We **were going to meet** at 2.00 but didn't arrive until 3.00.*

We use *be about to* to say that we were very close to doing something, but were prevented at the last moment.

*I **was about to leave** the house when the telephone rang.*

We use *would* to talk about the future in the past to report what somebody said they would do.

*Jane said that she **would work** that evening.*
*He promised he **would send** me the report.*

We use *would have* to refer to a future action in the past which didn't happen.

*I **would have bought** it, but I didn't have enough money with me.*

We use *supposed to* to talk about actions which people should have done, but didn't.

*They **were supposed to get** here at eight o'clock! Where are they?*

Practice

2 Complete the second sentence so it has the same meaning as the first. Use the words in bold.

1 He planned to tell you, but he didn't see you.
   going He ___was going to tell___ you, but he didn't see you.
2 'I'll work harder next week.'
   would John said that he _____ harder next week.
3 She intended to tell you, but she was too frightened to speak.
   would She _____ you, but she was too frightened to speak.
4 Marilyn was going to bring enough food for everyone! Where is it?
   supposed Marilyn _____ enough food for everyone! Where is it?
5 They intended to start studying tomorrow, but then they went out instead.
   going They _____ studying tomorrow, but then they went out instead.

6 He wanted to say something, but then decided not to.
   about He _____ something, but then decided not to.

7 Why didn't you ask her? She wanted to tell you.
   would She _____ you if you had asked her.

8 'I'll pass all my exams.'
   would Liz said that she _____ all her exams.

UNIT 12

Focus adverbs: *only, just, even, too, also, as well*

Form

only, just, even

Only, just and *even* always come directly before the word they are emphasising.

Only/Just *Dave knows how difficult it was for them to move.*
It is **only/just** *two days since I saw him.*
A lot of people don't **even** *have enough savings to pay the rent for a month.*

too, also, as well

- sentence + *too*:
  We can invest in that company **too**.
- sentence + *as well*:
  We bought a new iPad **as well**.
- *Also* + sentence:
  Also, *she runs a successful accountancy business.*
- *also* + main verb:
  Most people **also** *want to plan for their future.*
- *be* + *also*:
  He's good at tennis. He's **also** *a good badminton player.*
- auxiliary verb + *also* + main verb:
  They have **also** *got three cars.*

Use

We use focus adverbs to emphasise a particular piece of information. Sentences which include focus adverbs can all exist as complete sentences without the adverbs in them.

Only and *just* focus on one particular thing to the exclusion of all others.
Only/Just *she and I know her secret.*
It's **only/just** *banks that accept travellers cheques.*
He packed **only/just** *a toothbrush and one change of clothes.*

We use *even* to show that we think something is unusual or surprising.
The question was so easy that **even** *Bill knew the answer.*
Even *football doesn't interest him any more.*

We use *also, as well* and *too* to emphasise an additional piece of information in a sentence. *Also* comes before most verbs, but after the verb *to be*, or at the beginning of a sentence. *As well* and *too* come after the verb (and the object if there is one).
He likes outdoor sports, but **also** *enjoys playing chess.*
He likes outdoor sports, but enjoys playing chess, **as well/too**.

Practice

1 Choose the correct option.

1 I (only) / too heard about his financial situation yesterday.
2 Did you want to go to the stock exchange *even* / *too*?
3 He *even* / *too* asked the accountant about it!
4 He usually goes to the bank on Thursdays *even* / *as well*.
5 They have *only* / *as well* got a few thousand pounds left.
6 The sum has *just* / *even* been deposited in your account.
7 The boys *also* / *too* wanted some of the money.
8 The recession is a big problem for us *too* / *only*.

Causative *have* and *get*

Form

have/get + something + past participle
I **had/got my car repaired** *last week.*

have + someone + infinitive (without *to*)
I **had a gardener help** *me with the garden.*

get + someone + *to* + infinitive
I **got a gardener to help** *me with the garden.*

Use

We use *have / get something done* to explain that we asked someone to do something for us but we don't say who. We often pay for the work.
She **has her house cleaned** *by a cleaning company.*
We **get our car serviced** *every six months at the local garage.*

We use *have someone do / get someone to do* to explain that you have asked someone to do something for you. With these expressions, we say who does the job. Notice that with *get* we use *to* + infinitive. With *have* we use the infinitive without *to*.
I **have a gardener mow** *the lawn.*
I **get a window cleaner to clean** *the windows!*

Practice

2 Write sentences using the prompts. Use causative forms.

1 I / get / hair cut / yesterday
   I got my hair cut yesterday.

2 I / have / accountant / go over / my accounts / on Saturday

3 We / get / mortgage rate / fix / last week

4 She / get / neighbour / pay for / new fence / this afternoon

5 He / get / friend / open / an account / last summer

6 She / have / new credit card / send out / this morning

Unit 7

🔊 2.1

… so if you always keep these three things in mind, it's actually quite simple to make a difference to your own personal consumption of natural resources. Number one and most important is reduce. In other words, try to buy and use fewer goods. In the UK we throw away a third of the food we buy. If we only bought the food we really needed, this wouldn't happen. Umm … try to reduce the energy you use too, for example switching the lights off when you leave the room or umm … walking somewhere instead of taking the car. The second thing is to reuse. Mend things that are broken. Think how you can reuse old things, such as those old jeans you threw out. If you hadn't thrown them away, you could have worn them the next time there was some gardening or decorating to do. And lastly recycle. Only buy products that are made of recyclable materials: like glass bottles or certain plastics; and when you have finished with them, take them to a recycling point. OK so that's three things to remember: reduce, reuse, recycle.

🔊 2.2

Speaker 1
Liam from the United Kingdom
I live in Manchester, which is probably one of the wettest places in the UK. If I had been brought up somewhere like Saharan Africa, where I had to walk miles each day just to fetch water, I'd obviously be a lot more conscious of water conservation. But I'm afraid I don't set a very good example – er … I probably waste a lot – leaving the tap running when I brush my teeth and so on. Clearly we're not going to run out of water in the UK, but I know water conservation is important. If we all used less water, the water companies wouldn't have to use so much energy treating water to make it clean. And of course that would be more environmentally-friendly.

Speaker 2
Gemal from the United Arab Emirates
I'm not saying the idea of desalination plants is wrong. If desalination methods didn't exist, this country would not have been able to develop in the way it has. Nowadays we use water in our homes more or less as we want to. But I don't think we can continue like this. You see, the waste from the desalination process is a kind of brine with a dangerously high salt content … which will eventually destroy life in the sea. I am interested in discovering farming techniques that use salt water. There are grasses and other types of plant that can grow with sea water. If we were to use more of these, it would give our natural fresh water springs a chance to recharge.

Speaker 3
Daniel from the United States
Americans (and I'm as guilty as the rest) use water like there is no tomorrow. I think it's well-known that the Colorado River doesn't reach the sea anymore. If you had visited the area around the old delta in Mexico 100 years ago – rich wetlands, full of wildlife – you'd be shocked to see it now. It's all dried up … a kind of salt flat. The reason is agriculture. The river has been dammed and diverted in various places along its route to irrigate fields and provide enough water for people living in the desert areas of Nevada and California. Unless we change the way we think about water and stop wasting so much, the river will carry on getting smaller.

Speaker 4
Carmen from Mexico
My water needs are the same as most people's, I think: I have a small vegetable garden; I have to wash myself and my clothes. I don't have to save water, but I want to, you know. I collect rainwater for the garden, I fill a basin to wash in rather than running the tap, I wash my dishes every other day. But now governments are discussing big projects for transporting water from one part of the world to another using huge pipes and tankers. I think if more people thought and acted like me, things would not have come to this point, you know.

🔊 2.4

E = Erika; A = Andy; J = Jane; R = Ralph
A: Erika, what do you think about all these people who say that there's no proof that climate change is man-made?
E: OK, I'll tell you my position. I don't know if climate change is man-made and I'm not sure anyone can say for sure. Let me give you an example … umm … an analogy. Imagine you were losing your hair and I told you that some people had found that if they ate a banana every day it prevented hair loss. Even though you had no proof it worked, you would probably try eating a banana each day, wouldn't you? Well, it's the same with global warming. We don't know that we're causing it, but some people say we might be with all the fossil fuels we burn. And I, for one, am happy to be a little more careful in how I pollute in case they're right.
A: Mmm … well, I don't accept that. I used to believe in climate change, but the last few winters here in the UK have been much colder than normal. To be honest with you, I'd believe it more if I wasn't getting up in the morning and scraping ice off the inside of my windows rather than the outside.
E: Yeah, but that's not the point, Andy, is it? You know, regional temperatures may be lower, but average global temperatures carry on rising.
J: Mmm … Look – there's no doubt that the weather's changing, but I don't believe it's a man-made problem. It's just part of a natural weather cycle. Yeah, I know you'll say 'Oh, that's just your excuse to drive a big car and fly to exotic places for your holidays', but actually that's not the reason. I don't believe it simply because no scientist has successfully proved it yet.
R: We're approaching this debate all wrong by saying 'it's a big environmental problem that we need to address'. Because it's not just an environmental problem. It's an economic problem, a social problem, even an ethical problem.

Unit 8

🔊 2.7

N = Newsreader; M = Martha Cash
N: And in China, hundreds of parents of first-year students at the University of Wuhan have been sleeping on the floor of the university's gym so that they can be near their children in their first anxious days at college. As Martha Cash, our Far East correspondent, reports.
M: China's policy of urging families to have only one child has meant that parents, already ambitious for the success of their children, become even more intensely focussed on helping a single son or daughter to make it in the world. Going to university is of course seen as a necessary first step in this journey, but most Chinese families are not particularly well-off and they often make great sacrifices to support their children. So staying in a local hotel during their children's first days at college is not really an option. That was how, on a recent visit to Wuhan in the centre of China, we witnessed this extraordinary scene: a mass adult sleep-in on the university gym floor. It seems odd to us in the West to find parents so involved in their children's education and lives when they are already adults, but as an expression of parental concern, you can't help but be impressed by it.

🔊 2.8

And finally … it was thought that the large blue butterfly was extinct in Britain, but it seems to have made a remarkable return. The large blue, which disappeared 30 years ago, is only found in certain fields. What these fields have in common is that their grass is very short, because rabbits, sheep and cows graze there. Originally it was believed that greedy butterfly hunters had killed off the large blue butterfly, but it is now agreed that changes in farming techniques were responsible for its decline. As a result of recent efforts to protect its natural habitat, it is estimated that around 20,000 of these beautiful creatures will be seen in the British countryside this summer.

And finally, researchers believe they may have found a cure – or at least some relief – for the common cold. In tests it was reported that people who started taking zinc at the first signs of a common cold got well sooner. There have been many previous studies into the effectiveness of zinc but they were inconclusive. The new study, involving over 1,000 people of various ages, found that on average people who took zinc supplements recovered from their colds one day earlier than those who took nothing. The effectiveness of zinc in preventing a cold in the first place was less certain, although it was said that those who took it regularly suffered less serious symptoms than those who didn't.

And finally, believe it or not, eating chocolate might be good for you after all. In the past it was thought that eating sweets would result in tooth decay and putting on weight. But now it is claimed that a new chocolate bar, invented by the world's largest chocolate maker, can actually slow the ageing process of your skin. The special chocolate contains antioxidants, which help hydrate the skin and fight wrinkles. The market for healthy foods has grown by over five per cent a year in recent years and it seems now that even the sellers of traditionally unhealthy snacks are trying to get in on the act. However, doctors have warned against rushing out to buy extra chocolate – good skin and chocolate are not generally natural partners, they say.

And finally, Costa Rica today has the honour of being named the world's happiest nation. According to the latest Happy Planet Index, it is said that Costa Rica has the best balance of human well-being – that is to say, good health, a long life, low levels of poverty – and a low ecological footprint, in other words the amount of natural resources it uses. In fact, Latin American countries took nine of the top ten places, while richer, so-called developed countries, like the US at number 74, were much further down in the list.

🔊 2.10

J = Jess; P = Phil
J: Hi Phil. Did all that noise in the street wake you up last night?
P: No, it didn't but then I'm a deep sleeper. What happened?
J: Well, I didn't see it myself but I heard that it was an argument between two car drivers and supposedly it got quite heated.
P: Really?? Who told you about it?
J: Tara at number 42. It seems that both drivers got out of their cars and started shouting at each other. She says they almost started fighting.

P: Hmm ... well I'd take what Tara says with a pinch of salt if I were you. She tends to blow things out of proportion.

J: No, I believe her actually – people do get very frustrated by not being able to pass each other on this street. Anyway, the police were called ...

P: The police? It wasn't that serious, was it?

J: Well, no. The cars didn't crash or anything. But Tara says that they got out of their cars and started arguing. She reckons that if the police hadn't arrived there would have been a fight.

P: Did the cars make contact?

J: No ... they were just coming in opposite directions and they met where the street gets narrow and neither one would reverse to let the other pass. So they just stayed there, in the middle of the road, with neither one giving way.

P: How childish.

J: Yeah, it is rather. Someone said they'd seen one of the drivers before. Apparently he's a local politician.

P: It wasn't Tara getting her facts mixed up again, was it?

J: No it was Chris ... I think I'd take his word for it; he's not the type to spread gossip.

P: So what did the police do about it?

J: Well, according to Chris, they took them both away for questioning ... surprisingly ...

Unit 9

🎧 2.13

Both the mahout and the elephant start their training at a young age. A mahout generally begins to learn his trade when he's about ten years old and is assigned a baby elephant to look after. He'll probably be paired with this elephant for the rest of his life. It's traditionally a family trade, with knowledge being passed down from one generation to another. There are no formal qualifications for the job, but extreme patience is required. An elephant will learn up to 65 commands in its life – depending on what work it's expected to do – and the mahout has to teach these. The mahout must also develop an intimate understanding of his elephant – something that only comes with time and experience – so that he knows when it's sick or unhappy. In this way he can get the best out of his elephant. It's a very physical job and extremely hard work. The elephant must be fed and bathed daily and watched so that it doesn't run away.

🎧 2.14

A: Do you know this photo?

B: Of course. It's the first man on the Moon, Neil Armstrong. The guy who said 'That's one small step for man, one giant leap for mankind'.

A: That's what everyone thinks, but actually it's his fellow astronaut, Buzz Aldrin. Neil Armstrong took the photo – you can see his reflection in Aldrin's visor. But you're right. It was that mission: Apollo 11 in 1969.

B: Amazing to think that was over 40 years ago ... but what happened to Neil Armstrong after that?

A: He probably toured the world getting paid huge amounts of money for public speaking at corporate dinners and official openings and that sort of thing.

🎧 2.16

Q: Can you tell us something about the Emerging Explorers programme?

A: It's an award scheme set up by the *National Geographic Society* to encourage young adventurers, scientists, photographers and storytellers to continue their work and to realise their potential. Each year between eight and fifteen explorers, whose work is really outstanding, are selected and given money to help them continue their research and exploration.

Q: So Emerging Explorers are generally young people, are they?

A: Not necessarily. Emerging Explorers are generally people who are at an early stage of their careers. What they have in common is that they are all people who are pushing at the boundaries of their field, whether that's exploring undiscovered deep water caves or watching the stars through a telescope.

Q: And how does *National Geographic* encourage them?

A: Well, first of all *National Geographic* awards each one of them US $10,000, which is intended to go towards further research and exploration. Of course their profiles are also raised by the articles and news that appear in *National Geographic*. In other words, the magazine is a place where other interested people can read about their work.

Q: And what kind of fields do the winners come from?

A: We have so many different types of explorer, chosen from fields as diverse as anthropology, space exploration, mountaineering and music.

Q: You mentioned storytellers earlier. What did you mean by that, exactly?

A: Well, there are all these people doing important work out there in the various fields that I have described. And that's great but it's also very important that everyone hears about this work. That's the skill of the storytellers, communicating with pictures and words important facts about the planet and life on the planet in a way that grabs everyone's attention. A really good example is Alexandra Cousteau, whose grandfather Jacques Cousteau was well-known for his films about marine life. She works as a conservationist, trying to persuade people to protect scarce resources like water. Alexandra, inspired by her grandfather's success as a storyteller, is researching ways in which the environmental community can use new media – social networks, video games – to communicate its message.

🎧 2.17

S = Sarah; P = Phil

S: So, you're 24 years old, you graduated a year ago and you're looking for work with a charity. What attracted you to Shelterbox?

P: Well, I'm familiar with your work because I have a friend who volunteered for you last year – packing boxes – and I think it's a fantastic concept. But umm ... mainly I'm very keen on the idea of working abroad ... in different countries ...

S: Mm, I see ... and what makes you think you'd be suited to that? I see you studied economics at Cambridge ... Don't you think that's a rather different world?

P: Yes, it's true that I specialised in economics but, actually, I'm good at coping with difficult environments. I spent three months helping to build a school in Chennai in India last summer. And the year before that I trekked across the Mojave Desert. So I think I'd be suited to the work.

S: OK – well ... they're certainly not easy places to adapt to ... although in fact you'd also be spending a good part of the time here in the office doing paperwork.

P: Yeah, that's also fine. I was expecting that. I have quite a lot of experience of sitting at a desk ... for my studies. What sort of paperwork is it?

S: Well, each trip involves a lot of preparation and a certain amount of follow-up too.

Keeping spreadsheets, writing reports. Are you OK doing that sort of thing?

P: Yeah, I'm quite good with computers. I'm comfortable with all the usual programs – Excel, Word, some financial software ...

S: OK. There's just one thing that's worrying me though. You're clearly a bright person and you have a good degree. How do I know that you won't just do this job for a few months and then go and get a better paid job with a bank or consultancy business?

P: That's a good question. It's actually what a lot of my friends from university have done but I'll tell you why that's not for me. Firstly, I'm really serious about wanting to help people in need. Secondly, I think I need to become more knowledgeable about the world, before I use my economics degree to do something else ... If you put your faith in me, I will be absolutely committed to doing the best job that I can ... for two or three years at least.

Unit 10

🎧 2.20

Well a narrow view of this quotation is that you need to have good manners or you won't get far in life ... Good manners meaning the kind that we teach our children: you know the kind of thing – don't talk with your mouth full; don't interrupt when grown-ups are speaking; don't point or stare at people; don't slouch or chew gum; don't wear clothes that are inappropriate or offensive; in a nutshell, be polite, well-behaved and show courtesy to others.

But I think what William of Wykeham really meant is that each society creates its own code of behaviour and customs, and that is what makes people what they are. So each culture defines itself by the way it behaves socially – how we eat, how we dress, how we celebrate, how we interact with one another. In fact, the different ways we all find of doing essentially the same things.

🎧 2.21

1 I've seen this situation so many times in Mexico. What happens is children beg their parents for some sweets. At first the parent will say no. So then the child will pester and pester until the parent finally gives in – which they always do. It's against all the rules of parenting.

2 I teach in a school in San Francisco where we have quite a lot of ethnic Chinese and Japanese kids. By and large they will do what you tell them. But the other kids – wow – they are always misbehaving. You can tell them ten times to sit down before they do.

3 Where I live in India, it's common for young children to work. Kids still depend on their parents, but they have a different attitude to responsibility. Just as children in every culture play naturally, so children in India naturally assume responsibility for working and earning money.

🎧 2.22

Different people's diets rarely surprise me these days. We didn't use to think so much about what we ate. But today, well ... we live in an age where people are just very conscious of their diets. A day hardly ever passes without a story in the news about a particular food that's good for your health or bad for you if you eat too much of it.

So I was very interested to read a story the other day about the diet of the Nochmani tribe of the Nicobar Islands in the Indian Ocean. People used to think that these tiny islands – which are about 600 miles from the coast of India – that they were uninhabited by humans. But in 2004, aid workers in helicopters spotted some tribespeople on a mountainside.

Scientists were particularly surprised that there were inhabitants there, because people usually need mammals – you know, cows, goats and so on – and their produce – meat, milk, etcetera in order to live. But the Nicobar islands have almost no mammals. So what were the Nochmani surviving on? Fish, perhaps? No. Amazingly, their diet consisted largely of insects, in particular beetles, of which there were over 1,700 varieties on the islands, but also other insects and spiders.

This presented a problem for the aid workers, who'd brought with them standard survival meals, including chicken, beef and pork. The Nochmani, who weren't used to eating meat at all, were disgusted by these offerings. All they'd take from the aid workers were sweets and cakes. It wasn't just a matter of taste either. If you're used to a certain type of food – even insects – other types may be completely indigestible.

Insects are in fact very nutritious: high in protein and fat and low in carbohydrates, making them an ideal food source for humans. But what was even more amazing was that just as we usually help our animals to live by providing food for them, so the Nochmani cultivate certain fungi and mosses to attract and feed the insects they eat. Perhaps we can learn from this tribe. If more of us could get used to eating unconventional foods such as insects, it might help the world's food problems.

2.25

M = Marie; E = Esther

M: I know of henna painting as a custom from Indian weddings … but you came across it in Turkey, didn't you?

E: Yes, in eastern Turkey when I was travelling there. It takes place a few nights before the wedding.

M: Was it a bit like a hen night?

E: Well, in the sense that it marks the last evening that a bride spends with female family and friends, I suppose it is a bit like that. What happens is typically, the women from both families get together, with the bride, to celebrate with music, song and dance. But it's not just a party. It's an occasion for sadness too, because it symbolises the end of life as a single person and the start of another stage.

2.26

M = Marie; E = Esther

M: So what happens exactly?

E: Well, the ceremony begins with preparation of the henna. It's traditional for this to be done by the daughter of a couple who have had a successful marriage themselves. Then, after the bride's head has been covered in a red veil, her hands and feet are decorated with henna. After that, a gold coin is put into the remaining henna. While this is happening, the guests sing … umm … separation songs – these are rather sad, as you can imagine. The party continues well into the night. Then, on the morning of the wedding, a child presents the hennaed coin to the groom as a symbol of future prosperity and good fortune.

2.27

M = Marie; E = Esther

M: I know of henna painting as a custom from Indian weddings … but you came across it in Turkey, didn't you?

E: Yes, in eastern Turkey when I was travelling there. It takes place a few nights before the wedding.

M: Was it a bit like a hen night?

E: Well in the sense that it marks the last evening that a bride spends with female family and friends, I suppose it is a bit like that. What happens is typically, the women from both families get together,

with the bride, to celebrate with music, song and dance. But it's not just a party. It's an occasion for sadness too, because it symbolises the end of life as a single person and the start of another stage.

M: So what happens exactly?

E: Well, the ceremony begins with preparation of the henna. It's traditional for this to be done by the daughter of a couple who've had a successful marriage themselves. Then, after the bride's head has been covered in a red veil, her hands and feet are decorated with henna. After that, a gold coin is put into the remaining henna. While this is happening, the guests sing … umm … separation songs – these are rather sad, as you can imagine. The party continues well into the night. Then, on the morning of the wedding, a child presents the hennaed coin to the groom as a symbol of future prosperity and good fortune.

Unit 11

2.30

We rely on our intuition all the time. Let me give you a couple of examples. Imagine you're going to buy a second-hand car. You have a basic grasp of car mechanics. So, first you consult an authority on the subject … like a motoring magazine. You do a bit of research to find out what the best kind of car is, and try to pick up some tips from experts and journalists. Then you study the facts about the car – how big the engine is, how economical it is and so on – and make some reasoned judgements from the information you read about whether it's a suitable car for you or not. In other words, you process the information.

But when it actually comes down to buying a particular car from a particular person, then … in the end you have to trust your instinct or gut feeling. Do I trust this person? Is a car of this age going to give me any trouble? No one else can answer these questions. And that's how it is with many situations in life. Our knowledge is rarely perfect enough to mean we can make a purely objective decision.

2.31

I became interested in growing my own vegetables a few years ago because I was aware of how expensive vegetables were in the shops. It also struck me that a lot of the vegetables we buy are imported. It occurred to me that if more people grew their own, we wouldn't have to import so many. I was really ignorant of the subject – I couldn't grow a thing – but luckily I managed to discover a fantastic book written by woman called Joy Larkcom. That was six years ago and it's become more than a hobby. It never crossed my mind that I would become an expert, but now I get a lot of neighbours coming to ask me for my advice.

2.32

Do these situations sound familiar to you? Have any of these things happened to you? You were about to give a speech or make a comment at a meeting, and then your mind went blank. You were supposed to send a friend a card for their birthday, but then you forgot. You recognised someone in the street and would have spoken to them, but you didn't because you couldn't remember their name. You promised you would post a letter for someone and two days later you found it still in your pocket. You were going to write down a great idea you had, but when you found a pen and paper, the idea had gone. I could go on, … but I won't because I'm sure everyone recognises these common failures of memory.

2.33

Everyone would like to remember more but would it actually make us any happier?

I want to tell you the story of a 41-year-old woman from California known in medical literature as 'AJ,' who remembers almost every day of her life since the age of 11. She remembers that at 12:34 p.m. on Sunday, the 3rd of August 1986, a young man she was attracted to called her on the telephone. She remembers that on the 28th of March 1992, she had lunch with her father at the Beverly Hills Hotel. It's a bit like certain smells that evoke strong memories … AJ's memory is stimulated in the most intense way by dates.

You'd think that being able to retrieve facts and knowledge in this way would make us more confident and wiser. But in fact for AJ an incredible memory is as much a burden as it is a benefit. That's because most memories are selective: they remember mostly important things and mostly good things too. AJ remembers every detail good or bad, important or not.

So when we curse our poor memories for forgetting to send a birthday card, actually we should be grateful also for all the things that our memories hide away because they don't need to be remembered or thought about. Umm … technology of course helps us with this. We don't need to remember the precise content of a report or the exact time of a meeting, because it's stored on our computer or in our mobile phone.

But interestingly, the growth of this technology – what psychologists call our external memory – is having an effect on what and how much we remember. Even our memories of happy events – like parties or holidays – get stored in photo albums on our computers. So our internal memories are probably worse than those of people 100 years ago. Medical science is trying to address the problem of poor memory and this is what I want to talk about next …

2.34

Do these situations sound familiar to you? Have any of these things happened to you? You were about to give a speech or make a comment at a meeting, and then your mind went blank. You were supposed to send a friend a card for their birthday, but then you forgot. You recognised someone in the street and would have spoken to them, but you didn't because you couldn't remember their name. You promised you would post a letter for someone and two days later you found it still in your pocket. You were going to write down a great idea you had, but when you found a pen and paper, the idea had gone. I could go on, … but I won't because I'm sure everyone recognises these common failures of memory.

Everyone would like to remember more but would it actually make us any happier?

I want to tell you the story of a 41-year-old woman from California known in medical literature as 'AJ,' who remembers almost every day of her life since the age of 11. She remembers that at 12.34 p.m. on Sunday, the 3rd of August 1986, a young man she was attracted to called her on the telephone. She remembers that on the 28th March of 1992, she had lunch with her father at the Beverly Hills Hotel. It's a bit like certain smells that evoke strong memories … AJ's memory is stimulated in the most intense way by dates.

You'd think that being able to retrieve facts and knowledge in this way would make us more confident and wiser. But in fact for AJ an incredible memory is as much a burden as it is a benefit. That's because most memories are selective: they remember mostly important things and mostly good things too. AJ remembers every detail good or bad, important or not.

So when we curse our poor memories for forgetting to send a birthday card, actually we should be grateful also for all the things that our memories hide away because they don't need to be remembered or thought about. Umm … technology of course helps us with this. We don't need to remember the precise content of a report or the exact time of a meeting, because it's stored on our computer or in our mobile phone.

But interestingly, the growth of this technology – what psychologists call our external memory – is having an effect on what and how much we remember. Even our memories of happy events – like parties or holidays – get stored in photograph albums or on our computers. So our internal memories are probably worse than those of people 100 years ago. Medical science is trying to address the problem of poor memory and this is what I want to talk about next …

🎧 2.35

Do these situations sound familiar to you? Have any of these things happened to you? You were about to give a speech or make a comment at a meeting, and then your mind went blank. You were supposed to send a friend a card for their birthday, but then you forgot. You recognised someone in the street and would have spoken to them, but you didn't because you couldn't remember their name. You promised you would post a letter for someone and two days later you found it still in your pocket. You were going to write down a great idea you had, but when you found a pen and paper, the idea had gone. I could go on, … but I won't because I'm sure everyone recognises these common failures of memory.

🎧 2.37

A = Ahmad; L = Liz

A: Hi there, I'm interested in taking a class at your college – umm … the history of art course.

L: Is that the two year A-level course?

A: Sorry, what do you mean by A-level?

L: The A-level art history course is a two year pre-university course with examinations at the end of each year.

A: Oh no, no, no … I don't want to take any exams. It's just for interest.

L: OK. In that case, we have a one year art appreciation course.

A: Sorry. Could you speak up a little? I can't hear you very well.

L: Yes, we have a one year art appreciation course.

A: Umm … can you explain what the course involves?

L: Yeah, it's a two hour class once a week and, basically, it teaches you how to look at art so that you get the most from the experience.

A: No, sorry, I'm not really with you. Are you saying that it doesn't really deal with the history of art?

L: No … there's some history of art in it, of course, but it's mainly learning about composition, techniques, references and so on.

A: Hmm … Could you give me an example of the kind of thing students do in the class?

L: Sure. Typically, students look at works of art and then comment on them. Then they're told more about the artist, what he or she was trying to achieve and then they look at their work again, … with fresh eyes as it were.

A: Mmm, OK. It sounds quite interesting.

What was the course called again?

L: Art appreciation.

A: And when is it?

L: Every Tuesday – in term time, that is – from 7 p.m. til 9 p.m., starting on … one minute … yeah, starting on the 29th of September. The cost is £298 for the year, unless you're a registered student.

A: Hang on a second. That's too much to take in all at once. I'm trying to write it down. I didn't catch the start date. Did you say the 29th of November?

L: No, the 29th of September.

A: OK. Well, thanks. I'll have a think about it, but it sounds good.

L: No worries, bye.

Unit 12

🎧 2.39

Poverty is a relative concept. For some people being poor may mean not having enough to eat; others consider themselves hard-up if they can't afford to go on holiday. Much depends of course on the cost of living, in other words how pricey basic goods and services are. In the UK one definition of poverty is that you spend more than ten per cent of your earnings on energy – that is, the gas and electricity you use in your home. The trouble with this kind of definition is that something like energy might be much more reasonable in one country than another. So sometimes poverty is expressed as a percentage of average national income – for example, if you earn less than 60 per cent of the average, you are classified as poor. Wealth is also a relative concept. Being well-off doesn't necessarily mean being loaded and surrounded by luxuries – two cars and a second home in the country. Wealth can also be measured by people's quality of life. You can be considered rich if you have all that you need – the basic necessities – a good work-life balance and a happy family life.

🎧 2.40

I = Interviewer; D = Davis Stiles

I: Thirty years ago, the idea of getting a worker to hand wash your car would have been unthinkable – except to the very rich. Either you washed it yourself at home on a Sunday morning or you took it down to the automatic carwash at your local garage. Nowadays, you can have it washed inside and out by a team of willing and capable workers for as little as £6. So, what's changed? I have here with me David Stiles, author of *The Servant Economy*. David, are we just getting too lazy to do our own domestic chores or is this part of some new economic phenomenon?

D: Well, first of all hello and thanks for inviting me onto your programme … um so, yes in answer to your question, it's said that in Britain today there are more workers doing domestic jobs than there were in the 19th century – um … perhaps as many as two million: gardeners, nannies etcetera. And this is a direct consequence of globalisation and the freeing up of the labour market. You see, many of these workers are migrants – in the case of Britain mostly Eastern Europeans. Umm and I think that in capitalist economies, at any rate, the richer classes will always provide employment for the poorer classes. As the Victorian satirist Hilaire Belloc famously said, 'it is the duty of the wealthy man to give employment to the artisan'.

I: Yes, … but that's the point, isn't it? A 19th-century style servant economy actually emphasises the inequalities between rich and poor in a society.

D: Well, hmm … yes, it can do, but it also creates employment. You don't have to be

especially rich to have a cleaner come once a week and tidy your house. Quite a lot of working people do that. A lot of so-called ordinary people get their windows cleaned every few months. But there are some – er … rich – people who get it into their heads that they're too busy or important to do any domestic chores. So they'll hire a personal shopper, and have someone walk their dog every day. If they're having a party at home, they'll get an outside catering company to prepare the food. I know some people who even have their Christmas tree installed in their living room and then decorated for them. That really *is* a statement of wealth.

I: Hmm … it seems more a statement of confused priorities to me. Walking the dog and decorating the Christmas tree are supposed to be a pleasure, aren't they?

D: Mmm … of course, they are. But look at it another way … these are all things that create employment. As long as staff are treated well – you know, as employees, not as servants –and are fairly paid and their skills are valued, just as you would show respect to your hairdresser when you get your hair cut, then I don't see a problem.

🎧 2.43

LA = Letting agent; W = Woman

LA: So, you've had a look at the offices. What do you think?

W: Well, yeah, I really like the building. To be honest, it's absolutely perfect for our needs.

LA: That's wonderful. So you'd like to take it then?

W: Well, yes, ideally I would but … mmm a key thing for us is how long we'd be tied into the lease.

LA: Er … It's a fifteen-year lease. I think that was on the details I sent you.

W: Yes, it was but I was hoping we could negotiate that down. Because if you look at it from our point of view … we're a young business … umm … we don't really know how things are going to go over the next few years … who does? … and let's face it, fifteen years is a big commitment. So if your client could move a bit on that …

LA: Hmm … I think what you have to appreciate is that our client's main concern is to secure a rental for a reasonable length of time. You know, at the end of the day, it gives them some security. To tell you the truth, that's why the rent is so low. The fifteen-year period is a kind of compensation for that. So I'm not at all sure we're going to get anywhere there …

W: Oh … that's a bit of a sticking point then, isn't it? Is there not some way around that?

LA: Er … Not that I can think of offhand. What did you have in mind?

W: Well, perhaps if we signed a fifteen-year lease but with a get-out clause after, say, six years, then we could pay some kind of forfeit to get out of the contract.

LA: Um … well the normal forfeit would be that you paid the remaining nine years rent, so I don't really think that would work …

W: Oh, I see. Well, that's a shame because I really like it and we need somewhere pretty urgently.

LA: Look, we have other people interested in the premises, so someone will take it … If I were in your shoes … you know … and found the terms of the lease difficult, I think I'd just leave it. When all's said and done, it has to feel right for you.

W: But that's just the problem it does feel right for us. Give me a moment. I'm just going to call my business partner and see what he thinks …

LA: OK no problem …

Life

UPPER INTERMEDIATE
WORKBOOK

Paul Dummett

7a Solving the water problem

Solving the **water** problem

Conservation

This is perhaps the simplest and most cost-effective solution. Moreover, everyone can contribute, from the water companies to the end-user. The water companies can make sure that they minimise waste by repairing cracked pipes and by imposing restrictions on water usage – not allowing people to use hosepipes has been one traditional method. But more significantly, they can also limit water consumption by making people pay for what they use, rather than for their connection to the water supply. If everyone had a water meter, they would think more carefully when they turned on the tap. With metered water, the market for water-saving devices – low-flush toilets, efficient washing machines and dishwashers, and water butts for collecting rainwater – will grow by itself.

Desalination

In many parts of the world, there is not enough fresh water but an abundance of salt water. This has encouraged the building of desalination plants. On the face of it, this seems to be a very neat solution. However, these plants are incredibly expensive to build – a recent project in Hawaii cost US $35 million. This is why not many plants have been built in poorer regions. Also, their ecological footprint is heavy. The process requires huge amounts of electricity. There is also growing evidence that the high concentrations of salt which are returned to the earth or the sea have a very damaging effect on plant and wildlife.

New technologies

'Cloud seeding' is a new 'weather modification' technology that scientists are developing to solve global climate change. In this process, the clouds are sprinkled with tiny crystals of silver iodide, which encourage moisture to collect and condense, causing rainfall. Some sceptics wonder whether this technology will be effective and ask what use it is going to be in countries where there is very little cloud. Others worry that no one has properly researched the possible harmful effects of a concentration of silver on human health. As one scientist amusingly put it, 'Sometimes not every cloud has a silver lining.'

The conclusion would seem to be that new technologies are a long way from solving our water problems, particularly in poorer countries. For the moment, conservation still seems to be our best hope.

Reading water

1 Look at the solutions for solving the water problem. Read the text and tick (✓) the solutions that are mentioned.

- [ ] repairing broken water pipes
- [ ] stopping climate change
- [ ] reusing rainwater
- [ ] having fewer showers and baths
- [ ] turning salt water into fresh water
- [ ] making artificial rainclouds

2 Read the article and choose the best option (a–c).

1 Probably the most effective way for water companies to reduce water consumption is:
   a to fix broken water pipes.
   b to limit how much water people are allowed to use.
   c to charge people according to how much water they consume.

2 According to the author, people will buy water-saving devices:
   a if the devices are more efficient.
   b if they see there is financial benefit.
   c whether they have a meter or not.

3 Desalination plants have … main disadvantages.
   a two
   b three
   c four

4 'Cloud seeding' is a technology that:
   a manipulates natural weather patterns.
   b uses the natural elements in a cloud to produce rainfall.
   c encourages cloud formation.

5 The author says that new technologies:
   a will soon be able to provide a solution.
   b will never provide a solution.
   c cannot provide a solution at the moment.

Glossary
moisture (n) /ˈmɔɪstʃə/ water in the air or on the surface of something
restriction (n) /rɪˈstrɪkʃ(ə)n/ limit
sprinkle (v) /ˈsprɪŋkl/ to cover with little pieces of a thing

3 Read the article again and find words that mean:

a   a consumer (para 1) ....

b   something you use to water the garden or clean the car (para 1) ....

c   something that measures the amount of water you consume (para 1) ....

d   something that collects water, usually in the garden (para 1) ....

e   at first sight (para 2) ....

f   impact on the environment (para 2) ....

g   a person who isn't convinced (para 3) ....

h   'there is always some good, even in a bad thing' (para 3) ....

Grammar mixed conditional sentences

4 Complete the sentences. Put the verbs in the correct form. Use zero, first, second, third and mixed conditionals.

1   If the water companies .... (not / impose) restrictions on water use in the past, there .... (be) water shortages now.

2   If people .... (have) to pay according to how much water they used, they .... (use) less water.

3   If companies .... (introduce) water meters, then people .... (buy) more water-saving devices.

4   If there .... (be) more fresh water, we .... (not/ need) technologies like desalination.

5   If desalination plants .... (not / be) so expensive, more of them .... (be built) in poorer countries before now.

6   If some ecosystems .... (not / be) damaged by pollution, people .... (feel) more optimistic about this technology.

7   Cloud seeding only .... (work) if there .... (be) clouds in the sky.

8   If someone .... (think) of a better idea than conservation, it .... (be) in use by now.

🔊 **2.8** Listen to the contracted forms in these sentences. Notice how *I'd have* and *he'd have* sound like one word. Listen again and repeat.

1   If he asked me, I'd certainly offer to help him.

2   I'd come with you, if we could leave a little later.

3   If I'd known, I'd have told you.

4   If he was more thoughtful, he'd have remembered your birthday.

5   If it's not too late to be included, I'd like to come to the meeting.

Vocabulary conservation verbs

6 Complete the sentences about resources using these verbs.

conserve   consume   preserve   protect
run out of   save   spend   waste

1   We've .... milk. Can you go and buy some from the shop?

2   It's very important to .... money in good times, so that you have some for the bad times.

3   Don't .... your energy trying to persuade the council. They are going to build on that green space anyway, even though they promised to .... it for wildlife.

4   Using salt to .... food is a very old practice.

5   The WWF has launched a campaign to .... the tiger from the threat of extinction.

6   We need to return to a simpler way of life. We .... too much time shopping and we .... too many goods.

7b Oil

Vocabulary oil

1 Label the pictures using these words.

> oil barrel   oil field   oil pipeline   oil refinery
> oil rig   oil slick   oil tanker   oil well

1 _____

2 _____

3 _____

4 _____

5 _____

6 _____

7 _____

8 _____

Listening alternatives to oil

2 🔊 **2.9** Listen to an interview with an oil industry expert. Does he think there is a reasonable alternative to oil?

3 🔊 **2.9** Listen again and answer the questions.

1 Peak oil means … .
   a the maximum amount of oil that can be extracted
   b the oil which is still in the ground
   c the high point in oil reserves

2 The conventional way to extract oil is to … .
   a drill deep under the surface of the Earth
   b drill a little way under the surface
   c drill only on land

3 The speaker says that unconventional drilling methods can be … .
   a very expensive
   b unsafe
   c not environmentally-friendly

4 What surprises the presenter?
   a that no one has found an alternative to oil
   b that the price of oil continues to rise
   c that people have not chosen another source of fuel

5 What makes petrol so convenient, according to the expert?
   a the amount of energy that petrol produces
   b the easy storage and delivery of petrol
   c both these things

6 What problem do electric cars share with petrol cars?
   a they have a limited range
   b the basic material needed to power them is limited
   c they have the potential to explode

Grammar *wish*, *would rather* and *if only*

4 Complete these sentences from the interview by putting the verb in the correct form.

1 We wish oil _____ (go) on forever.

2 I wish I _____ (be able) to give you a straight answer.

3 A lot of people wish that we _____ (not / start) to go down this route.

4 I'm sure people would rather _____ (have) a cheaper and cleaner alternative.

5 If only there _____ (be) a cheaper, cleaner and more efficient alternative.

6 Would you rather we _____ (run) out of oil or lithium?

5 Complete the short conversations using the correct form of the verbs given.

1 **A**: Would you like to drive or shall I?
   B: I'd rather you _____ (drive).

2 **A**: Are you going to buy that new electric car?
   B: If only I _____ (have) enough money, then I'd get it tomorrow, but it's over £20,000!

3 **A**: Some people think that cheap petrol is a basic human right.
   B: I know. I wish people _____ (stop) complaining and use their cars less.

4 **A**: Your new car is amazing. Doesn't it use a lot of petrol, though?
   B: Yes, it does. I wish I _____ (buy) one with a smaller engine.

5 **A**: The oil spill was terrible. What do you think happened to all the oil in the sea?
   B: I'd rather _____ (not / think) about it. It's probably still out there.

6 **A**: We all depend too much on the countries who produce oil.
   B: I know. I wish each country _____ (become) more independent in its energy needs.

7 **A**: Did you see the programme about alternative energies last night?
   B: No, but I wish I _____ (see) it. It looked really interesting.

8 **A**: Shall I speak to the neighbours about parking their car in front of our garage?
   B: I'd rather you _____ (not / speak) to them. I don't want to have an argument.

6 Pronunciation contractions with *wish* and *would rather*

🔊 **2.10** Listen to the contracted forms in these sentences. Notice how *I'd* = *I had* and *I would*, and how *we'd* = *we had* and *we would*. Listen again and repeat.

1 I wish I'd known earlier.
2 Actually, I'd rather you didn't smoke.
3 If only we'd taken the train.
4 We'd rather not wait, if possible.
5 I wish I'd left my job.

7 Dictation Canada's oil sands

🔊 **2.11** Listen and complete the description of an article about Canada's oil sands.

_____

in the tar sands of Alberta _____

_____

However, _____

_____

as conventional methods of extraction.

As a result, _____

_____

_____

7c An emotive subject

Listening conservation stories

1 🔊 **2.12** You are going to hear three people talking about conservation projects. Listen and complete the table.

	What needs to be protected?	Has the conservation work been successful?
1	The mangrove _____ in _____	
2	The West African _____	
3	The black poplar _____ in _____	

2 🔊 **2.12** Listen again. Are the sentences true (T) or false (F)? Or is there not enough information (N) to say if the statements are true or false?

1 Every inhabitant of Cancún misses the beautiful mangrove forest.
2 Waste water has badly damaged the coral reef along this part of the coast.
3 In West Africa, conservationists needed to find out where the giraffe went for food.
4 Farmers were killing the giraffes who fed on their land.
5 People associate the word 'conservation' with work in developing countries.
6 The decrease in the numbers of black poplar trees has been quite sudden.

3 🔊 **2.12** Complete the sentences about the conservation projects using these words. Then listen and check.

> classic heroic rarest rotting sale small wonderful victims

1 Today that forest is buried and _____ underneath 500 hotels.
2 This place is a _____ example of how not to build a tourist resort.
3 Nature is for _____ here.
4 The mangroves are not the only _____ .
5 A _____ effort on the part of conservationists has saved the giraffe.
6 The conservationists could then begin to educate local people about the dangers facing these _____ creatures.
7 But in fact, many conservation efforts are _____ in scale.
8 The black poplar is one of Britain's _____ species of tree.

4 Find words and expressions in Exercise 3 that have these meanings:
1 very typical _____
2 a period of ten years _____
3 a person or thing against which a crime is committed _____
4 placed under the ground _____
5 you can buy it _____
6 decaying or going bad _____

Vocabulary strong feelings

5 Look at these words. Tick the emotive words.

> back-breaking criticise deplore desperate
> interested in keen on majestic obsessed with
> tall tiring

6 Rewrite the text about the black poplar tree. Replace the words in bold with a more emotive word from the box.

> deprived exploit giant most threatened
> over-developed plummeting rescue wonderful

If you mention the term 'conservation efforts', people often think of attempts to [1] **save** endangered animals; or to protect [2] **poor** communities from [3] **big** corporate organisations which are trying to [4] **use** their land. But in fact, many conservation efforts are small in scale and many have [5] **positive** outcomes. The black poplar tree is one of Britain's [6] **rarest** species and its numbers have been [7] **declining** for decades. That's mainly because much of its natural habitat – the floodplain – has been [8] **built on** with new housing.

1 _____   5 _____
2 _____   6 _____
3 _____   7 _____
4 _____   8 _____

7d Is globalisation good?

Real life making your point

1 🎧 **2.13** Listen to four people speaking about globalisation. Are the speakers in favour (F) or against globalisation (A)?

	F	A
Speaker 1	☐	☐
Speaker 2	☐	☐
Speaker 3	☐	☐
Speaker 4	☐	☐

2 🎧 **2.13** Listen again to the four speakers and complete the summaries.

Speaker 1:   Globalisation helps us all to

Speaker 2:   Globalisation just helps people

Speaker 3:   Globalisation is just a

Speaker 4:   Globalisation has just increased

3 🎧 **2.13** Complete these phrases used by the speakers. Then listen and check.

1   That's _____ the _____ .
2   Sorry, I _____ don't _____ that.
3   To _____ , I could live without flowers that are imported from Africa.
4   We're _____ this debate all _____ .
5   _____ if we had to grow our own coffee in England.
6   _____ me _____ you another example.
7   There's no _____ that it has helped the rich.

4   Which techniques did the speakers use in their arguments? Match the speakers (1–4) with the techniques (a–e). There is one extra technique.

Speaker 1 _____
Speaker 2 _____
Speaker 3 _____
Speaker 4 _____

a   humour
b   challenging the question itself
c   speaking clearly and slowly
d   illustrating with examples
e   anticipating counter-arguments

5 Pronunciation sentence stress

a 🎧 **2.14** Underline the words that you think are most stressed in these sentences. Then listen and check.

1   Globalisation may have helped the rich, but it hasn't helped the poor. (2 words)
2   Globalisation is not something that has been invented; it's a natural phenomenon. (2 words)
3   I like having things that I can't buy locally, but I don't actually need them. (2 words)
4   Globalisation doesn't harm poor countries; it helps them. (2 words)
5   I wish you were right, but the facts show the opposite. (4 words)

b 🎧 **2.14** Practise saying the sentences. Listen and compare your pronunciation.

6 Listen and respond making your point

🎧 **2.15** Listen to a friend asking you to give your opinion about globalisation. Look at the points below. Respond with your own words. Then compare your response with the model answer that follows.

- Stress what your opinion is.
- Reject their argument.
- Give an example.
- Challenge the question itself.

1

> *What do you think about globalisation?*

> *To be honest with you, I think it's probably a good thing.*

7e Waste

Writing a letter to the press

1 Read the letter below and answer the questions

1 What caused the writer to send the letter?

....

....

2 What does she say will happen if nothing is done?

....

....

Daily Times

Published: January 12

Sir,

I am very tired of seeing so much waste in a world where many people [1] ....
.... suffer shortages of food, energy and other basic necessities.

Each day at my local supermarket, enormous quantities of food [2] ....
are thrown away when it could easily be given to charities for the homeless. People often throw away electronic equipment, [3] ....
.... when the item is only four or five years old. Cars [4] ....
sit in traffic jams with their engines running, burning fuel unnecessarily. Clothes, [5] ....
...................., are so cheap nowadays that people think nothing of wearing something once or twice and then throwing it away.

How have we allowed ourselves to become so careless about precious resources? Are we simply too rich to care? If we do not change the way we behave, a change of behaviour will be forced upon us because there will be no more resources left for us to waste.

H. Henby, Oxford

2 Writing skills giving vivid examples

a Use these words and one of the details (a–e) to add information that makes the letter more vivid. Insert the information in the spaces (1–5).

such as   with   especially   which   who

a items of fashion clothing
b flat-screen TVs, computers or mobile phones
c is near its sell-by date
d live in more difficult circumstances than us
e only one person in them

b Make the short letter below more vivid by giving more information or examples in the spaces (1–5). Use these notes to help you.

- give more details of the building
- give examples
- describe what people do here
- give examples
- give reasons

Sir,

I agree totally with James Needham (*Daily Times*, 4th May). The decision to build a new block of flats [1] ....
on part of what is now Summerdine Park is shocking. This park not only contains many species of trees [2] ...., it is also one of the few green spaces in the area, [3] .... There are certainly other more suitable places to build new housing [4] .... It would be better to develop areas like this [5] ....

Word focus *better*

3 Match the beginning of the sentences (1–5) with their endings (a–e).

1 You had better
2 We would be better off
3 I think it would be better
4 He always tries to go one better
5 He should know better

a than me.
b if we kept this car until it gets too expensive to maintain.
c not mention the question of waste to him. He gets very emotional.
d than to cut down a tree in a conservation area.
e to send a letter to the local paper.

4 Complete the dialogue using the verbs in the correct form: *to* + infinitive, infinitive or *-ing*.

Andy: I still haven't heard back from the company that interviewed me last week for a job. Do you think I should call them or would it be better [1] .... (wait)?

Fran: I think you'd be better off [2] .... (call) them. It shows you're interested, at least.

Andy: Yeah, you're right. I'd better [3] .... (do) that this afternoon. It's better [4] .... (know) than not.

Wordbuilding collocations related to one word

1 Look at these noun + noun collocations. Match them to the definitions below.

air: air bridge   air force   air vent

water: water jug   water leak   water lily

wind: wind chill   wind farm   wind instrument

1   e.g. clarinet, oboe, flute
....

2   used for getting from the airport terminal to the plane ....

3   a place where renewable energy is generated
....

4   the drop in temperature cause by a cold wind
....

5   an escape of water from a pipe or tank
....

6   part of the military, along with the army and navy ....

7   used for serving water at the dinner table
....

8   a place (e.g. in a wall) where air can enter or exit ....

9   a flower that grows in lakes and ponds
....

2 Some noun + noun collocations become one compound noun. Look at these collocations with *sun*. Which two words are opposites?

sunglasses   sunlight   sunrise   sunset   suntan

Learning skills improving your listening

3 🔊 **2.16** A key to understanding fast native speech is to understand stress and linking in English pronunciation. Listen to this sentence and note the stress and linking in it.

1   **Stress:**   Sorry I just <u>don't</u> ac<u>cept</u> that.
2   **Linking:** Sorry‿I just don't‿accept that.

4 🔊 **2.17** Look at these sentences. Underline the stressed syllables and indicate where the sounds are linked. Then listen and check.

1   Globalisation helps people in rich countries.
2   They can have goods out of season.
3   But to be honest, I don't need flowers imported from Africa in December.

5 🔊 **2.18** Read these steps for improving your listening skills. Listen again to the first speaker from 7d, Exercise 1 and follow the steps (1–5).

1   Write down the words you hear.
2   Read your transcript back. Does it make grammatical sense?
3   Compare your transcript with the audioscript.
4   Note the words and sounds which have the strongest stress. These should be the key words that convey the meaning.
5   Note which words are clearly linked. This will help you to distinguish them the next time you hear them.

Check!

6 Complete the crossword using phrases about natural resources. All the answers are in Student's Book Unit 7.

Across

1   resources which can be replaced in nature (9)
4 and 5   with its special plants and wildlife, Madagascar has one of these (6,9)
5   see 4 Across
7   the substance which is removed from water in the desalination process (4)
10   this American river does not reach the sea anymore (8)
12   another word for 'conserve' (4)
13   see 11 Down

Down

1   the three Rs in conservation: reduce, …, recycle (5)
2   people whose job it is to cut down trees (7)
3   Ecuador wanted to be paid not to do this with its oil (7)
6   the opposite of abundant (6)
8   this sea is a tenth of the size it was in the 1960s (4)
9   producing half a kilo of this uses 85,000 litres of water (4)
11 and 13 Across   the point where oil is taken from the ground (3, 4)

Unit 8 The news

8a Photojournalism

Vocabulary the news

1 Complete the crossword with words related to news reporting.

Across

1 and 8 a story which is both serious and urgent (4, 4)

3 news which is less serious and not urgent (4)

7 a piece expressing the opinion of the newspaper (9)

Down

2 any piece written in a newspaper or magazine (7)

4 a special or prominent piece in a magazine or newspaper (8)

5 the title of the main news story, written in big letters (8)

6 a section of the newspaper dedicated to a particular writer (6)

(crossword grid with clues: 1 H, 2 A, 3 S, 4 F, 5 H, 6 C, 7 E, 8 N)

Listening re-touching reality

2 🔊 **2.19** Listen to an interview with a journalist talking about altering photos. What two examples do they discuss? Complete the descriptions.

1 The _____ of the February _____ edition of *National Geographic* magazine.

2 A photo of _____ Reagan and Raisa Gorbachev in *Picture* _____ magazine.

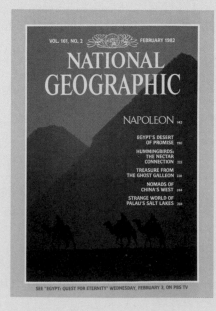

3 🔊 **2.19** Listen again. Are the sentences true (T) or false (F)?

1 Photo editors changed the size of the pyramids in the photo.

2 An editor said that the changes to the photo were OK because it was a cover photo.

3 He also said that technology had made altering images more acceptable.

4 Editors have said that it's acceptable to alter covers because they advertise the book or magazine.

5 The photographer thinks that there's no difference between manipulating cover images and altering news photos.

6 *Picture Week* changed two photos to suggest the people in them had friendly faces.

7 People thought that the *Picture Week* photo was unacceptable.

8 People are not able to distinguish between reality and fiction.

Glossary
alter (v) /ˈɒltə/ change
digitally enhanced (adj) /ˈdɪdʒɪt(ə)li ɪnˈhɑːnst/ improved using digital technology
touch up (v) /tʌtʃ ˈʌp/ make small changes to improve an image

4 Pronunciation long vowel /əʊ/

🔊 **2.20** Listen to these words. Pay attention to the long /əʊ/ sound. Then listen again and repeat.

b<u>oa</u>t	d<u>o</u>n't	fell<u>ow</u>	g<u>o</u>ing	gr<u>ow</u>ing	h<u>o</u>tel
kn<u>ow</u>	l<u>o</u>cal	opp<u>o</u>sed	<u>ow</u>n	ph<u>o</u>to	s<u>o</u>fa

Grammar reporting verbs

5 Rewrite these sentences using the reporting verbs given.

1 People said that the magazine had manipulated reality.

People **accused** the magazine ....

2 The editor said they had altered the image.

The editor **admitted** ....

3 But he said they hadn't done anything wrong.

But he **denied** ....

4 He said modern technology made it easy to alter images.

He **blamed** ....

5 Some editors tell their designers that it is OK to alter images for covers.

Some editors **persuade** ....

6 People weren't happy and said they had been given a false impression.

People **complained** ....

7 Some people say, 'Don't trust a photo if there's anything important riding on it.'

Some people **warn** you ....

6 Complete the text using the correct form of the verbs. Use prepositions where necessary.

In the past, photographers have been criticised [1] .... (invade) people's privacy or [2] .... (take) pictures that did not reflect the reality of a situation. But nowadays, in the age of digital photography, there is a new problem. How do we know that the photo has not been altered after it has been taken? It would be wrong to blame the photographer [3] .... (manipulate) some of the photos that appear in our newspapers and magazines. A photo editor might be asked [4] .... (alter) a photo digitally in order to make a good story. For example, someone might suggest [5] .... (touch) up the photo of a film star's face to make them look more attractive. Or they might urge the photo editor [6] .... (add) an image of a frightened child into a photo of a street protest. You can perhaps forgive the editor [7] .... (make) the first alteration, but what about the second? That is a practice people should possibly refuse [8] .... (accept).

Vocabulary photography

7 Match the verbs in Box A with the nouns in Box B and write the collocations.

A	**B**
capture	events
open	the lens
record	the moment
see through	a photo
take	a snaphot
take	the shutter

1 ....

2 ....

3 ....

4 ....

5 ....

6 ....

8 Dictation digital photography

🔊 **2.21** Listen to someone talking about analogue and digital cameras. Then complete the text.

1 Like many of his fellow professionals, photographer Fritz Hoffman ....

....

2 A digital camera ....

...., but an analogue camera ....

3 Hoffman also claims ....

....

4 That's so that ....

....

8b News in brief

Reading good news stories

1 Read the four newspaper stories below and match the headlines (a–d) with the stories (1–4).

a Better to give than receive
b A sense of community
c A charmed life
d An old secret

2 Write the number of the story (1–4) next to the statements (a–f).

This story shows that:
a you can help people without spending a lot of money. ....
b there is not one right way to do something. ....
c you can inspire other people by your actions. ....
d miracles do happen. ....
e there is a good and a bad side to every situation. ....
f people's faith in human nature can be restored. ....

News in brief

1 ....

In the UK street riots of 2011, it is estimated that rioters caused over £100 million of damage to their own communities. But for every negative, there's often a positive, as the case of Mr Biber, a London barber, shows. Mr Biber's barber shop in London, where he has been cutting hair for 40 years, was among those wrecked, and the 89-year-old thought he had lost everything. But word got around and a website to support him was set up. Donations raised £35,000, enough to make the necessary repairs. Moreover, people's generosity gave Mr Biber the encouragement to carry on doing what he loves.

2 ....

Some people believe that the secret to a long life is a glass of red wine every day. For others, it is plenty of exercise. But few people would claim that eating fast food contributed to longevity. They obviously haven't met 100-year old Catherine Reddoch from Matamata, New Zealand. Every day, using her zimmer frame to support her, she walks a kilometre – a journey which takes her one hour – to her local hamburger café. Here she eats a cheeseburger and drinks a cup of hot chocolate. Mrs Reddoch is not concerned about the fat content of the meal. 'I eat anything and everything – I like my cheeseburgers,' she says. It was reported that on her 100th birthday, the café put a plaque with her name on it on her usual seat.

3 ....

Secret Agent L is the brainchild of one woman, Laura Miller. Laura's mission is to spread kindness in the world. She does this by doing small acts of kindness, like leaving a flower on someone's car windscreen or making a nice walking stick for someone to find when they are on a long walk.

The idea is that when someone finds these secret gifts, it brightens up their day. It is believed that Secret Agent L now has over 1,800 followers around the world, all creating and sharing their ideas for similar kind acts.

4 ....

A 21-year-old man who drove his car over the edge of the Grand Canyon escaped with only a few minor injuries. Witnesses said that his car had plunged 200 feet into the mile-deep canyon before hitting a tree which stopped it falling further. It is not thought that he was speeding, but the cause of the accident remains unknown. Another visitor found him lying in the road after he had apparently climbed back out of the canyon. The emergency services said he was an extremely lucky man.

Glossary
plaque (n) /plæk/ a small metal sign
riot (n) /ˈraɪət/ a violent protest

3 Read the stories again and find words that mean:

1 destroyed (para 1) ....
2 gifts of money (para 1) ....
3 living a long time (para 2) ....
4 a walking aid for old people (para 2)
   ....
5 an original idea (para 3) ....
6 make more cheerful (para 3) ....
7 fell or dived (para 4) ....
8 driving too fast (para 4) ....

Grammar passive reporting verbs

4 Find an example of a passive reporting verb in each story on page 106 and underline it.

5 **Grammar extra tenses in passive reporting verbs**

> ▶ **TENSES IN PASSIVE REPORTING VERBS**
>
> Note how these tenses are transformed from active to passive.
>
> People say ...   → It is said that ...
> People have said ...   → It has been said that ...
> People said ...   → It was said that ...
> People had said ...   → It had been said that ...

Look at the grammar box. Rewrite these phrases using passive reporting verbs.

1 People say that ...   → It *is said that ...*
2 Everyone understands that ...
   It ....
3 Everyone knew that ...
   It ....
4 People believed that ...
   It ....
5 People have estimated that ...
   It ....
6 People think that ...
   It ....
7 People had hoped that ...
   It ....
8 Everyone supposes that ...
   It ....

6 Rewrite the sentences using passive reporting verbs.

1 People say that for every negative, there is always a positive.
   It is said that for every negative, there is always a positive.
2 People expect Mr Biber to carry on doing what he loves.
   It .... that Mr Biber
   .... what he loves.

3 People used to think that a glass of red wine a day helped you to live longer.
   In the past, ...
   ....
4 Most people don't recommend eating fast food if you want to live longer.
   It .... that you
   ....
5 People hoped that secret gifts would brighten up someone's day.
   It .... that secret
   gifts ....
6 People supposed that the tree prevented the car falling further.
   It ....
7 People considered the man lucky to survive the accident.
   It .... that the man
   ....
8 People have reported great success with the idea.
   It .... the idea
   .... very successful.

Vocabulary the feel-good factor

7 Match the adjectives describing good news stories in box A with the words that have the opposite or a near opposite meaning in box B.

A	**B**
amusing	ordinary
charming	depressing
inspiring	pessimistic
quirky	serious
encouraging	dreary
optimistic	uninspiring

8 **Pronunciation weak forms in verbs**

🔊 **2.22** Listen to the auxiliary verbs in these sentences. Note how they are pronounced using the weak form. Listen again and repeat.

1 It was estimated that £100 million worth of damage was caused in the riots.
2 It is believed that Secret Agent L has more than 200 followers.
3 It was thought that the driver had fallen asleep at the wheel of his car.
4 It was expected that the injured man would make a full recovery.
5 It has been estimated that 50% of the population will be overweight by 2020.
6 It had been thought that diet was more important than exercise.

8c Balanced reporting

Listening news reports

1 💿 **2.23** Listen to a journalist talking about balanced reporting. Are the sentences true (T) or false (F)?

1 *National Geographic* likes to report on endangered environments.
2 The main article was about a gas pipeline.
3 The speaker thinks that journalists should give equal space to both sides in a debate.

2 💿 **2.23** Listen to the report again and choose the correct option.
1 Journalists have to try to give a balanced *view / opinion* and tell a good story.
2 *National Geographic* tries to find places where we can marvel at the *joys / wonders* of nature.
3 The main article described the *beauty / nature* of the white Kermode Spirit Bear.
4 A smaller article described the building of a gas *platform / pipeline*.
5 *Technically / Strictly* speaking, it was inaccurate to say the government had given its approval.
6 The journalists and editors in question *shot / jumped* the gun in order to make their point.
7 The article highlights the *dilemma / problem* for journalists.
8 Ideally the people involved would like to have *the say-so / the last word*.

3 Look at the words and expressions in Exercise 2 and find words that mean:
1 in actual fact (2 words)

2 amazing and beautiful things (1 word)

3 have the final decision (4 words)

4 an impartial opinion (2 words)

5 a difficult choice (1 word)

6 be too hasty (3 words)

Word focus *word*

4 Look at these expressions with *word* and choose the correct definition (a or b).

1 *From the word go*, the restaurant was full every night.
   a from when we had permission
   b from the start

2 Jamie has been behaving very strangely recently. Can you *have a quiet word with* him?
   a be very strict with   b talk privately to

3 Please *don't say a word* to Sarah about the cup I broke. It's her favourite.
   a don't mention   b lie

4 He said I would never be a professional artist but he had to *eat his words*.
   a admit he was wrong   b apologise

5 Complete the sentences using the expressions with *word*.

> don't take my word for it   eat my words
> from the word go   gave his word
> have the last word
> one person's word against another's
> was lost for words   word of mouth

1 Our magazine gets most of its new customers by _____ or because someone has read a copy in a doctor's waiting room.
2 I assured them that it would be easy to find a good wildlife photographer. I hope I don't have to _____ .
3 It is just _____ . In the end, the reader will have to decide who they believe.
4 If you don't believe what I'm telling you, then _____ . Go and check the facts for yourself.
5 He _____ that he would not publish the story before I had read it.
6 _____ , the journalist involved the company in the research for the article.
7 I didn't know what to say – I _____ .
8 She's very argumentative and always has to _____ .

8d Guess what

Real life reporting what you heard

1 Complete the sentences. Use a verb in each space. Do the sentences express belief (B) or disbelief (D)?

	B	D
1 I think I'd _____ her word for it.	☐	☐
2 He generally _____ his facts right.	☐	☐
3 He's not the type to _____ gossip.	☐	☐
4 _____ no notice of what she says.	☐	☐
5 It's been _____ out of proportion.	☐	☐
6 I'd _____ that with a pinch of salt.	☐	☐

2 🔊 **2.24** Listen to a conversation between two friends, Jane and Annie, and answer the questions.

1 What is the news about Patrick that Jane wants to share?

_____

_____

_____

2 Who did she hear this news from?

_____

3 What does Annie ask Jane to do with the news? Why?

_____

_____

3 🔊 **2.24** Complete the sentences from the conversation. Then listen again and check.

> *verbs*: guess   heard   reckons   seems
> *prepositions*: about   according to
> *adverbs*: apparently   supposedly
> *nouns*: gossip   pinch

1 Did you hear the good news _____ (*preposition*) Patrick? _____ (*verb*) what?

2 Well, _____ (*adverb*) he was spotted by someone from a big theatrical agency.

3 She _____ (*verb*) that it won't be long before we see him on TV.

4 Well, I'd take that with a _____ (*noun*) of salt if I were you.

5 No, _____ (*preposition*) Kate, it's more than that.

6 That'd be fantastic. I _____ (*verb*) that it was really difficult to get that kind of work.

7 Don't worry. I'm not the type to spread _____ (*noun*). Does the agency take a big fee?

8 It _____ (*verb*) that they only take 10% or 15%, _____ (*adverb*).

4 Pronunciation the schwa

🔊 **2.25** Listen to these words from the conversation. <u>Underline</u> the stressed syllable and circle the schwa / ə / sounds.
Example: s(u)ppos(e)dly

1	comedy	5	according
2	festival	6	difficult
3	apparently	7	agency
4	reckon	8	theatrical

5 Listen and respond reporting what you heard

🔊 **2.26** Listen to someone giving you some news about government taxes. Respond after the tone with your own words. Then compare your response with the model answer that follows.

1

> *Did you hear the good news about taxes?*

> *Good news about taxes? No, what happened?*

8e Group action

Vocabulary meetings

1 Write two verbs that collocate with each noun.

> attend   discuss   draft   hold   make (x2)
> put forward   reach   weigh up   write

1 _____ , _____
  a meeting

2 _____ , _____
  a suggestion

3 _____ , _____
  a decision

4 _____ , _____
  the options

5 _____ , _____
  a letter

2 Writing skill impersonal language

Rewrite the sentences using impersonal language. Use the words given.

1 We all got together to discuss how to raise the money.
  A _____ (held)

2 We discussed all the things that we could do.
  All _____ (options)

3 Julian suggested that we should ask the local council for help.
  One _____ (suggestion)

4 Pete said it was better to have some fun events.
  Another _____ (idea)

5 Several people said organising events would take too long.
  It _____ (agreed)

6 No one could decide what to do about funding the project.
  _____ (decision)

Writing minutes from a meeting

3 Read the minutes from a local meeting about a waste incinerator (a plant where rubbish is burned) in the area. Answer the questions.

1 What are the main advantages and disadvantages of the incinerator? _____

2 What action was decided on? _____

3 What action was rejected? _____

St Paul's Residents' Association

From: Kathy Barbosa

Re: New waste incinerator

Here are the minutes from the meeting which was held on 3 September.

▶ Following the government's decision to build a new waste incinerator on the old factory site in Quibble Street, <u>we met to decide</u> what action residents could take to oppose this new source of pollution.

▶ <u>Karen suggested</u> that we should get everyone in the area to sign a petition against the proposal. <u>Everyone agreed</u> that this was a good first step.

▶ <u>Tom thought</u> we should present the government with some alternative locations, but no one at the meeting was able to suggest any so the action was rejected.

▶ <u>Jo made the point</u> that the government wanted to use the incinerator to generate electricity for the area, which was a good thing for the community.

▶ <u>Kevin proposed</u> that we could have another kind of plant which sorted the waste for recycling. <u>Harry said he would research this option and discuss it</u> at the next meeting.

Next meeting date: **26 September**

---

4 Replace the underlined phrases with more impersonal ones.

1 *a meeting was held to decide*

2 _____

3 _____

4 _____

5 _____

6 _____

7 _____

Wordbuilding forming adjectives from verbs

1 Complete the sentences using the verbs + -ing.

charm   confuse   depress   inspire
refresh   tire   touch   worry

1   It is _____ that she is so late – she's normally very punctual.
2   The article was rather _____ . You couldn't work out why the daughter had left her family.
3   It's very _____ to hear a story about a business which doesn't just do things to make money.
4   He is a really _____ man – polite, interesting and kind.
5   The story about two friends overcoming their difficulties was very _____ .
6   Environmental news is often _____ , but in this case the story offered hope.
7   The news featured the _____ story of a 14-year-old girl who got a part-time job to help support her family.
8   It's very _____ to follow a film with subtitles for three hours.

2 Make adjectives using verbs + -ive.

1   good at **inventing**   _inventive_ (from _invent_)
2   good at **persuading**   _____
3   good at **creating**   _____
4   liking to **compete**   _____
5   **producing** a lot   _____
6   **talking** a lot   _____
7   wanting to **protect**   _____
8   not **responding**   _____

Learning skills keeping a learning diary

3 What is a learning diary and why is it a good idea to keep one? Look at these reasons and compare them with your own ideas.

• To learn from your mistakes and your successes

• To track your progress

• To make clear targets for the next stage of your learning

• To record what you have learnt

4 Read the following actions which can help you to evaluate and personalise your learning.

Actions

1   Write down your experiences of learning after each lesson: what you found easy, what you found difficult, what was the most important thing you learned.

2   Note down mistakes that you have made before.

3   Make a note of an extract, even a sentence, that you particularly liked and try to memorise it.

4   Set yourself a small task based on the language you learned in your last lesson, e.g. describe a good news story, report what someone said to you, or describe a situation where somebody's reputation was questioned.

5 Apply the actions (1–4) for Unit 8. Then remember to do it for your next lesson!

Check!

6 Do the quiz. You can find all the answers in Student's Book Unit 8.

Quiz Time

1   Complete these quotations.
   a   'A picture is worth a thousand w_____ .'
   b   'Good news doesn't s_____ .'
   c   'Bad news travels f_____ .'

2   Complete these sentences about the characters in Unit 8.
   a   The pilot Peter Burkill went from hero to z_____ .
   b   Sharbat Gula's photo is one of the most i_____ images of our time.
   c   It was believed that the large blue butterfly was e_____ in Britain.

3   Complete the phrases about the news.
   a   The best form of advertising is when news travels by word of m_____ .
   b   Good news stories generate a f_____ factor among people.
   c   It's not a good thing to s_____ gossip.
   d   There was an amazing f_____ about India in _National Geographic_ this month.

Unit 9 Talented people

9a The great communicator

Listening

1 🔊 **2.27** Read the questions. Then listen to the description of Ronald Reagan and complete the answers.

1 Where was Ronald Reagan raised?
In a _____

2 What jobs did he have before he entered politics?
He worked as a _____
and _____

3 What important historical event occurred during his presidency?
The collapse of _____

4 How did people make fun of him as President?
They said he _____

5 What made him a great communicator?
His ability to _____

6 What other factor worked in his favour as president?
It was a time of _____

2 🔊 **2.27** Look at the words and phrases in bold from the description of Ronald Reagan. Choose the correct meaning (a or b). Then listen again and check.

1 His skills as **an orator** were noticed and he was persuaded to run for Governor of California.
a a politician
b a public speaker

2 He took a **hard line** against communism.
a strict approach
b difficult road

3 He understood the **fundamental essence** of leadership.
a real meaning
b basic problem

4 He made people feel that they **mattered**.
a were lucky
b were important

5 The economy **thrived** during his presidency.
a did badly
b did well

6 Reagan's style of communication **stands out**.
a is noticeable
b is old-fashioned

Vocabulary careers

3 🔊 **2.27** Complete the sentences with the correct verb. Then listen again to the description and check your answers.

1 Ronald Reagan _____ from Eureka College, Illinois with a degree in economics and sociology.

2 He _____ for a short time as a radio broadcaster in Iowa.

3 He moved to Los Angeles to _____ a career as an actor in films and television.

4 After _____ the Republican Party in 1962, his skills as an orator were noticed.

5 He _____ a good job as Governor of California.

6 He went on to _____ President of the United States between 1981 and 1989.

Grammar articles: *the* or zero article?

4 Complete with *the* or zero article (–).

Countries:	_____ Japan, _____ United Arab Emirates, _____ Netherlands, _____ Thailand
Places:	_____ Amazon River, _____ countryside, _____ Moon, _____ Mount Everest
Times:	_____ weekend, _____ Saturday, _____ April, _____ spring
Other:	_____ breakfast, _____ police, _____ poor, _____ biology

5 Complete the sentences with *the* or zero article (–).

1 After joining _____ Republican Party in 1962, his skills as an orator were noticed and he was persuaded to run for _____ Governor of _____ California.

2 He then went on to become President of _____ United States between _____ 1981 and 1989.

3 He remains one of _____ most popular American presidents of _____ past 50 years.

4 Ronald Reagan understood _____ fundamental essence of _____ leadership: that is, that you have to be able to communicate.

5 Reagan always gave _____ impression that he was listening when he was speaking to you.

6 He looked you in _____ eye, smiled at you, made you feel special.

7 He presided over a time of _____ great economic growth in _____ America.

8 _____ things weren't great for most Americans and he gave them _____ hope.

9 It obviously helped that _____ economy thrived during his presidency.

10 If you can connect with _____ ordinary person, there's very little you can do wrong.

6 Pronunciation linking vowels

a 🔊 **2.28** Listen to these phrases. What sound links the words: /w/, /j/ or /r/?

	/w/	/j/	/r/
1 one idea‿at a time	☐	☐	☐
2 he‿often spoke to ordinary people	☐	☐	☐
3 do‿a good job	☐	☐	☐
4 the beginning of the‿end	☐	☐	☐
5 an area‿of outstanding beauty	☐	☐	☐
6 China‿and India	☐	☐	☐
7 look someone in the‿eye	☐	☐	☐
8 too‿expensive	☐	☐	☐
9 it's so‿exciting	☐	☐	☐

b 🔊 **2.28** Listen again and check. Then practise saying each phrase.

7 Dictation careers

🔊 **2.29** Listen to three people describing their careers. Write down the words you hear. Be careful – many of the sentences contain the linking sounds /w/, /j/ or /r/.

1 I guess I _____

2 It's not easy _____

3 I was always told _____

Vocabulary qualifications

8 Complete the job interview between an interviewer (I) and an applicant (A) using these words.

background	experience	knowledge
qualifications	qualities	talents

I: So can you tell me first a little bit about your ¹ _____ ?

A: Sure. My mother's French and my father's English. I was brought up in France and …

I: And do you have any previous ² _____ of journalism?

A: Yes. At university I was editor of the student magazine and after that I worked for a local radio station …

I: What ³ _____ do you have?

A: I have a degree in media studies and a diploma in …

I: What would you say are your best ⁴ _____ ?

A: I'm a very organised person, I'm hard-working and I think I …

I: Do you have any ⁵ _____ of European politics?

A: Well, I read the papers regularly and I take a great interest in current affairs …

I: And lastly. Do you have any particular ⁶ _____ ? Things that might make you different from other candidates?

A: I'm good at learning languages and I'm a good photographer.

9b An inspirational scientist

Reading

1 Read the text quickly and underline the part of the text that answers these questions.

1 What is the aim of Hayat Sindi's work?
2 What is the problem with medicines used to fight diseases like hepatitis?
3 What is the tool that can prevent this?
4 Why did Sindi move to England?
5 What is her hope for other women like her?

2 Read the text again and answer the questions. Choose the correct option (a–c).

1 Which of the following is NOT a quality of the new tool?
   a small   b powerful   c high-tech

2 Where is more health monitoring needed?
   a in developed countries
   b in developing countries
   c everywhere

3 Compared to results from a diagnostic laboratory, this tool's results are … .
   a more accurate   b more positive
   c quicker

4 Sindi's family was not … .
   a rich   b academic   c traditional

5 Sindi studied hard in England because she was afraid of … .
   a her parents   b failure   c feeling lonely

6 Sindi would like women to use their education to … .
   a go abroad
   b help their own countries
   c become scientists

3 Look at these words and phrases from the text. Choose the best definition (a–c).

1 entire (para 1)
   a complete   b modern   c sophisticated

2 detect (para 2)
   a have   b find   c solve

3 low-tech (para 2)
   a cheap   b small   c not sophisticated

4 daunting (para 3)
   a medical   b very difficult
   c personal

5 against the odds (para 3)
   a unsurprisingly   b unfairly
   c unexpectedly

6 guidance (para 4)
   a teaching   b comfort   c advice

Something the size of a postage stamp, costing just a penny apiece, could be a medical breakthrough that will save millions of lives. According to biotechnology scientist Hayat Sindi, this tiny piece of paper has the same power as an entire diagnostic laboratory. 'My mission is to find simple, inexpensive ways to monitor health,' Sindi says. She believes technology pioneered by a team at Harvard University will make it possible, and she co-founded the charity 'Diagnostics For All' to produce and distribute the innovation.

In the developing world, powerful drugs are used to combat diseases like HIV/AIDS, tuberculosis and hepatitis. But these medicines can cause liver damage. In developed countries, doctors monitor liver function frequently and change the medication if they detect problems. But in isolated, rural corners of the world, health monitoring simply doesn't exist. The tragic result is that millions are dying from the same drugs intended to save them. The small piece of paper is a low-tech tool which detects disease by analysing bodily fluids. Positive results, which show up in less than a minute, are indicated by a change in colour on the paper.

Sindi's determination to solve daunting problems should come as no surprise. Despite coming from a modest background, never travelling outside Saudi Arabia or speaking a word of English, she moved to England to attend university. Alone, homesick, and worried that she would fail and dishonour her family, she learned English by watching BBC news. She studied up to 20 hours a day for college entrance exams. Against the odds, she became the first Saudi woman to study biotechnology at Cambridge University. She went on to get a PhD and become a visiting scholar at Harvard University.

Sindi's passion and accomplishments have made her a role model for young women across the Middle East, an inspiration to a new generation. 'I want all women to believe in themselves and know they can transform society. When I lecture at schools, the first thing I ask children is to draw a picture of a scientist. 99.9% of them draw an old bald man with glasses. When I tell them I'm a scientist, they look so surprised.' A new foundation that she has launched gives guidance and money to encourage young women who attend university abroad to bring their skills back to their homelands.

Grammar relative clauses and reduced relative clauses

4 Look at the article again and find examples of the following.

1 a defining relative clause using *which* (para 2)

2 a defining relative clause using *who* (para 4)

3 a non-defining relative clause using *which* (para 2)

4 a reduced relative clause using a present participle (para 1)

5 a reduced relative clause using a past participle (para 1)

5 Write sentences using relative clauses. Use the relative pronouns *who, which, whose, where* and *when*. Use commas where necessary.

1 The piece of paper is the size of a postage stamp. It could save thousands of lives.

2 The charity 'Diagnostics for All' produces the tool. It was co-founded by Sindi.

3 The tool will be used in developing countries. It is difficult to find clinics there.

4 People take powerful drugs to combat diseases. These drugs can cause liver damage.

5 The results show up on the paper. The paper's colour changes if there is a problem.

6 Sindi went to England. She was a young woman at the time.

7 Sindi later went to Harvard. She was the first Saudi woman to study biotechnology at Cambridge.

8 Sindi has become a role model for other women. They want to follow her example.

6 Replace the relative clauses in these sentences with reduced relative clauses. Number 6 has two clauses.

1 Sindi's low-tech tool helps people who are suffering from the negative effects of the drugs.

2 People who live far away from hospitals and clinics will benefit from this technology.

3 The same medicines, which have been designed to fight disease, can also harm people.

4 Sindi, who was determined to succeed, studied up to twenty hours a day.

5 Sindi uses her own experience to inspire other women who wish to become scientists.

6 A new foundation, which was launched recently by Sindi, offers help to young women who want to follow a career in science.

Vocabulary personal qualities

7 The adjectives below describe Sindi's qualities. Find the nouns in the article from which the adjectives are derived.

Adjective	Noun
1 determined	
2 accomplished	
3 inspirational	
4 passionate	

8 Complete the summary about Sindi Hayat. Use these adjectives.

adaptable	analytical	articulate	daring
easy-going	independent	passionate	patient

Sindi Hayat is [1] _____ about helping people in developing countries. She also is an [2] _____ speaker and supporter of women's right to education. To be a scientist, you have to have an [3] _____ mind and to be very [4] _____ , as it can take a long time to get positive results from an experiment.

Sindi has an [5] _____ spirit, demonstrated by the fact that she went to England alone to study at university. Living in a different culture also requires you to be [6] _____ . For Sindi, to take these risks showed what a [7] _____ individual she is. Despite everything, Sindi remains a very relaxed and [8] _____ person.

9c Women leaders

Listening

1 🔊 **2.30** Look at the qualities of leaders below. Which do you associate with men (M) and which with women (W)? Listen to an interview with an author and compare your answers.

	M	W
1 happy to take risks	☐	☐
2 good at getting things done	☐	☐
3 care more what others think	☐	☐
4 insisting on a point	☐	☐
5 good at persuading people	☐	☐
6 giving orders	☐	☐
7 including others in decisions	☐	☐
8 good organisers	☐	☐

2 🔊 **2.30** Listen again. Are the sentences true (T) or false (F)?

1 The interviewer thinks that whether a leader is male or female is not the issue.

2 The author says that her claims are supported by research.

3 The author is surprised that women, not men, take more risks.

4 According to the author, men care more about what others around them think.

5 The interviewer thinks that the author is stereotyping women.

6 The author thinks that people want a more co-operative style of leadership than in the past.

3 🔊 **2.30** Complete the adjectives to describe the qualities in Exercise 1. Then listen and check.

1 adventur........
2 effect........
3 sensi........
4 car........
5 assert........
6 persuas........
7 autocrat........
8 inclu........

4 Pronunciation word stress in adjectives ending -ive

a 🔊 **2.31** Listen to the adjective words ending -ive from Exercise 3. The stress falls in the same place in each one, except for one word. What rule can you make? Which is the odd one out?

b 🔊 **2.32** Look at these adjectives. Listen and underlined the stressed syllable.

1 protective
2 creative
3 perceptive
4 imaginative
5 responsive
6 impulsive

Word focus *long*

5 Look at the sentence from the interview and its definition. Then match the sentences (1–10) with the correct definition (a–j).

> 66 It doesn't matter what gender a leader is, **as long as** they are a good leader. 99
> = It doesn't matter what gender a leader is, **if/provided that** they are a good leader.

1 'It's been great to see you. I hope we can meet up again **before long**.'

2 He stood there for what seemed like hours and **at long last** someone opened the door.

3 She wasn't angry that the company paid her poorly, but she **longed for** recognition.

4 They arrived **long after** they had intended to.

5 Jake and I **go back a long way**.

6 **The long and short of it** is that we need to reduce our spending or we'll be in trouble.

7 He **put on a long face**, so I asked him what the matter was.

8 He **has come a long way** since he was working as a washer-up in his local café.

9 '**So long**,' she said, 'I'll write to you soon.'

10 **In the long term,** I think we will see benefits from all these efficiencies.

a after much waiting
b are old friends
c desired very much
d goodbye
e the main message
f looked sad
g made a lot of progress
h much later than
i over a long period of time
j soon

9d Your own talents

Real life describing skills, talents and experience

1 Complete these expressions using the correct preposition.

1 At university, I specialised _____ photojournalism.
2 I'm very familiar _____ your magazine.
3 I'm good _____ spotting an interesting story.
4 I have some experience _____ news photography.
5 I think I'd be suited _____ working in this kind of environment.
6 I feel quite comfortable _____ tight deadlines.
7 I'm very keen _____ the idea of working closely with other journalists.
8 I'm serious _____ wanting to become a full-time news photographer.

2 🔊 **2.33** Listen to three people describing their skills at a job interview. What job are they applying for?

_____

_____

3 🔊 **2.33** Listen again and answer the questions about each of the applicants.

1 What are the skills or talents of each applicant?
  Applicant 1

  _____

  Applicant 2

  _____

  Applicant 3

  _____

2 What does each speaker lack experience of?
  Applicant 1

  _____

  Applicant 2

  _____

  Applicant 3

  _____

4 Grammar extra adjective + -ing or to + infinitive

> ▶ **ADJECTIVE + -ING or TO + INFINITIVE**
>
> Some adjectives can be followed by a preposition + -ing or by an infinitive.
>
> I'm interested **in learning** French.
> I'm happy **to show** you how it works.

Look at the grammar box. Complete the sentences. Use the correct form of the verb: -ing form or to + infinitive.

1 I'd be keen on _____ (participate) in one of your trial days.
2 I'll be sad _____ (leave) this place.
3 I'm interested in _____ (travel) to new places.
4 I'm excited about _____ (do) field research in India.
5 I'm very keen _____ (work) abroad.
6 I'd be interested _____ (find out) more about the job.

5 Pronunciation difficult words

🔊 **2.34** Practise saying these pairs of words. Then listen and check your pronunciation.

1 although also
2 clothes cloth
3 private privacy
4 knowledge know-how
5 suit sweet
6 island Iceland
7 receipt recipe
8 thorough through

6 Listen and respond describing skills, talents and experience

🔊 **2.35** Listen to questions at an interview for a job as a journalist with a local newspaper. Respond with your own words. Then compare your response with the model answer that follows.

1

So what did you study at university?

I studied media, but I specialised in newspaper journalism.

9e Networking

Writing an online profile

1 Complete the personal profile using the information below (a–f).
  a Current
  b Freelance marketing consultant and translator
  c London Business School, UK
  d Media and food
  e Summary
  f Past

Mitsuko Uchida

¹ ....

Location: Tokyo
Industry: ² ....
³ .... : Advising British supermarket on market plan for Japan

....

⁴ .... :
• Marketing Manager, Disney, Japan – responsible for 'Winnie the Pooh' account;
• Marketing assistant, Coca Cola, Japan;
• Translated marketing documents for various British and US companies.

....

Education:
Seisen International School; Tokyo University;
⁵ ....
Currently doing distance learning MBA.

....

⁶ ....

I love projects which combine my language skills with my experience in marketing. I am interested in cross-cultural issues and in fun or exciting marketing projects. You can see some examples of my work by clicking on the links below.

---

2 Answer the questions.

1 What kind of work is Mitsuko interested in? ....

2 What languages can she speak? ....

3 How would you describe her level of education? ....

3 Writing skill writing in note form

a Look at these shortened phrases from the profile and put them into full sentences.

1 advising British supermarket on market plan for Japan

....

2 responsible for 'Winnie the Pooh' account

....

3 translated marketing documents for various British and US companies

....

4 currently doing distance learning MBA

....

b The personal profile below has no shortened phrases. Find the places where it would be appropriate to use them and rewrite the sentences in a shortened form.

Harry Ross

I am a specialist website designer

....

Current: I am designing an interactive website for a local sports and leisure centre.

....

Work history: I used to work for British Telecom as a computer programmer. Afterwards I worked for a local hospital designing their patient communications website. I set up my own company in 2010.

....

....

Education: I went to Buckingham Grammar School and Liverpool University.

....

....

I specialise in websites that use video and special effects. I think that most websites are too static and my aim is to create websites that are fun and exciting to use. I have many good recommendations from customers and you can see some of the websites I have created by clicking on the links below.

Wordbuilding verb (+ preposition) + noun collocations

1 In each of these groups, one of the verbs does NOT collocate with the noun on the right. Put a line through this verb.

1	follow/do/have	a career
2	make/do/attend	a course
3	acquire/learn/get	a skill
4	take/make/pass	an exam
5	get/win/acquire	promotion
6	gain/win/get	experience
7	own/have/nurture	a talent
8	do/work/get	a job
9	gain/earn/get	a qualification
10	join/set up/take on	a company

2 Complete the description of someone's career by putting a suitable verb in each space.

When I was 19 I ¹ .... an exam to get into a drama school in London, but I was unsuccessful. At that point, I had to decide whether to try to ² .... a career in acting or just abandon the idea and ³ .... a completely different kind of job. All my friends told me that I ⁴ .... a natural talent for acting and that I didn't need to ⁵ .... a qualification to prove it. So instead, I ⁶ .... a small theatre company and ⁷ .... experience of acting that way. Just by working with other actors I was able to ⁸ .... new skills and two years ago I was asked by the National Theatre to perform in a production of Shakespeare's *The Tempest*. I have never looked back!

Learning skills the language of learning

3 When you learn a language, you often need to ask questions about it. Look at the terms (1–8). Then match the terms with the definitions (a–h).

1 a part of speech
2 past participle
3 an idiom
4 a colloquial expression
5 a false friend
6 a collocation
7 register
8 a euphemism

a two words that naturally go together
b a phrase whose meaning is not clear from the individual words it is composed of
c the level of formality
d e.g. noun, verb, adjective, adverb, preposition
e a word that looks similar in two languages but has different meanings
f the third form of the verb, e.g. 'go, went, <u>gone</u>'
g a word or phrase that expresses an idea more politely or gently
h a phrase used in everyday informal speech

4 Answer these questions about words from Unit 9.

1 What is the past participle of *feel*? ....
2 What part of speech is *the*? ....
3 What verb collocates with *knowledge*?
....
4 Is *grab someone's attention* an idiom? ....
5 What register is the online profile on page 118 of the Workbook? ....

Check!

5 Answer these questions. You can find all the answers in Student's Book Unit 9.

1 What are these people's jobs?

a ....   b ....

2 Complete this famous quotation of Neil Armstrong.

'That's one small .... for man, one giant .... for ....'

3 Which of these places have *the* in front of them?
a .... Atlantic Ocean
b .... Korea
c .... Florida
d .... USA
e .... Moon

4 What type of clause is the underlined clause in the quotation?
a a defining relative clause
b a non-defining relative clause
c a reduced relative clause

Kira Salak, <u>known as the real-life Lara Croft,</u> doesn't want to tell travel stories you have already heard.

10a Child behaviour

Listening growing up

1 🔊 **2.36** Listen to four people talking about growing up and child behaviour. Match the speakers (1–4) with the topic they are talking about (a–f). There are two extra topics.

Speaker 1 ....   a   Being the youngest in the family

Speaker 2 ....   b   Being the eldest

Speaker 3   c   Learning from each other

Speaker 4 ....   d   Sibling rivalry

                                e   Home schooling

                                f   Discipline in the home

Glossary

intervene (v) /ˌɪntəˈviːn/ get involved

sibling (n) /ˈsɪblɪŋ/ a brother or sister

2 🔊 **2.36** Listen again. Write the number of the speaker (1–4) next to the view they are expressing.

a   Family arguments are perfectly healthy. ....

b   The best results are when children learn for themselves. ....

c   Having to fight to get your parents' attention can have a positive effect. ....

d   Children need to mix with lots of other children. ....

e   Your position in the family – e.g. first child, second child – is influential. ....

f   Parents should try to be less involved in their children's upbringing. ....

3 Look at the words and phrases in bold from the interviews and choose the correct definition.

1   Schools don't **stretch** children enough.
    a   discipline
    b   challenge
    c   teach

2   I'm sure they **mean well**, but they're missing the point.
    a   have good intentions
    b   have good ideas
    c   have good qualities

3   Children often **squabble** over toys.
    a   have small arguments
    b   lose interest
    c   make friendships

4   Eldest children are organising and **bossy** types.
    a   showing leadership qualities
    b   independent
    c   telling others what to do

5   Younger children are often the **clowns** of the family.
    a   ones who aren't taken seriously
    b   ones who like to joke
    c   the less intelligent ones

6   It's normal just to leave the children to **get on with it**.
    a   manage by themselves
    b   make friends with each other
    c   grow up

Grammar habitual actions: present tenses, *will*

4 Complete the short passages about growing up and child behaviour. Use the present simple, present continuous and *will*.

1

Some parents ¹ .... (take) their children out of school because they ² .... (think) that they are not being challenged enough. These parents then ³ .... (teach) their children at home, giving them structured lessons each day. Some ⁴ .... (follow) a programme specially written for home schooling, others ⁵ .... (design) their own programme of lessons and activities.

2

Parents complain that their children
⁶_____ (always / fight) and
⁷_____ (squabble). It is of course
the case that most children do this when they are
young. Even older siblings ⁸_____
(argue) and fight as they struggle for their parents'
approval. But psychologists ⁹_____
(say) that this is normal behaviour and it
¹⁰_____ (help) to prepare them
for other relationships later in life.

3

There is quite a lot of literature written about the
personality traits of children according to their
birth order. First-borns ¹¹_____ (tend)
to be model children: conscientious and reliable
and high-achievers. They ¹²_____
(generally / follow) a career that their parents
approve of and ¹³_____ (be)
successful at it. Middle children are more difficult
to categorise, but they ¹⁴_____
(always / follow) a different path from their elder
brother or sister. Last-borns are sociable and fun-
loving and ¹⁵_____ (often / get) all
the attention when in a group.

5 Look at these examples of annoying behaviour.
Complete the sentences using the present
continuous of the verbs with *always*.

ask	leave	play	spend	~~talk~~	talk

1 A girl is on her mobile phone all the time.
  She*'s always talking* to her friends on the phone.

2 In the car, a young boy says: 'Are we nearly
  there yet?'
  He _____ we're
  nearly there yet.

3 A teenage girl spends ages in the bathroom
  so no one else in the family can get in.
  She _____ in the
  bathroom.

4 At mealtimes, a young boy never swallows his
  food before speaking.
  He _____ with his
  mouth full.

5 A teenage boy is obsessed with computer
  games.
  He _____ computer
  games.

6 A young girl never tidies her bedroom up.
  She _____ her room
  in a mess.

Vocabulary raising children: verbs

6 Complete the sentences using the correct verbs.
The first letter has been given for you.

My father worked abroad for most of my
childhood so we were ¹**b**_____ up by
my mother. When he came home, he used to
²**s**_____ us quite a lot, buying us presents
and taking us out. He never ³**p**_____ us
if we were naughty, because he wanted to enjoy
his time with us. He left it to my mum to
⁴**d**_____ us. That was tough on her,
because we used to ⁵**d**_____ her quite a
lot – playing outside when she had told us not to.

It's difficult to be a single parent looking after
your children. You are always ⁶**n**_____
them to do things, when really you want to enjoy
the time you have with them. My elder sister
⁷**r**_____ against my parents completely and
went off to live in London when she was 17.

It isn't easy being a parent. My own kids are always
⁸**p**_____ me to buy them things that other
children have, but I try not to ⁹**g**_____
in to these demands. Of course when they do
something good, I might ¹⁰**r**_____ them
with a present, but I don't want them to be spoilt!

**7 Dictation cultural differences in raising
children**

🔊 **2.37** Listen to a psychologist talking about
raising children and complete the paragraphs.
Which aspect of bringing up children do you
sympathise most with?

Everything depends on _____
_____ .

In other words, what _____
_____
_____ ?

Do you want them _____
_____ ?

If so, _____
_____
_____ .

Or do you want them to be successful individuals?
If so, _____
_____
_____ .

Or is it important that they are good family
members? Then _____
_____
_____ .

10b Globalisation of the food market

Reading global food

1 Read the article. Who has the globalisation of food brought benefits for?
  a Everyone from the UK to Kenya.
  b People in developing countries in particular.
  c The richer people in the world, but not those in under-developed countries.

2 Read the article again and answer the questions.

  1 The author thinks that the weekly family menu in Britain 50 years ago:
    a was very boring for those who had to eat it.
    b used food resources carefully.
    c was not very nutritious.

  2 The main difference with a weekly family menu in Britain these days is that:
    a people don't plan what they are going to eat.
    b people have more money to eat out.
    c there is a greater choice of food.

  3 The phrase 'homogenisation of taste' means:
    a we all eat similar things.
    b everything tastes more and more the same.
    c each type of food doesn't taste as strong as it did in the past.

  4 The main reason that the price of food has increased globally is:
    a people in developing countries want more western-style food.
    b climate change has badly affected food production.
    c the general economic depression.

  5 Higher food prices have caused people in the West to:
    a eat less meat.
    b not eat in restaurants.
    c economise on the food they eat.

GLOBALISATION OF THE FOOD MARKET

Globalisation has had a huge impact on eating habits all over the world. From the UK to Kenya to China, the food we eat today is determined by global markets and world economic events.

If you go back 50 years, a typical working family in Britain ate the same things every week – not that anyone complained about it. The weekly menu was built around the Sunday roast, when a large piece of meat – beef or lamb, for example – was served up with seasonal vegetables as a treat. On the following days, people used to eat leftovers from this 'feast' in a way that clearly avoided waste. On Monday they would have cold cuts of meat and on Tuesday a dish made from the remains, such as shepherd's pie. Wednesday and Thursday were less predictable, but Friday was 'Fish and Chips' day. Saturday was usually sausage and mash because this was quick and easy, and then it was back to the Sunday roast again.

Look at today's average weekly family menu in Britain and there is no comparison. For a start, there is no average: the element of predictability has disappeared, because what is on offer now is not just British but international cuisine. Chinese stirfry on Sunday, Italian lasagne on Wednesday, Mexican tortillas on Thursday. Secondly, seasonality is no longer a factor. If I want strawberries in December or asparagus in March, I can buy them, because even if it's not the season to grow them in the UK, it is in South Africa or Chile. Eating out is not the exceptional treat it used to be. It's fairly normal to eat out at least once a week and to have a takeaway – perhaps a curry – when you can't be bothered to cook.

But while globalisation may have brought more variety to our table, at the same time global food brands have brought a homogenisation of taste, particularly in snack foods and fast foods. You can buy a Kit Kat anywhere from Berne to Beijing, and no one is surprised any more when they see MacDonald's in some provincial town far from the USA.

This demand for Western foods, such as hamburgers and pizza, in countries where there is rapid economic development has had a dramatic effect on the price of wheat and other basic food commodities. Add to this crop failures from unfavourable weather conditions and the result is that we are all paying more for our food. In the West, this may cause us some inconvenience: eating chicken, which is less expensive, instead of beef for example, or cutting back on the number of times we eat out, but in under-developed countries the effect has been devastating. For a poor family in Kenya who are used to a diet of corn, rice and beans with meat maybe once or twice a week, the choice is not between goat or chicken, but rather rice with beans or rice without beans.

Glossary
treat (n) /triːt/ something special to reward people
mash (n) /mæʃ/ mashed potatoes

Grammar *used to, usually, be used to* and *get used to*

3 Choose the correct option according to the facts in the article.

1 Families in Britain *usually eat / were used to eating / used to eat* the same thing every week.

2 British families *were used to using / got used to using / used to use* the Sunday roast to make meals for the next two days.

3 Today people in Britain *are used to eating / get used to eating / used to eat* a variety of international foods.

4 They *usually eat / have got used to eating / used to be eat* whatever they want, whether it is in season or not.

5 They *usually eat out / got used to eating out / used to eat out* at least once a week.

6 People *usually see / are used to seeing / got used to seeing* MacDonald's everywhere in the world

7 People in Kenya *are used to eating / have got used to eating / used to eat* rice, corn, beans and a little meat.

8 Nowadays, in tougher times, they *usually eat / are used to eating / got used to eating* just beans and rice.

4 Read about an English person living 100 years ago. Which of the underlined verbs can be replaced with *used to, would* or *was/were used to*? Write the alternative.

'We ¹ didn't cook on a stove, because we didn't have one. We ² cooked everything over a fire. For example, if we ³ wanted to cook sausages, we ⁴ hung them on hooks over the fire. But if it ⁵ was a special occasion and we had a lot of things to cook, then we had to take it down the road to the hotel which ⁶ had a proper oven and for a few pennies they ⁷ cooked it for us. It seems strange now, but we ⁸ did that whenever all the family got round the table.'

1	*didn't use to cook*	5	
2		6	
3		7	
4		8	

5 Pronunciation /uː/ and /juː/

a 🔊 **2.38** Listen to the words. Write the words in the table.

blue	consume	fortune	humanity	humour
lunar	menu	rude	suit	truce	used
usually				

/uː/	/juː/

b 🔊 **2.39** Now listen and check.

Vocabulary food types

6 Look at what these people ate for lunch. Which of the following did they have? Write staple food (S), dairy product (D), processed food (P) and fresh fruit and vegetables (F).

1 **Simon**
cheese sandwich
....
packet of crisps
....

2 **Kerry**
mixed salad ....
grapes ....
can of cola ....

3 **Will**
rice and stir-fried vegetables ....
instant coffee with milk ....

4 **Katie**
hamburger and chips ....
strawberry milkshake ....

10c Body language

Listening Desmond Morris

1 🔊 **2.40** Listen to a description of the work of Desmond Morris. Are the sentences true (T) or false (F)?

1 Desmond Morris studied as a zoologist and a psychologist.

2 More than 90% of human communication is made using speech.

3 The first example describes the body language of Desmond Morris and a radio presenter.

4 Postural echo involves imitating someone's facial expressions.

5 In the second situation, it would be right to use postural echo.

6 Leaning back in your chair shows that you feel in control.

2 🔊 **2.40** Look at the diagrams and answer the questions. Then listen again and check.

1 In the first situation, how are Desmond Morris and the presenter sitting? Choose the correct diagram.

2 How should the boss and the interviewee be sitting? Choose the correct diagram.

a    b

c    d

3 🔊 **2.40** Choose the correct option to complete the sentences. Then listen again and check.

1 Morris's lifelong interest has been human *more / rather* than animal behaviour.

2 *Unlike / As* the traditional experts in human behaviour, he is not so interested in what people say, but rather in what they do.

3 In fact, he gives *few / little* attention to human speech.

4 In another situation, though, *that / such* postural echo might be inappropriate.

5 *The worst / At worst*, the boss would find it deeply insulting.

4 Pronunciation unstressed syllables

🔊 **2.41** Look at these words. In each word, the second syllable is unstressed and contains the schwa /ə/ sound. Listen and repeat.

action	common	elder	forward	human
little	other	posture	rather	verbal

Word focus *common*

5 Look at the two expressions in bold in the sentence below. Match the expressions with the correct definition (a or b).

"It may be in the **common interest** of both the foreign and the national company to build a dam here, but I am not sure it is for the **common good**."

a something which benefits the public

b something which benefits those involved

6 Complete the crossword with expressions with *common*.

Across

4 an area where both parties agree: *common …*

5 something we should all possess: *common …*

Down

1 things that we all know: *common …*

2 things that we all make: *common …*

3 something that both parties benefit from: *common …*

4 something that benefits everyone: *common …*

10d Wedding customs

Vocabulary weddings

1 Write the words for these definitions.

1 a post-wedding holiday _____

2 promises the couple make to each other
_____

3 a pre-wedding party for men only is a
'_____ night'

4 a covering for the bride's face _____

5 what you hear when a wedding is approaching
_____

6 the man on his wedding day _____

7 an offer of marriage _____

Real life describing traditions

2 🔊 **2.42** Listen to the description of the custom of dowry-giving and answer the questions.

1 What is a big dowry a sign of?
_____

2 What did the dowry act as compensation for?
_____

3 Which family normally gives the dowry?
_____

4 Which family gives the dowry in Nigeria?
_____

5 What do the guests at a Nigerian engagement party do, as well as dancing and having fun?
_____

6 What two things does a Nigerian dowry consist of?
_____

3 🔊 **2.42** Complete the sentences with the words in the box. Then listen again and check.

customary	marks	occasion	on	place
rule	symbolises	traditional		

1 Dowry-giving _____ different things, for example, a sign of wealth.

2 As a _____ , in the past, brides did not go out to work.

3 It's _____ for a dowry to be given by the bride's family.

4 The engagement ceremony in Nigeria _____ the beginning of the wedding celebrations.

5 The ceremony is an _____ for people to have fun.

6 It takes _____ on the evening or a couple of nights before the wedding itself.

7 It used to be _____ for money to be thrown at the couple's feet.

8 _____ the night of the wedding, the bride goes back to her own house.

4 Pronunciation the letter *s*

🔊 **2.43** Look at these words. Is the 's' sound /s/ or /z/? Listen and check.

		/s/	/z/			/s/	/z/
1	things	☐	☐	7	suit	☐	☐
2	house	☐	☐	8	kiss	☐	☐
3	brides	☐	☐	9	delivers	☐	☐
4	social	☐	☐	10	increase	☐	☐
5	sign	☐	☐	11	realise	☐	☐
6	clothes	☐	☐	12	is	☐	☐

5 Listen and respond describing traditions

🔊 **2.44** Listen to some questions about wedding traditions and customs. Respond with your own words. Then compare your response with the model answer that follows.

1

> *What does the groom wear on his wedding day?*

> *It's traditional for the groom to wear a morning suit and a top hat, but these days, he can also wear an ordinary suit.*

10e Cultural differences

1 Writing skill elision in informal writing

Read the formal email (1) and the informal version (2). There are 16 differences. Find and underline as many as you can.

1

Dear Annabelle

It was very good to see you the other day. I hope you had a safe journey back to Leipzig. I forgot to mention that I am travelling to Poland next month on business to visit a supplier. I am unfamiliar with business customs in Poland and wondered if there was anything that I ought to be particularly aware of. For example, should I take some gifts with me? Will they be offended that I do not speak any Polish? I certainly do not want to offend my hosts in any way.

I do not want to inconvenience you, but if you have a moment to write a few words of advice, I would be most grateful.

With kind regards
Paul

2

Hi Annabelle

Very good to see you the other day. Hope you got back to Leipzig safely. I forgot to mention that I'm travelling to Poland next month on business to visit a supplier. I've really got no idea about business customs in Poland and wondered if there was anything I should know especially. For example, should I take some gifts with me? Will they be put out that I don't speak any Polish? I certainly don't want to put my foot in it with my hosts in any way.

I don't want to bother you, but if you've got a moment to write a few words of advice, I'd be really grateful.

All the best
Paul

Writing an informal email

2 Look at Annabelle's reply. Rewrite the underlined words and phrases so that they are in a more informal style.

---

[1] Dear Paul

[2] I enjoyed seeing you also and [3] thank you very much for [4] assisting me with my English CV. [5] I regret to say I don't know very much about Polish business customs but [6] here is a little advice.

A small gift – a souvenir of England perhaps – would be appreciated, I think. But [7] do not give them anything too [8] substantial as that would [9] cause embarrassment for them. [10] You will find that Polish business people [11] appear to be quite formal at a first meeting. [12] That is perfectly normal. Just spend time getting to know them and I [13] have no doubt that [14] they will relax. [15] Regarding the language, 'Milo mi' means [16] 'It is nice to meet you' and 'Dziekuje' means 'Thank you'.

[17] I hope it all goes well. Do [18] inform me about it [19] on your return.

[20] Yours sincerely

Annabelle

---

1 _____	11 _____
2 _____	12 _____
3 _____	13 _____
4 _____	14 _____
5 _____	15 _____
6 _____	16 _____
7 _____	17 _____
8 _____	18 _____
9 _____	19 _____
10 _____	20 _____

Wordbuilding word pairs

1 Make matching pairs. Match the words in box A with their 'partners' in box B.

> **A** bride   husband   friends   suit   food
> singing   bits   time   plans   pomp*
> fun   life

Glossary
***pomp** (n) /pɒmp/ magnificent display

> **B** arrangements   dancing   drink   ceremony
> family   games   groom   pieces   soul
> tie   trouble   wife

2 Complete the sentences with matching pairs from Exercise 1.

1 We wanted a simple wedding, without the _____ of a normal wedding.

2 Planning the wedding took ages, but it was worth all the _____ .

3 There's so much to organise at a wedding, including all the _____ that you never think about beforehand.

4 I'm so glad we invited James – he's always the _____ of the party.

5 It was a small wedding. We just invited a few _____ .

6 The woman usually wears a white dress and the man wears a _____ .

Learning skills making full use of your teacher

3 Use your teacher as a resource. Read these tips to help improve your English.

1 Pay attention to the way your teacher pronounces words and phrases and try to imitate them.

2 Every teacher uses certain idiomatic phrases and expressions. Ask them what they mean.

3 Ask the teacher to correct your mistakes, particularly your pronunciation. Even teachers can feel shy about doing this.

4 Ask your teacher what they think your main fault in English is and how you can correct it.

5 Tell your teacher what kinds of books you like to read and ask them to recommend some in English.

6 Make sure that you have the vocabulary you need (e.g. to describe your job). Ask your teacher to supply these words.

4 Answer these questions. Then check with your teacher. Does your teacher agree with you?

1 Can you pronounce these words from Unit 10?
   a disobey
   b dairy
   c future

2 Which one of these do you think you have most difficulty with?
   a using the right tense
   b lack of vocabulary
   c pronouncing things correctly

3 What can you do well in English?
   a study
   b communicate at work
   c get around in a foreign country

Check!

5 Complete these phrasal verbs and idiomatic phrases. You can find all the answers in Student's Book Unit 10.

Quiz Time

1 Try not to give _____ to all your children's demands. (preposition)

2 We don't eat _____ much these days because restaurants are so expensive. (preposition)

3 Parents who are very relaxed and laid-_____ don't push their children to be high achievers. (preposition)

4 Sarah and I have a lot _____ common. (preposition)

5 Bringing up children is complicated, but if you use your common _____ you won't go far wrong. (noun)

6 We didn't agree at first, but in the end we found some common _____ . (noun)

7 Can you tell me what I should take as a present? I don't want to put my _____ in it. (noun)

8 In the UK, the party that a bride has with her friends before the wedding is called a _____ night. (noun)

11a Conserving languages

Listening enduring voices

1 🔘**3.1** Listen to a description of the work of Dr K. David Harrison and the 'Enduring Voices' team at *National Geographic*. Which sentence (a–c) best summarises their work?

a to help different people in the world to communicate with each other
b to increase the number of languages spoken in the world
c to save dying languages from extinction

2 🔘**3.1** Read the questions. Then listen again and choose the best option (a–c).

1 How many languages will there be in the world in 2050?
   a about 7,000
   b about 3,500
   c about 700

2 Bolivia is used as an example of a country with many languages because … .
   a they are so different
   b it has a large population
   c it has as many languages as Europe

3 Yuchi is a language spoken in Oklahoma which … .
   a has only 70 speakers
   b is a dead language
   c people are trying to revive

4 According to Dr Harrison, when we lose a language, we lose a culture's … .
   a knowledge of the world
   b important monuments
   c stories

5 Speakers of Yupik have helped us to understand better … .
   a the geography of the Arctic
   b their language and culture
   c the effects of climate change

6 The speaker thinks that globalisation highlights the importance of … .
   a diversity
   b finding common interests
   c saving dying languages

3 🔘**3.1** Complete the sentences from the description using the correct form of these verbs. Then listen again and check.

document	express	record	save	seek out
store	trace			

1 He is part of a *National Geographic* project called 'Enduring Voices' whose aim is to ———— languages which are little known.
2 The race is on to ———— and ———— these languages.
3 Dr Harrison ———— these language 'hotspots'.
4 All cultures ———— their genius through their languages and stories.
5 These languages ———— knowledge which can be of huge benefit to people today.
6 Dr Harrison and his team aim to ———— as many languages as they can.

Grammar *could, was able to, manage to* and *succeed in*

4 Look at these sentences from the description. Choose the correct option.

1 Studies in the Oklahoma region of the USA *could discover / succeeded in discovering* 26 languages.

2 By highlighting this fact, researchers *could help / were able to help* the community to keep this dying language alive.

3 Some ancient cultures *could build / managed to build* large monuments by which we can remember their achievements.

4 A book written a few years ago by Yupik elders and scientists *was able to help / managed to help* other scientists to understand how climate change is affecting the polar ice.

5 One of the original arguments for globalisation was that it *could bring / managed to bring* us all closer together.

6 He *could save / couldn't save* Ubykh – a language spoken near the Black Sea – from extinction.

5 Complete the sentences about learning a language using *could, was/were able to, manage to* or *succeed in* and the verb in brackets. Sometimes more than one answer is possible.

1 The video I got was in Turkish, but I _____ (find) English subtitles on the main menu.

2 My sister is an amazing linguist: she _____ (speak) four languages fluently by the time she was twelve.

3 Esperanto was invented to be a world language, but supporters of it _____ (never / convince) enough people to use it.

4 When I first moved to England, I _____ (not / understand) native speakers because they seemed to mumble when they spoke.

5 I had a friend who was brought up speaking three different languages, but I was never sure if he _____ (express) himself clearly in any of them!

6 I spent eight years learning Italian, but when I tried to use it a couple of years ago, I found that I _____ (remember) the grammar but not the vocabulary.

Vocabulary learning

6 Match the expressions (1–8) with the correct definition (a–h).

1	pick up	a	become involved in
2	take in	b	not know about
3	learn by trial and error	c	learn as you go along
4	inspire	d	understand simply
5	have a basic grasp of	e	know about
6	engage with	f	absorb
7	be ignorant	g	motivate
8	be aware of	h	learn by making mistakes

7 Complete the sentences using a verb or expression from Exercise 6.

1 Don't worry about explaining. I'm sure I'll _____ it _____ .

2 She's a great teacher. She really knows how to _____ her students.

3 I used to be completely _____ about art, so I went on an art appreciation course.

4 I _____ of car mechanics, but I couldn't repair an electronic fault.

5 Mathematics is a difficult subject for some people to _____ because it's so theoretical.

6 Sorry, that's too much information to _____ all at once. Can you go through it more slowly?

8 Dictation languages

a 3.2 Listen to someone talking about languages, place names and words. Write the words that they spell.

1 a _____ b _____

2 a _____ b _____

3 a _____ b _____

4 _____

5 _____

b 3.2 Listen again and match the words from Exercise 8a with the correct meaning:

a a very long word in English _____

b the name of a college in the USA _____

c a word for an animal in a Siberian language _____

d an extinct language from the USA _____

e a new language found in India _____

11b Memory loss

Reading memory loss

1 Read the description of three types of memory loss quickly. Match the descriptions (1–3) with the summaries (a–c).

a When you can't recognise someone you know ....

b When your mind chooses to forget something it doesn't want to remember ....

c When you deceive yourself with a false memory ....

2 Read the descriptions again. Are the sentences true (T) or false (F)? Or is there not enough information (N) to say if the statements are true or false?

1 Lacunar amnesia is when people have had a bad shock and don't remember what happened.

2 In these cases, the memory is erased from the mind.

3 Sarah only remembers the moment when the truck hit the house.

4 Prosopamnesia is a condition some people inherit from their parents.

5 Philippa was concerned that the man who approached her was William Child.

6 William Child was upset that she didn't recognise him.

7 In source amnesia, people intentionally change the source of the memory.

8 In Jon's profession it is common to meet people with this condition.

9 The woman wanted her neighbour to be punished for the crime.

① Lacunar amnesia

This literally means a gap in the memory. People who suffer from lacunar amnesia fail to remember a very specific event. It usually occurs when a person has suffered a traumatic event and their mind chooses to blank this out. The memory is still there in fact, but our psychological defences stop us remembering the event to protect us from suffering further psychological trauma.

Sarah's story: 'When I was a child, something extraordinary happened at our house. My sister and I were just about to go to bed and I was downstairs saying goodnight to our parents. My sister was going to say goodnight to them too, but had gone to the kitchen to get a glass of water. At that moment, a truck ran into the ground floor of our house. I know that because my sister, who was unhurt, told me afterwards. All I remember was saying goodnight, then waking up in hospital.'

② Prosopamnesia

Prosopamnesia is an inability to remember faces. It is something that many people have in a mild form, but in severe cases sufferers can forget the faces of even close friends or associates. People can be born with this syndrome or it can be acquired during their lives.

Philippa's story: 'I'm terrible at remembering faces. I recall being at a conference at Berkeley University in California and another academic came up and started chatting to me. I would have asked his name, but knowing my inability to remember faces I didn't in case he was someone I was supposed to know. Anyway, it turned out that we had a friend and colleague in common. "Oh yes, I know Wiliam Child," I said. "We collaborated on a research project last year. He came to dinner at my house many times. How do you know him?" "I am Willliam Child", the man replied.'

③ Source amnesia

Also called 'memory distrust syndrome', source amnesia occurs when a person is unable to recall the context in which they learnt about something. Subconsciously, they then attribute the fact to some other, usually reliable, source. This can happen when the real source is not reliable and the person very much wants to believe that the fact is true.

Jon's story: 'I work as a lawyer, and in my line of work I often come across people who have persuaded themselves of a version of events that may not be true. I had a witness who was going to give evidence in court that her neighbour had thrown a brick at her car. She clearly believed that this had happened, and was determined that her neighbour wouldn't get away with it. But it turned out that it was not her own memory of events, but what another neighbour had told her.'

3 Find phrasal verbs in the text on page 130 with the following meanings:

1 erase (especially a memory) (para 1)

2 collided with (para 2)
3 approached (para 4)
4 was found (para 4)
5 find something (without expecting to) (para 6)

6 escape without punishment (para 6)

Grammar future in the past

4 There are six examples of the 'future in the past' forms in the text on page 130. Underline the examples. Which of the other future in the past forms could be used in each case?

> was/were about to do   was/were going to
> was supposed to   would do   would have done

1 *My sister and I were just about to go to bed … or were just going to go to bed …*

2

3

4

5

6

5 Complete the sentences using a future in the past form. Sometimes more than one form is possible.

1 'I'm so sorry. I _____ (write) you a letter, but I lost your address.'
2 'I _____ (just / book) tickets to visit Munich, but then I remembered that it was Oktoberfest and all the hotels _____ (be) full.'
3 'I promised her I _____ (speak) to my boss about finding her a job, but I forgot.'
4 'The meeting _____ (last) only an hour, but just as we _____ (finish), Julian remembered that we hadn't discussed the move to our new offices.'
5 'I _____ (take) my driving test sooner, but I didn't feel ready.'
6 'That's funny. I _____ (just / ask) you exactly the same question.'

6 Pronunciation contrastive sentence stress

a ⬥ **3.3** Underline the words in the first half of the sentences that are most strongly stressed. Then listen and check.

1 I was going to email him, but I decided it would better to speak face to face.
2 He was supposed to get here early, but he's already ten minutes late.
3 I would have come by train, but there's a strike on at the moment.
4 She said she would be pleased if I talked to him, but she seemed really angry.
5 I was about to buy a flat, but Katie said I could rent hers for six months while she was away.
6 Liz was going to be in charge of the project, but now she's just acting as an advisor.

b ⬥ **3.3** Underline the words in the second half of the sentences that are most strongly stressed. Practise saying each sentence. Then listen again and check.

7 Grammar extra future phrases

> ▶ **FUTURE PHRASES**
>
> Notice that we use other phrases with the infinitive to talk about the future.
> She's **bound to** want to leave early.
> He's **likely to** change his mind.
> You're **unlikely to** find the information here.

Look at the grammar box. Then look at phrases (1–5) which talk about the future. Match the phrases to the correct definition (a–e).

1 I'm sorry, but I always thought it was a terrible idea. It was **bound to** fail.
2 The plane was **due to** take off at 7 a.m., but poor weather meant it was delayed.
3 We thought that it was **unlikely** to be cold, so we didn't take any warm clothes with us.
4 It was **about to** rain so we decided to eat inside.
5 The political situation was **likely** to get worse, so we left the country for our own safety.

a not probable
b probable
c certain
d scheduled / expected
e on the point of

11c Intelligent animals

Listening

1 Match the name of the animal with the correct picture.

> Bonobo monkey   border collie   crow
> dolphin   scrub-jay

1 _____   2 _____

3 _____

4 _____   5 _____

2 🎵 **3.4** Listen to a description of five intelligent animals. Write the number of the description (1–5) next to the intelligent behaviour that this type of animal is known for.

a   They are good at copying what they see.   ☐

b   They are good at communicating.   ☐

c   They like to follow instructions.   ☐

d   They make plans for the future.   ☐

e   They make implements to get different jobs done.   ☐

3 🎵 **3.4** Listen again and write the number of the description next to the intelligent action each animal did.

a   found a clever way to reach some food   ☐

b   did acrobatics in time with one another   ☐

c   made food disappear   ☐

d   learned to match a two-dimensional image to a real object   ☐

e   cooked himself a treat   ☐

4 Match the words from the descriptions with the adjectives below (1–5).

> inventive   mischievous   smart   expressive   playful

1   intelligent _____
2   creative _____
3   fun-loving _____
4   communicative _____
5   naughty _____

Word focus *learn*

5 Complete the sentences using expressions with *learn*.

1   You have to learn to w_____ before you can run.
2   It's never too l_____ to learn.
3   In life, you have to learn from your m_____ .
4   I learnt a few t_____ of the trade.
5   Never again. I've learnt my l_____ .
6   Just learn to l_____ with it!
7   I learnt the hard w_____ .
8   I've learnt the whole poem by h_____ .

11d Ask the teacher

Real life getting clarification

1 Complete these phrases with the correct verb.

1 What do you _____ by 'difficult'?

2 Can you _____ up a little? I can't hear you.

3 Can you _____ what the exam at the end of the course involves?

4 I'm sorry. I _____ not really with you.

5 Are you _____ that learning the historical dates isn't important?

6 Could you _____ me an example of an important historian of the last century?

7 There's a lot of information to _____ in.

8 I didn't _____ that last word. Can you repeat it?

2 🔊 **3.5** Listen to a conversation between a student and a college lecturer. Answer the questions.

1 What is the course?

2 What is the student worried about?

3 What does the lecturer recommend?

3 🔊 **3.5** Listen again and complete the student's questions.

1 Can you explain _____ ?

2 And are you saying that _____ ?

3 Sorry, I'm not really with you. You mean _____ ?

4 Could you give me an example of _____ ?

5 Did you say _____ ?

4 Grammar extra verbs with indirect objects

> ▶ **VERBS WITH INDIRECT OBJECTS**
>
> Some verbs, e.g. *tell* and *show* can be followed by an indirect personal object. Other verbs, e.g. *say* and *explain*, don't always need an indirect personal object. If you use an indirect personal object with these verbs, you must put *to* before the object.
>
> He told **me** about the history course.
> I showed **him** a copy of the lecture notes.
> They explained (**to me**) that I could find the reading list online.

Look at the sentences below and write the pronoun *me* where necessary.

1 Can you tell _____ how many hours of study we're expected to do each week?

2 Do you recommend _____ that I should read Stephen Hawking's book?

3 She said _____ that I could get most of the books from the library.

4 She also explained _____ that the library was open until 10 p.m.

5 Can you show _____ how that works?

6 He taught _____ that I didn't always need to write such long essays.

5 Pronunciation linking in question forms

🔊 **3.6** Practise saying these sentences. Then listen and compare your pronunciation.

1 Did you say 'Africa'?

2 Could you explain that?

3 What do you mean by 'difficult'?

4 Can you give me an example?

5 What are you saying?

6 Listen and respond getting clarification

🔊 **3.7** Listen to a conversation between a teacher and a student (you). Respond with your own words. Then compare your response with the model answer that follows.

1

> *So you wanted to ask me a question about the exam at the end of this course?*

> *Yes. Can you explain what the exam involves?*

11e A letter to a college

Writing an email about a misunderstanding

1 Match the two parts of the sentences about a misunderstanding over an application for a course. What seems to be the problem according to the writer?

1 The website said the deadline for entries was 20 August.

2 Despite the fact that my application arrived in time,

3 I am not someone who does things at the last minute.

4 While I appreciate that you have a lot of applicants for this course,

5 Whereas most colleges seem to select applicants on the merits of their application,

a you choose people on a 'first come, first served' basis.

b I cannot understand why you have chosen to ignore those people who applied after July.

c In fact, I sent in my application at the end of July.

d On the contrary, I am always careful to observe deadlines.

e I was told that I had missed the deadline.

2 Writing skill linking contrasting ideas

Rewrite these sentences from the reply to the applicant's letter using the words given.

1 We sympathise with your situation, but it is too late to do anything about it now. (while)

2 Despite the fact that you sent your form in before the deadline, we had already received too many applications. (although)

3 You say in your letter that we have no right to do this, but the college has the right to close the application process early. (in actual fact)

4 We are very careful to follow the rules. We don't 'make up the rules as we go along' as you suggest. (on the contrary)

5 Most colleges would keep your application fee, but we are refunding it to you. (whereas)

3 Look at the notes and write a letter to a college. Include the following points.

a Reason for writing: you can't attend the accountancy course this term.

b Misunderstanding: you thought it was an evening class, but it's during the day.

c Effort on your part: your company would like to give you time off, but they can't.

d Apology: probably your mistake, but these things happen.

e Action required: want the college to refund the money paid for the course fee.

Dear Sir / Madam

a

b

c

d

e

I look forward to

Yours

Wordbuilding idiomatic expressions

1 Read the story. What do the idiomatic expressions in bold (1–6) mean? Match the idiomatic expressions with the definitions (a–f).

> I don't know when ¹**it first dawned on me** that it would be a good idea to grow my own vegetables. I know ²**it struck me** some time ago that vegetables in the shops were getting very expensive. ³**It occurred to me** that if more people grew their own, we wouldn't have to import so many. I ⁴**didn't have a clue** about growing plants, but then I read a fantastic book written by woman called Joy Larkcom. The book really ⁵**opened my eyes.** That was six years ago and it has become more than a hobby. ⁶**It never crossed my mind** that I would become an expert, but now a lot of neighbours come and ask me for my advice.

a I had a strong impression ....
b helped me to see the truth ....
c was ignorant ....
d I realised ....
e I had the idea ....
f I didn't ever think ....

Learning skills techniques for memorising

2 People remember things in different ways. Some remember better by hearing (auditory learners), some by seeing (visual learners) and some by doing or by action (kinaesthetic learners). It is important to know how you remember things. What do you remember of the following items in Unit 11?

1 Maria Fadiman's work on conservation of plants. ....

2 How *could* is different from *managed to*. ....

3 The intelligence of Alex, the grey parrot. ....

4 Useful phrases for checking understanding. ....

5 Idiomatic expressions containing the word *learn*. ....

3 How did you remember the information? Was it through something:
a you heard?
b you saw?
c you did?

4 Look at these tips for memorising. Tick (✓) the one(s) you feel suit you best.

a **Auditory**: Record five words that you need to learn, giving each a translation or putting them into a sentence. Then listen to them again last thing at night.

b **Visual**: Draw a picture of the words that you need to learn. Look at the pictures the following day and see if you can remember the words.

c **Kinesthetic**: Work with another student and simulate a situation that illustrates the meaning of the word. Or think of an action that would help you remember the word.

5 Try to memorise these words and expressions from Unit 11 using the tips in Exercise 4.

> absorb   grasp   gut feeling   learn your lesson
> a misunderstanding

Check!

6 Complete the crossword.

Across

1 Maria Fadiman's stories help students to .... with the subject (6)

5 a .... memory remembers only what it wants (9)

7 another word for advice (8)

8 the opposite of your 'internal' memory (8)

10 'Sorry I didn't .... your name.' (5)

Down

2 if you understand something in a simple way, you have 'a basic ....' of it (5)

3 you can *manage to do* or .... *in doing something* (7)

4 a person who studies plants (8)

6 the opposite of knowing is being .... (8)

8 one way of learning is by trial and .... (5)

9 'It's never too .... to learn.'

12a Economics

Listening character and economics

1 🔊 **3.8** Listen to an economist giving his opinion about how character affects economics. Answer the questions.

1   Concerning attitudes to money, what two types of people does the economist describe?

....

2   Can we apply these stereotypes to particular countries? Why? / Why not?

....

....

2 🔊 **3.8** Listen again and choose the best option (a–c) to complete the sentences.

1   People who are prudent spend money ... .
    a   when they see something they really want
    b   when it's for something of lasting benefit
    c   on what's necessary

2   People who are extravagant with money say that they want to ... .
    a   enjoy life while they can
    b   save but can't
    c   increase their possessions

3   Some commentators said that certain countries who had borrowed money ... .
    a   hadn't worked hard enough
    b   hadn't paid enough tax
    c   hadn't been careful with the money

4   A lender faces the possibility of losing money and ... .
    a   creating problems for the borrower
    b   going out of business
    c   waiting a long time for payment

5   In most developed economies people want to ... .
    a   be able to borrow money
    b   live more comfortably
    c   reduce their debts

6   We need ... to behave more responsibly.
    a   spenders
    b   savers
    c   spenders and savers

3 Match the words in box A with a synonym in box B.

A	fund	prudent	transaction	wages
	wasteful			

B	careful	deal	extravagant	finance
	salaries			

Vocabulary rich and poor

4 Find and circle the words in the word search that mean the following:

1   poor
2   have enough money
3   inexpensive (2 words)
4   expensive
5   income
6   comfortable
7   very rich

R	H	P	I	M	O	I	N
E	A	R	N	I	N	G	S
A	R	I	C	C	F	O	T
S	D	C	H	E	A	P	O
O	U	E	S	O	F	U	L
N	P	Y	B	A	F	L	E
A	W	E	L	L	O	F	F
B	I	L	E	F	R	A	T
L	O	A	D	E	D	E	S
E	S	T	O	N	R	I	A

Grammar focus adverbs *only, just, even, too, as well, also*

5 Complete the sentences with these adverbs. Sometimes more than one adverb is possible.

also	as well	even	just	only	too

1 Let's _____ consider people's attitude to money at its simplest level.
2 Of course, savers spend money _____ , but _____ when they can afford it.
3 People in these countries would have to work longer hours, pay more taxes and _____ accept lower wages.
4 You risk losing the money but you _____ risk putting the borrower in a difficult situation.
5 We need both types of person, but _____ if they lend and borrow responsibly.

6 Write the focus adverbs in the correct place in the sentences.

1 Some people believe that if you go through life saving money, you will never have any fun. ONLY
2 Some people carry on spending money when they can't afford to. EVEN
3 You can guard against bad times by putting aside a small amount of money each week. JUST
4 If a few people save money, the banks won't have any to lend. ONLY
5 I'm not the only person who has debts. Other people have them. ALSO
6 Attitude to money is partly a cultural thing, but it has something to do with your upbringing. AS WELL
7 Some people are careful with money in hard times and in good times. TOO
8 Borrowers admit that they sometimes borrow money irresponsibly. EVEN

Vocabulary money

7 Complete these sentences with the correct noun. Use the verbs in brackets to help you.

1 To buy the car, I had to make _____ of £70 a month for five years. (pay)
2 We need to cut back on our _____ because the cost of living has become so high. (spend)
3 They say that gold is a good _____ at the moment. (invest)
4 We took out a _____ from the bank to finance the purchase of our apartment. (lend)
5 If you can't afford university fees, then the government gives you a _____ . (give)
6 We wanted to increase our _____ so that we could build an extension on our house. (borrow)
7 The public _____ of the USA are counted in trillions of dollars rather than billions. (owe)
8 Public sector workers are protesting because their _____ have been frozen for the last two years. (earn)

8 Dictation money and lifestyle

🔊 **3.9** Listen to someone talking about money and lifestyle, and write down the words you hear.

I think that _____

It's a lifestyle _____

This desire _____

12b Cheap labour

Reading the slave economy

1 Read the article. What is the main message?
   a Business does well from using cheap labour.
   b All industries use cheap labour.
   c The American economy has always relied on cheap labour.

2 Look back at the article. Are the sentences true (T) or false (F)? Or is there not enough information (N) to say if the sentences are true or false?

1 It is only in recent years that businesses have started moving to where labour is cheaper.

2 The colonists of the Americas needed a lot of labour to take economic advantage of their new territory.

3 Native Americans as well as African people were used as slaves.

4 The practice of slavery was quite common around the Mediterranean, even before the colonisation of America.

5 African slaves seemed to work harder than slaves from other regions.

6 The African slave population of the Americas outnumbered the Europeans by more than five to one.

7 The slaves in cities were treated better than those living on the plantations.

8 A kind of slavery – not paying people a fair amount of money for the work they do – still exists in the world today.

The history of successful industries has always been a story of cheap labour. Clearly, if you can get people to work for very little, your business will be more profitable. Even in more recent times, you can track the movement of industry – textiles and tuna canning are two striking examples – to the places where the work can be done more cheaply.

But imagine the profits if your labourers work for nothing. In other words, if you use slaves as the European colonial powers of the 16th to the 19th centuries did. Those countries which had colonised the Americas became dependent on enslaved labour for their survival. Colonial officials believed that the land they had 'discovered' in the Americas was useless without sufficient labour to exploit it. However, since there were not sufficient European or Native American workers, large numbers of African people were captured and transported to the Americas to work.

The trans-Saharan slave trade had long supplied slaves from central Africa to work on sugar plantations in the Mediterranean. Having proved themselves competent workers in Europe, enslaved Africans became the labour force of choice in colonial America.

Of the 6.5 million immigrants who survived the crossing of the Atlantic and settled in the western hemisphere between 1492 and 1776, only one million were Europeans. The remaining 5.5 million were African. 80 percent of these enslaved Africans were employed as field-workers. Women as well as children worked. Only the very young and infirm escaped. Their 'owners' put them to work first on the sugar plantations, then on tobacco plantations and, following the invention of the cotton gin in 1793, on cotton plantations. These products brought great riches to the United States.

Even though the majority of slaves were employed in agriculture, there were many in other jobs – as butlers, waiters, maids, carriage drivers, blacksmiths and stable boys. In urban areas, such as New Orleans and Philadelphia, where they accounted for up to a third of the population, their owners forced the slaves to learn the trades of carpenter, stonemason, baker, etc. And so not just agriculture, but the whole economy came to depend on this free labour. At the same time, the British textile industry grew rich making clothes from America's cheap imported cotton.

Unfortunately, even though slavery was abolished a long time ago, the temptation to exploit people for extra profit by employing them on low wages has not gone away.

Glossary
cotton gin (n) /ˈkɒt(ə)n dʒɪn/ a machine that separates cotton fibre from the seeds
plantation (n) /plænˈteɪʃ(ə)n/ a farm where a crop such as cotton is grown
stable boy (n) /ˈsteɪbl bɔɪ/ a boy who looks after horses

3 Find words or expressions in the article with the following meanings.

1 follow (para 1)

2 making a strong impression (para 1)

3 enough (para 2)

4 good at one's job (para 3)

5 favoured or preferred (para 3)

6 weak, sick or disabled (para 4)

7 someone who works with iron and metal (para 5)

8 a skilled manual job (para 5)

Grammar causative *have* and *get*

4 Put the words in brackets into the right form to complete these sentences.

1 It's evident that if you can _____ (have / people / work) for very little money, your business is going to be more profitable.

2 Companies are always searching for a country where they can _____ (get / their work / do) more cheaply.

3 Imagine how much more profitable it is if you _____ (get / your labourers / work) for nothing.

4 The traders who sent slaves to the Mediterranean also _____ (have / 10,000 slaves a year / send) to serve owners in America.

5 The slave 'owners' _____ (get / the slaves / work) first on the sugar plantations, then on tobacco plantations.

6 On the plantations, the owners _____ (have / their slaves / work) as butlers, waiters, maids, etc.

7 In urban areas, their owners _____ (get / them / learn) various trades.

8 In the 19th century, the British textile industry _____ (have / cheap cotton / ship) over from America.

5 Pronunciation the sounds /ʃ/, /tʃ/, /ʒ/ **and** /dʒ/

a 🔊 **3.10** Listen to these words from the article and complete the table.

abolished	carriage	cheap	decision
riches	sugar	usually	wages

/ʃ/	/tʃ/	/ʒ/	/dʒ/
wash	watch	pleasure	change

b 🔊 **3.11** Now listen and check.

Vocabulary domestic jobs

6 Complete the sentences about repairs to a house. The first letter of each verb has been given.

1 We need to get someone to f_____ this carpet. The shape of the room is so irregular.

2 I've asked John to p_____ up some new shelves in the living room. He's a professional carpenter.

3 I think we can d_____ the room ourselves. We don't need to have it done by a professional painter.

4 The kitchen units came in pieces and I had to a_____ them by myself. It took me about seven hours.

5 Can you call a roofer? The roof's still leaking and we need to get it f_____ .

6 You know that guy who t_____ our bathroom walls – he did a terrible job. There are cracks everywhere.

7 Do you know anyone who can p_____ a ceiling? We have cracks in our living room and I'm worried the ceiling's going to come down.

8 Can you help me to h_____ this picture on the wall?

7 Look at these DIY jobs and match each one with the professional who does it.

1	fixing a leaky tap	a	a gardener
2	rewiring a house	b	a plumber
3	cutting the grass	c	a carpenter or joiner
4	demolishing a wall	d	a general builder
5	fitting a new front door	e	a decorator
6	painting the outside of a house	f	an electrician

12c The world of barter

Listening an interview

1 🔘 **3.12** Listen to an interview with a member of the Barter Society. What is the advantage of barter, according to him? Choose the correct option (a–c).

a   You can exchange things without paying tax.
b   It opens up a whole new world of people to do business with.
c   You get a much better deal than you would if you used cash.

Glossary
GDP (n) /ˌdʒiːdiːˈpiː/ gross domestic product
spear (n) /spɪə/ a long, pointed weapon used in hunting
tree surgeon (n) /ˈtriː ˌsɜːdʒ(ə)n/ a specialist in cutting off damaged parts of trees

2 🔘 **3.12** Listen again and choose the best option (a–c) to complete the sentences.

1   The example of barter given by the interviewer is an exchange of a chicken for:
a   an item of clothing.
b   some food.
c   a weapon.

2   Barter is a system of trade that:
a   all primitive societies use.
b   is still used widely today.
c   has always had a small group of followers.

3   'Exchange barter' is a system:
a   that involves two people exchanging goods with one another.
b   that involves being a member of a club of other barterers.
c   where you exchange goods up to a certain value.

4   Barter exchanges:
a   aren't taxed.
b   are taxed if they are above a certain value.
c   are taxed in some countries.

5   The advantage of direct barter groups is that they:
a   mean you can reach a big group of potential customers.
b   allow you to pay less tax.
c   avoid currency exchange.

Word focus *hard*

3 Complete the text using an expression with *hard*. There are two extra expressions.

| hard bargain | hard work | hard feelings | hard up |
| hard-headed | hard luck | hard done by | |

If you are ¹ _____ and short of cash, then barter may be a good solution for you. You don't have to be a ² _____ business person to make it work, because exchanges are done in a spirit of co-operation. In direct barter, the negotiation is friendly and there is no question of trying to drive a ³ _____ . So there are never any ⁴ _____ between the barterers, with one person feeling they have 'won' in the deal and the other feeling ⁵ _____ .

4   Grammar extra *hard* and *hardly*

> ▶ **HARD** and **HARDLY**
>
> The adjective *hard* has two different adverb forms: *hard* and *hardly*.
> *I'm trying **hard** to see the advantage of it.* (I'm making a big effort.)
> *It **hardly** seems worth the effort.* (It's almost NOT worth the effort.)
>
> Note the position of the *hard* and *hardly* in relation to the verb.

Look at the grammar box. Then complete the sentences using *hard* and *hardly* and the verbs in the correct form.

1   runs / hard
a   He _____ . He'll be very fit if he manages to keep it up.
b   He _____ . It's more of a walk.

2   works / hard
a   She _____ now. She goes in to the office once a week, I think.
b   She _____ now. She has a new boss who's very demanding.

3   know / hard
I _____ him. We've met twice, I think.

4   thought / hard
a   I _____ about it. It wasn't an easy decision.
b   I _____ about work when I was away on holiday.

5   tried / hard
a   The team _____ . It was as if they didn't care.
b   The team _____ , but they weren't good enough to win.

12d Organising an event

Real life negotiating

1 Match the expressions (1–6) with phrases with the same meaning (a–f).

1	to be honest	a	in your shoes
2	the key thing	b	what's important
3	let's face it	c	when all's said and done
4	if I were you	d	to tell you the truth
5	at the end of the day	e	you must understand
6	you have to appreciate	f	be realistic

2 🎵 **3.13** Listen to two people in a negotiation and answer the questions.

1 What event are they discussing?

2 What does the client try to negotiate?

3 🎵 **3.13** Complete the phrases from the negotiation. Then listen and check.

1 We want some food but, to be _____, nothing too fancy.

2 OK, so what did you have in _____ ? A few canapés, some sandwiches?

3 Well, I was _____ we could have something a bit more exciting than sandwiches.

4 Yes, that _____ be much more like it.

5 That's quite a lot, but let's _____ it, it is an important occasion.

6 If I were in your _____ , I'd like to put on an event that people would remember.

7 You have to _____ that we have to come and set it all up and take it away anyway.

8 I see. Well, the _____ thing for us is that it's a nice relaxing event.

4 Pronunciation sentence stress in idiomatic phrases

🎵 **3.14** Listen to these phrases used in a negotiation. Underline the words that are stressed. Then practise saying them.

1 Can I just explain our position?

2 To tell you the truth, …

3 If you look at it from our side, …

4 That's going to be a bit of a sticking point.

5 To be perfectly honest, …

6 What you have to bear in mind is …

5 Grammar extra *would*

> ▶ **WOULD**
>
> The function of *would* is to make what you say sound more polite or diplomatic, so it is often used in negotiations.
> Yes, that **would** be much more like it.
> **Would** that reduce the price a bit then?

Rewrite these sentences using *would* to make the sentences more diplomatic.

1 I'm afraid that will be difficult for me.

2 Can you move a bit on the price?

3 Are you willing to negotiate?

4 I need to have some kind of guarantee.

5 When do you need to know?

6 I don't want to put you to any trouble.

6 Listen and respond negotiating

🎵 **3.15** You are hiring a caterer to provide food at a party. Listen to what the caterer says and respond with your own words. Then compare your response with the model answer that follows.

1

> So what kind of food did you have in mind? Some sandwiches?

> I was hoping we could have some hot food too.

12e A proposal

1 Writing skill sub-headings and bullet points

Look at the first extract from a report. What is the report about?

....

> I have now spoken on the phone to two different caterers about the food to be served at the Annual General Meeting (AGM). One was Angel Foods, which is a local firm, and the other is Carrick's, a much bigger chain of caterers that do catering in London and other major cities all over the country.
>
> **Summary**
> Two caterers have been approached about food for the AGM:
> • Angel Foods, a local firm
> • Carrick's, a national catering chain

2 Rewrite these extracts from the rest of the report. Use bullet points and concise language.

> **1**
> There are several things that we ought to think about before we make a decision. How much food do we need to provide? How much is it going to cost us? Do people have any special dietary needs that we should take into consideration?
>
> **Three factors to consider**
> • ....
> • ....
> • ....

> **2**
> The caterer has suggested various types of food – some hot food which will cost about £10 per person (quite pricey, I think) and cold food which costs about £7 per person.
>
> **The caterer**
> • ....
> • ....

> **3**
> I suggest that we should go with Angel Foods, because they seemed to understand better what we want, and I think they will do it all for a better price.
>
> **Recommendation**
> ....
> ....

Writing a report

3 Read the report. Then rewrite it in the framework given, making the language more concise and using sub-headings and bullet points.

> I met a caterer, Party foods Ltd., yesterday and we discussed the food and arrangements for our office party on 12th December and this was what they proposed. They suggested that we have a range of different types of sandwiches and also hot and cold canapés. Sandwiches on their own would cost £6 per person and a mixture of sandwiches and cold canapés would be £8 per person. If the canapés were hot this would be an extra £2 per person – so a total of £10 per person.
>
> Also, if we want, they can provide drinks. Alternatively, we can buy our own and they will charge a small amount for serving them – I think she said an extra £1 per person.
>
> I think we should go for the mixture of sandwiches and cold canapés, and then provide our own drinks. I'd be happy to organise that part of it.

> **Subject: Office party 12th December**
>
> **Summary**
> ....
> ....
> ....
>
> **Food**
> • ....
> • ....
> • ....
>
> **Drinks**
> • ....
> • ....
>
> **Recommendation**
> ....

Wordbuilding *the* + adjective

1 Can you think of the right adjective for these groups of people in society?

1 People with a lot of money ____*the rich*____
2 People without a job _____
3 People with very little money _____
4 People with nowhere to live _____
5 People over 70 _____
6 People who are well known _____
7 People who can't see _____
8 People who can't hear _____
9 People who can't read or write
_____
10 People who are unwell _____

2 Which of the answers in Exercise 1 describe people in a positive situation (P), a negative situation (N), or neither positive or negative (X).

Learning skills using the internet

3 The following ideas are ways you could use the internet to help you learn. Tick (✓) the ideas you could use.

1 Listen to or watch the news in English, e.g. on the BBC website. Note down key words as you listen to each story. Check their meaning online or in a dictionary. Then listen again.

2 Search for articles relevant to your interests on newspaper websites. Read the title and the first paragraph. Either mentally or on paper, note down two questions you would like answered by the article. Then read the article and find the answers.

3 If you are not sure how to pronounce a word, check in an online dictionary. Then practise saying it.

4 If you listen to English or American songs, search for the lyrics online. Follow them as you listen to the song. Look up any words you don't know.

5 Search for interesting quotations, sayings and anecdotes on websites. Try to memorise them.

4 Use the internet to find the following:

1 What does the word 'spin' mean in the context of political news?

_____

2 How do you pronounce 'rhythm'?

_____

3 What are the opening lyrics to 'Big Yellow Taxi' by Joni Mitchell?

_____

4 A good quotation on the subject of 'success'.

_____

Check!

5 Complete the sentences about the economy using information from Unit 12. Then use the first letters of each word to make something that many of us dream of having!

1 Poverty is a _____ concept. You can be classified as poor if you earn less than 60% of the average person.

2 Norway is a country that has saved money for the future rather than _____ it all in its infrastructure.

3 The servant economy is growing in developed countries; even people who are not very well-off have a _____ come and tidy the house once a week.

4 In the Stone Age, _____ gatherers had a kind of gift economy. This was because they had a lot and needed little.

5 'At the _____ of the day' is a commonly used phrase in negotiations.

6 The opposite of saving money is _____ it.

Word: _____

🎧 **3.16**

LISTENING TEST

Please note that the page reference on the audio refers to the full edition. Stay on this page.

SECTION 1   *Questions 1–10*

Questions 1–3

Choose the correct letter, A, B or C.

Example

How did Martin first hear about the careers day?
A his tutor made an announcement
B he saw a notice advertising it
Ⓒ a friend told him about it

---

1   The careers day will be held
    A in the college where Martin studies.
    B in a public building.
    C in the open air.

2   How long does Martin plan to spend at the careers day?
    A a couple of hours
    B half the day
    C the full day

3   The Careers Day Website is available
    A to anyone who pays an additional fee.
    B only to those enrolled at the college.
    C for a limited period of time only.

Questions 4–5

Choose **TWO** letters *A–E*.

Which two activities are available during the lunch break?

    A advice on CV writing
    B talks by previous graduates
    C personal interviews with careers advisers
    D group discussions with recruitment agencies
    E video on opportunities to do voluntary work overseas

4   ....

5   ....

Questions 6–10

Complete the notes below.

Write **NO MORE THAN TWO WORDS AND/OR A NUMBER** *for each answer.*

	CAREERS DAY Scheduled Talks		
Time	Faculty	Speaker	Topic
10.00	Law	Professor **6**	contracts of employment
11.00	**7**	Professor Smith	internships
12.00	Languages	Dr Sally Wentworth	**8** ....
13.00	Lunch break		
14.00	Engineering	Dr Shah	opportunities in the **9** ....
15.00	Sports Science	Professor Bellucci	Olympic Games
16.00	**10**	Dr Fulton	interview techniques

Please note that the page reference on the audio refers to the full edition. Stay on this page.

SECTION 2   *Questions 11–20*

Questions 11 and 12

*Choose the correct letter, **A**, **B** or **C**.*

11 If you visit Jodrell Bank, you can
  A walk close to the telescope.
  B go on a guided tour of the buildings.
  C meet the scientists who work on the site.

12 A family ticket in the winter costs
  A £19.50.
  B £20.
  C £25.

Questions 13 and 14

*Choose **TWO** letters A–E.*

Which two facilities are currently available at the visitor centre?

  A cinema
  B lecture theatre
  C interactive displays
  D refreshments
  E planetarium

13 ....

14 ....

Questions 15–20

Complete the table below.

Write **NO MORE THAN TWO WORDS AND/OR A NUMBER** *for each answer.*

History of Jodrell Bank	
Year	Event
1939	The site was purchased by the university's **15** .... department.
1945	Bernard Lovell moved some radar equipment to the site. Installation coincided with a **16** ...., which Lovell observed.
17	Giant Transit telescope built at Jodrell Bank.
1957	The telescope was replaced by one originally called the **18** .... telescope.
1972	Arboretum created featuring a scale model of the **19** ....
2011	New visitor centre opened. Jodrell Bank proposed as a possible **20** .... site.

Please note that the page reference on the audio refers to the full edition. Stay on this page.

SECTION 3   *Questions 21–30*

Questions 21–24

*Choose the correct letter, **A**, **B** or **C**.*

21 When asked if the elective is like a holiday, Damian
    A suggests that this depends on the individual.
    B admits that he spent too much time enjoying himself.
    C denies that his placement was unusual in this respect.

22 Why did Damian find it hard to organise his elective?
    A He had never travelled alone.
    B He was unfamiliar with other cultures.
    C He wasn't sure what he wanted to specialise in.

23 How does Damian feel about splitting his elective between two places?
    A He wishes he hadn't decided to do that.
    B He thinks he spent too long in one place.
    C He insists that he made the right decision.

24 When choosing a company to help him find an elective placement, Damian
    A relied on word-of-mouth recommendations.
    B did thorough research on the Internet.
    C tried not to be influenced by price.

Questions 25 and 26

Complete the sentences below.

*Write **NO MORE THAN TWO WORDS** for each answer.*

Damian decided to look for an elective placement specialising in **25** .... medicine.

Damian chose Belize because he was impressed by pictures of the **26** .... there.

Questions 27–30

Complete the notes below.

*Write **NO MORE THAN THREE WORDS** for each answer.*

BELIZE

Total Population: **27** ....

Area where Damian worked: **28** ....

Nationality of most doctors: **29** ....

What Damian would do if he returned to Belize: **30** ....

Please note that the page reference on the audio refers to the full edition. Stay on this page.

SECTION 4   *Questions 31–40*

Questions 31–35

Complete the notes below.

*Write **NO MORE THAN THREE WORDS** for each answer.*

Antiguan Racer Snake	
Length:	**31** ....
Colouring of male:	**32** ....
Colouring of female:	**33** ....
Preferred habitat:	**34** ....
Diet:	**35** ....

Questions 36–38

Complete the sentences below.

Write **NO MORE THAN TWO WORDS** *for each answer.*

Until 1995, the snake was thought to be extinct.

In 1995 it was rediscovered living on **36** .... island.

A **37** .... was commissioned by the Antiguan Forestry Unit.

An estimated **38** .... racer snakes were found to be living on the island.

In 1996, a long-term conservation project was founded.

Questions 39 and 40

What still poses a threat to the snakes?

Choose **TWO** *letters A–E.*

    A disease
    B the extent of its habitat
    C severe weather events
    D predation by rats
    E expansion of tourism

39 ....

40 ....

READING TEST

SECTION 1
Questions 1–16

You should spend about 20 minutes on Questions 1–10, which are based on the text below.

How to get a grant for scientific research
In applying for a research grant, it's essential to start by identifying the appropriate granting body to contact for your proposal, as each body usually has its own particular priority areas. Once you've done this, check you can meet both the eligibility criteria and the deadline for the submission of applications. Your proposal should be written out in the format stipulated by your chosen organisation. Almost all granting bodies now have electronic application forms posted on the Internet, although these can sometimes be both complex and cumbersome.

A grant request is generally broken down into the following components:

Objectives
Succinctly describe your research goal, and what you propose to do to achieve this. It's a good idea to propose only those objectives that you feel relatively confident of achieving within the grant period. A proposal with too many objectives to be included in a relatively short time is likely to be considered over-ambitious, and might well be rejected, even if it involves cutting-edge science or a revolutionary new idea.

Background and rationale

Introduce the problem that the research intends to address. The length of your description is dictated by the length limitations on the application form. You should cover what is already known about the problem in the scientific literature, and highlight the major gaps or limitations in the current knowledge base. The final paragraph should state precisely what you will have achieved if the project succeeds, and the likely impact of a successful research project. In addition, many application forms, even for basic research grants, now have a section in which you're required to describe how the research is likely to contribute to economic development.

Experimental design and methods

You must describe in detail exactly what you're going to do to achieve your stated objectives. You should provide sufficient details to enable the review panel to critically evaluate your project. In particular, you must show how the experimental design will answer the questions that you're setting out to address; poor experimental design is the downfall of many applications.

Critical appraisal and limitations of the proposed approach

Describe the possible limitations of your proposed approach. For example, one of your proposed methodologies may have certain disadvantages that could impact adversely on your findings. A reviewer will certainly point this out and might find it sufficient grounds for rejecting your proposal. To meet such concerns, you should therefore state clearly that you're aware of the limitations of your approach, and if possible propose an alternative strategy if your first approach fails to deliver. You should also describe briefly any particular strengths of your laboratory likely to contribute to the success of the project if it is funded.

Questions 1–10

Do the following statements agree with the information given in the text?

In boxes 1–10 on your answer sheet, write

TRUE	*if the statement agrees with the information*
FALSE	*if the statement contradicts the information*
NOT GIVEN	*if there is no information on this*

1 Find the granting body which is best suited to the type of research you want to do.

2 Find out the date by which proposals must be sent in.

3 It's a good idea to lay out your proposal in an imaginative way.

4 Your proposal should have a long-term aim that extends beyond the timescale of the grant.

5 Make sure you fill all available space on the application form.

6 Your application should refer to other work already carried out on your topic.

7 It's essential to say how your research is relevant to economic and social issues.

8 The review panel may contact you with questions about your experimental design.

9 It's better to be honest if you have any doubts about aspects of your proposal.

10 You should give a full description of any laboratory facilities available to you.

Questions 11–16

The text on this page has six sections, **A–F.**

*Choose the correct heading for sections **A–F** from the list of headings below.*

Write the correct number (i–ix) in boxes 11–16 on your answer sheet.

List of Headings

i	Research experience
ii	Laboratory investigations
iii	Preliminary data
iv	Background reading
v	Description of the study area
vi	Data analysis
vii	Subject recruitment
viii	Collaboration
ix	Data collection

---

11 Section **A** ....

12 Section **B** ....

13 Section **C** ....

14 Section **D** ....

15 Section **E** ....

16 Section **F** ....

Experimental design and methods

Within this section of your research proposal, there should be several sub-sections, some of which are required for all types of grants, others of which are dependent on the topic of the research.

A Granting bodies like to see a concise description of the results of any work you have already carried out towards the research. Focus on the results that suggest that the proposed work will probably succeed.

B If the proposed research involves field studies, your application should include latitude and longitude, elevation, vegetation, rivers, rainy and dry seasons, mean rainfall and temperatures, and distance from the capital city.

C Describe how you plan to find people to take part in experiments and what criteria you will use for including or excluding particular individuals. Most importantly, include how you will obtain informed consent from these people, and which national authority or authorities have given ethical approval for your research.

D It is important to provide sufficient detail in this section for the reviewer to agree that the proposed work is feasible. There is no need to go into a lot of detail if the laboratory procedures that you plan to use are standard and widely described in scientific literature. However, you must still provide some details of your proposed procedures. Make sure you include a brief description of the various analytical techniques that you will carry out.

E This should include how it will be entered into a computerised database and what software will be used. In the case of trials, you should include how various variables, either continuous or discrete, will be compared among different groups studied using a variety of statistical methods, and how you intend to control for confounding variables.

F It is important to identify the partners with whom you intend to work, either in your own country or overseas. The choice of research partner or partners is crucial for your research project. They should provide complementary, rather than identical, expertise and/or facilities, and it must be clear how their presence will strengthen your proposal.

SECTION 2

Questions 17–27

You should spend about 20 minutes on Questions 17–27, which are based on the text below.

The world's oldest mattress

A study published in *Science* by Lyn Wadley of the University of Witwatersrand and her colleagues throws new light on the behaviour of early man in South Africa. The focus of the research is a cave in a natural rock shelter called Sibudu, situated in a sandstone cliff, 40 kilometres north of Durban. Dr Wadley has found evidence for at least 15 separate occasions when it acted as a home, with periods in between when it was abandoned, as is often the case with such shelters. Each occupation left debris behind, though, and as this accumulated, the cave floor gradually rose. All told, these layers reveal occupation over a period of about 40,000 years.

Among the things Dr Wadley's team found in the floor of the cave was evidence of mat making throughout the period of habitation. The oldest stratum, dating from 77,000 years ago, predate other known instances of plant matting by approximately 50,000 years. They consisted of compacted stems and leaves of plants stacked in layers within a chunk of sediment three metres thick.

'The inhabitants would have collected the plant matter from along the river, located directly below the site, and laid the plants on the floor of the shelter,' said Wadley. The lower part of these layers, compressed to a thickness of about a centimetre, consists of sedges, rushes and grasses. The upper part, just under a millimetre thick, is made of leaves from *Cryptocarya woodii*, a tree whose foliage contains chemicals that kill biting insects. Dr Wadley thus thinks that what she has found are mattresses on which the inhabitants slept, although they may also have walked and worked on them.

The upshot is another piece of evidence of how, around this period, humans were creating a range of hitherto unknown artefacts. Adhesives, arrows, needles, ochre-decorated pictograms and necklaces made from shells are all contemporary with Dr Wadley's finds, and stone tools became more delicate and sophisticated during this period.

Indeed, given the age of the mats and other artefacts at the site, it's clear that *Homo sapiens* was the hominid who slept in the cave. The earliest hominids had very different sleeping accommodations. Even though they had evolved an efficient way to walk on the ground, hominids such as *Australopithecus* were still small, not much bigger than a chimpanzee. They probably settled in trees at night, for if they slept on the ground, they would have been vulnerable to nocturnal predators looking for a midnight meal. The fossils of early hominids indicate this was possible; they still retained features useful for climbing, such as curved fingers and long arms. Once in the trees, they probably built nests of branches, twigs and leaves, just as chimpanzees do today.

The first hominid to try the ground as a bed might have been *Homo erectus*, starting almost two million years ago. Richard Wrangham, a biological anthropologist at Harvard University, suggests that once hominids learned how to control fire they discovered they could sleep on the ground while the flames kept predators away. It was also useful for cooking and processing foods, allowing *Homo erectus* to expand its diet. Adaptations for arboreal life were eventually lost, and *Homo erectus* became bigger and taller, the first hominid with a more modern body plan. Although there's no evidence in the paleontological record that hints at what type of bedding *Homo erectus* used, modern humans were certainly not the only hominids to construct 'mattresses'. Neanderthals were also building grass beds, based on evidence from a cave site in Spain dating to between 53,000 and 39,000 years ago.

Questions 17–19

Choose the correct letter, A, B, C or D.

Write your answers in boxes 17–19 on your answer sheet.

17 Dr Wadley believes that the cave at Sibudu was lived in
  A continuously over many thousands of years.
  B on a surprising number of different occasions.
  C intermittently during a long period of pre-history.
  D at times when other dwellings had to be abandoned.

18 Why is the evidence of mat making at Sibudu particularly significant?
  A It reflects findings in similar caves elsewhere.
  B It's older than other examples of similar craft skills.
  C It proves that the caves were actually once inhabited.
  D It helps establish the period when the caves were in use.

19 What leads Dr Wadley to think that the mats were used for sleeping?
  A one of the materials from which they were made
  B the thickness of the strata that were created
  C the use of plant matter collected nearby
  D the fact they were constructed in layers

Questions 20–22

What other artefacts from the same period as Sibudu are mentioned in the text?

Write the correct three letters A–G in boxes 20–22 on your answer sheet.

  A illustrations
  B building materials
  C weapons
  D sewing equipment
  E fastenings for clothing
  F cooking equipment
  G cleaning materials

20 ....

21 ....

22 ....

Questions 23–27

Complete the sentences below.

Choose NO MORE THAN TWO WORDS from the passage for each answer.

Write your answers in boxes 23–27 on your answer sheet.

Australopithecus probably used 23 .... as places to sleep.

Early hominids had physical features that suggest they were good at 24 ....

Early hominids may have constructed nests similar to those made by **25** ....

Homo erectus used **26** .... for protection whilst sleeping.

Neanderthals may have used **27** .... to make a surface to sleep on.

SECTION 3

You should spend about 20 minutes on Questions 28–40, which are based on the text below.

BRIGHT LIGHTS, BUG CITY

In the heart of Africa's savannah, there is a city built entirely from natural, biodegradable materials, and it's a model of sustainable development. Its curved walls, graceful arches and towers are rather beautiful too. It's no human city, of course. It's a termite mound.

Unlike termites and other nest-building insects, humans pay little attention to making buildings fit for their environments. As we wake up to climate change and resource depletion, though, interest in how insects manage their built environments is growing, and we have a lot to learn. 'The building mechanisms and the design principles that make the properties of insect nests possible aren't well understood,' says Guy Theraulaz of the Research Centre on Animal Cognition in France. That's not for want of trying. Research into termite mounds kicked off in the 1960s, when Swiss entomologist Martin Lüscher made groundbreaking studies of nests created by termites of the genus *Macrotermes* on the plains of southern Africa.

It was Lüscher who suggested the chaotic-looking mounds were in fact exquisitely engineered eco-constructions. Specifically, he proposed an intimate connection between how the mounds are built and what the termites eat. *Macrotermes* species live on cellulose, a constituent of plant matter that humans can't digest. In fact, neither can termites. They get round this by cultivating gardens for fungi, which can turn it into digestible nutrients. These areas must be well ventilated, their temperature and humidity closely controlled – no mean feat in the tropical climates in which termites live. In Lüscher's theory, heat from the fungi's metabolism and the termites' bodies causes stagnant air, laden with carbon dioxide, to rise up a central chimney. From there it fans out through the porous walls of the mound, while new air is sucked in at the base.

This simple and appealing idea spawned at least one artificial imitation: the Eastgate Centre in Harare, Zimbabwe, designed by architect Mick Pearce, which boasts a termite-inspired ventilation and cooling system. It turns out, however, that few if any termite mounds work this way.

Scott Turner, a termite expert at The State University of New York, and Rupert Soar of Freeform Engineering in Nottingham, UK, looked into the design principles of *Macrotermes* mounds in Namibia. They found that the mounds' walls are warmer than the central nest, which rules out the kind of buoyant outward flow of CO_2-rich air proposed by Lüscher. Indeed, injecting a tracer gas into the mound showed little evidence of steady, convective air circulation.

Turner and Soar believe that termite mounds instead tap turbulence in the gusts of wind that hit them. A single breath of wind contains small eddies and currents that vary in speed and direction with different frequencies. The outer walls of the mounds are built to allow only eddies changing with low frequencies to penetrate deep within them. As the range of frequencies in the wind changes from gust to gust, the boundary between the stale air in the nest and the fresh air from outside moves about within the mounds' walls, allowing the two bodies of air to be exchanged. In essence, the mound functions as a giant lung.

This is very different to the way ventilation works in modern human buildings, where fresh air is blown in through vents to flush stale air out. Turner thinks there's something to be gleaned from the termites' approach. 'We could turn the whole idea of the wall on its head,' he says. 'We shouldn't think of walls as barriers to stop the outside getting in, but rather design them as adaptive, porous interfaces that regulate the exchange of heat and air between the inside and outside. Instead of opening a window to let fresh air in, it would be the wall that does it, but carefully filtered and managed the way termite mounds do it.'

Turner's ideas were among many discussed at a workshop on insect architecture organised by Theraulaz in Venice, Italy, last year. It aimed to pool understanding from a range of disciplines, from experts in insect behaviour to practising architects. 'Some real points of contact began to emerge,' says Turner. 'There was a prevailing idea among the biologists that architects could learn much from us. I think the opposite is also true.' One theme was just how proficient termites are at adapting their buildings to local conditions. Termites in very hot climates, for example, embed their mounds deep in the soil – a hugely effective way of regulating temperature. 'As we come to understand more, it opens up a vast universe of new bio-inspired design principles,' says Turner. Such approaches are the opposite of modern human ideas of design and control, in which a central blueprint is laid down in advance by an architect and rigidly stuck to. But Turner thinks we could find ourselves adopting a more insect-like approach as technological advances make it feasible.

Questions 28–34

Complete the notes below.

Choose **NO MORE THAN THREE WORDS AND/OR A NUMBER** *from the text for each answer.*

Write your answers in boxes 28–34 on your answer sheet.

Liischer's model of *Macrotermes* mounds

Termites rely on **28** .... as their source of food.

Termites create areas of fungi called **29** ....

The fungi produce **30** .... for the termites.

Both fungi and termites produce **31** .... and stale air.

Stale air goes up a structure called the **32** ....

Carbon dioxide escapes through the walls of the mound.

Fresh air then enters at the **33** .... of the mound.

The whole process provides ventilation for the fungi, and manages both the **34** .... and temperature of their area.

Questions 35–40

Do the following statements agree with the information given in the text?

In boxes 35–40 on your answer sheet, write

TRUE	*if the statement agrees with the information*
FALSE	*if the statement contradicts the information*
NOT GIVEN	*if there is no information on this*

35 Pearce's design in Zimbabwe was an attempt to put Liischer's ideas into practice.

36 Turner and Soar's research disproved Liischer's theory.

37 Turner and Soar built a model termite mound to test their ideas.

38 Turner likens the mechanism for changing the air in the mound to an organ in the human body.

39 Turner thinks it unlikely that the termites' way of ventilating their mounds would work in a human building.

40 Turner believes that biologists have little to learn from architects.

WRITING TEST

TASK 1

You should spend about 20 minutes on this task.

> *You have recently gone to live in a new city.*
>
> *Write a letter to your English-speaking friend. In your letter*
> - *explain why you have gone to live in the new city*
> - *describe the place where you are living*
> - *invite your friend to come and see you*

Write at least 150 words.

You do not need to write any addresses.

Begin your letter like this:

Dear Anna,

TASK 2

You should spend about 40 minutes on this task.

Write about this topic.

> *The ownership of cars should be restricted to one per family in order to reduce traffic congestion and pollution.*
>
> *To what extent do you agree or disagree?*

Give reasons for your answer and include any relevant examples from your own knowledge or experience.

Write at least 250 words

SPEAKING TEST

PART 1 – INTRODUCTION AND INTERVIEW

Let's talk about how you keep in touch with world events.
- How do you usually find out what is happening in the world?
- Are you more interested in national news or world news? Why (not)?
- What do you do if you want to find out more details about a news item (and why)?
- Do you think reading or listening to the news in English is a good idea?

PART 2 – INDIVIDUAL LONG TURN

Candidate Task Card

Describe a time when you took part in an experiment or a piece of research.

You should say:
   what the aim of the experiment or piece of research was
   why you became involved in it
   what your role in it was
and explain how you felt about taking part.

You will have to talk about the topic for one to two minutes.

You will have one minute to think about what you are going to say.

You can make some notes to help you if you wish.

Rounding off questions
- Do you know what the outcome of the experiment/research was?
- Would you take part in that sort of experiment/research again?

PART 3 – TWO-WAY DISCUSSION

Let's consider first of all the role of scientific research.
- How important is scientific research?
- Which type of scientific research do you think is most important (and why)?
- Do you think too much money is spent on exploring outer space? Why (not)?

Finally, let's talk about how scientific research is reported by the media.
- Do you think that the media reports scientific research accurately? Why (not)?

Audioscripts

Unit 7

💿 **2.9**

P = Presenter, E = Expert

P: Even though we wish oil would go on forever, sooner or later it's going to run out. The question is not 'if' but 'when'. A lot of people have talked about peak oil in recent years – the point when oil stocks start to decline. Some people say we've reached this point already; others say it's still fifteen years away. Terry Pritchard, an expert from the oil industry, is here in the studio. Mr Pritchard, what's the truth?

E: I wish I was able to give you a straight answer – but the fact is no one knows. It depends on how you look at it. We passed the peak for oil extracted by conventional methods – that is, drilling a hole into a reservoir 200 metres below the surface of the Earth – in around 2006. But these days, people extract a lot of oil using unconventional means – deep-water drilling and so on. And the peak for that kind of oil is still a few years away. Of course, a lot of people wish that we hadn't started to go down this 'unconventional' route because the new methods are dangerous – the oil spill in the Gulf of Mexico in 2010 is an example.

P: OK, but either way the peak is not far in the future. And the price of oil is going to rise as reserves become smaller. So why hasn't anyone managed to replace oil with something else? I'm sure people would rather have a cheaper and cleaner alternative.

E: If only there was a cheaper, cleaner and more efficient alternative. The problem is transport. You see, petrol is incredibly convenient: it produces a lot of energy, it's easily stored and it can be delivered from a tank to an engine very simply – with just a few pipes. You read a lot about electric and hydrogen vehicles, but these technologies have their drawbacks.

P: Such as?

E: Well, hydrogen has to be stored under very high pressure, so the car becomes a bit like a moving bomb. And electric vehicles have a limited range – around 200 miles maximum.

P: That doesn't sound bad at all.

E: No, but if everyone had electric cars, we'd need a lot of lithium batteries and lithium is also scarce. So it becomes a choice. Would you rather we ran out of oil or lithium?

💿 **2.11**

The recent discovery of oil in the tar sands of Alberta has put Canada in third place in the world in oil reserves.

However, extracting this oil creates two to four times the quantity of greenhouse gases as conventional methods of extraction.

As a result, Canada has been under a lot of pressure to limit the environmental impact of its new oil industry.

💿 **2.12**

Speaker 1

In the 1970s, Cancún was just a small fishing village – a few huts on the edge of a mangrove forest. Today that forest is buried and rotting underneath 500 hotels. Only a few inhabitants remember the forest and the seven million tourists that visit each year don't know it ever existed. This place is a classic example of how not to build a tourist resort. Nature is for sale here. The mangroves are not the only victims. The coral reef all along the coast is also slowly being destroyed by all the tourists' pollution. Very little waste water is treated: it's either pumped into the sea or injected into the land, from where in time it returns to the surface. Up to now, conservationists have failed to stop this development or the pollution it's caused.

Speaker 2

The story of the West African giraffe is a conservation success story. A heroic effort on the part of conservationists has saved the giraffe from extinction – from numbers as low as 50 giraffes 20 years ago to over 200 today. The main job was to track the giraffe's movements, since they travel huge distances looking for food. This was done by fitting them with GPS satellite collars – easy with their long necks, you'd think, but actually it's a delicate operation because the giraffes have to be anaesthetised first. Once they knew where the giraffes were going, the conservationists could then begin to educate local people about the dangers facing these wonderful creatures, and to compensate farmers when their land had been damaged by them.

Speaker 3

If you mention the term 'conservation efforts', people tend to think of attempts to save endangered animals, like the tiger; or to protect poor communities from big corporate organisations who are trying to use their land. But in fact, many conservation efforts are small in scale and many have positive outcomes. I'll give you an example: the black poplar tree in Britain. The black poplar is one of Britain's rarest species of tree and its numbers have been declining for decades. That's because much of its natural habitat – the floodplain – has been built on with new housing. Less floodplain means less protection against flooding. So conservationists persuaded local authorities to stop building on the floodplain and reintroduce the trees. As a result, black poplar numbers are rising again.

💿 **2.13**

1

Globalisation is a force for good. It brings us all closer together. You'll say, 'Yes, it makes us all watch the same TV programmes and want to buy the same brands,' but that's not the point. The point is that it helps us to understand each other better: our differences and our similarities, our hopes and our fears.

2

Sorry, I just don't accept that. All it helps is people in rich countries to have cheaper goods and also goods out of season. To be honest with you, I could live without flowers that are imported from Africa in December or my computer technical support team being based in India.

3

We're approaching this debate all wrong. Globalisation is just a natural economic phenomenon. It gives countries a much bigger market so that they can concentrate on producing the things they're good at producing. Imagine if we had to grow our own coffee in England. That would be nonsense.

4

And that's a silly example. Let me give you another example: people in China making cheap toys for us to give to our children. These people would be much better off making things that were really useful to them. There's no doubt that it's helped the rich countries, but overall globalisation has just increased the gap between the world's rich and poor.

2.14

1 Globalisation may have helped the rich, but it hasn't helped the poor.
2 Globalisation is not something that has been invented; it's a natural phenomenon.
3 I like having things that I can't buy locally, but I don't actually need them.
4 Globalisation doesn't harm poor countries; it helps them.
5 I wish you were right, but the facts show the opposite.

2.15

F = Friend, MA = Model answer

1
F: What do you think about globalisation?
MA: To be honest with you, I think it's probably a good thing.
2
F: But don't you think that it just makes the gap between rich and poor wider?
MA: No, I don't accept that.
3
F: What makes you say that?
MA: Well, take India for example. They have a lot of skilled workers who are making good money working for western companies.
4
F: And what do you think of people who say globalisation's just making us all the same?
MA: That's not the point. The point is whether it's making us all richer and improving our standard of living.

2.18

Globalisation is a force for good. It brings us all closer together. You'll say, 'Yes, it makes us all watch the same TV programmes and want to buy the same brands,' but that's not the point. The point is that it helps us to understand each other better: our differences and our similarities, our hopes and our fears.

Unit 8

2.19

P = Presenter, J = Journalist
P: … that's just one aspect of photojournalism. The question I'd really like to put to you is: When is altering a photo OK and when is it not?
J: Well, … that's a good question. In 1982, *National Geographic* magazine published on its cover a photo of the pyramids in Egypt. In order to fit the tops of the two pyramids onto its cover, photo editors digitally decreased the space between them. People said that this was a manipulation of reality and was wrong. Several years later, an associate editor defended the action. He said that although the magazine had altered the image, they hadn't done anything wrong. He said that he was opposed in general to manipulation of images, but that the cover was a graphic item, not a photo in a news story. He also said that photo editors had always touched up photos, but that this practice was now becoming more sophisticated with tools like Photoshop and Scitex.
P: So he said it was the fault of modern technology that people were altering images?
J: No … He was saying that the cover of a magazine was more like a piece of advertising, and it had to look aesthetically pleasing to help the magazine sell.
P: You mean the cover has to look good?
J: Yes, that's right. Other editors have used the same argument to alter images for book covers.
P: And what about cases of manipulation in hard news stories – you know, really serious and important ones?
J: That is, of course, a far more serious thing. Again in the 1980s, there was a case with *Picture Week* magazine.

The magazine put together two different photos – one of Nancy Reagan, the other of Raisa Gorbachev – put them together in such a way that they appeared to be great friends. This wasn't actually the case and of course people complained, saying that they had been given a false impression.
P: So what's the rule?
J: Well, some people say, 'Don't trust a photo if there's anything important riding on it.' Personally, I think that's going too far. We live now in a world of digitally enhanced visual images and alternative realities. But the public's not stupid – they know that and can make up their own minds about what's real and what's not.

2.21

1 Like many of his fellow professionals, photographer Fritz Hoffman recommends using an analogue camera.
2 A digital camera encourages you to look at the preview before you take a photo, but an analogue camera keeps you in the moment.
3 Hoffman also claims that with a digital camera you need more time to edit the images after they've been taken.
4 That's so that you can make them look like the image as you saw it.

2.23

The difficulty with journalism is trying always to make sure that you give a balanced view, to get your facts right and at the same time tell a good story. *National Geographic* tries to find places where we can marvel at the wonders of nature and places where it thinks that natural ecosystems are in danger.

In the August 2011 issue, the magazine brought the world's attention to such a place, the Great Bear Rainforest in Canada. The main article was a full feature entitled 'The Wildest Place in North America, Land of the Spirit Bear' and described the beauty of the white Kermode Spirit Bear. A smaller article, called 'Pipeline through Paradise', described the building of a gas pipeline through 'Great Bear' country to a gas terminal on the coast at a place called Kitimat. Here huge tanker ships will be loaded up with liquefied natural gas. The article stated that, 'The government has already approved a fleet of liquefied natural gas tankers to call at nearby Kitimat in 2015.'

Strictly speaking, this was factually inaccurate and it upset the company building the pipeline a great deal. Building of the terminal had in fact already begun, and the local government had given its verbal approval to the pipeline. But the company had not received an official licence at the time of publication of the article. Even though it's very probable that a licence will be granted, the journalists and editors in question clearly jumped the gun in order to make their point.

The article highlights the dilemma for journalists. They want to write an interesting article and one that gives definite, not probable, news. They also want to get the story first, before it appears in other newspapers or magazines. The people involved, on the other hand – in this case the company representatives who were interviewed for the article – want **all** the facts to be presented, not only the ones that interest the journalist. They also want any comment to be balanced: in other words, for the same amount of space to be given to their own views as to the journalist's. Ideally, they'd like to have the last word, but of course no journalist should allow that.

2.24

A = Annie, J = Jane
J: Hi Annie.

A: Hi Jane. Did you hear the good news about Patrick? Guess what?

J: What?

A: Well, you know he was doing a comedy routine ...

J: You mean that show that he and his friends took to the Edinburgh Festival.

A: Yes. Well, apparently he was spotted by someone from a big theatrical agency and they want him to sign a contract with them.

J: Really? Who told you about it?

A: Er ... Kate. She reckons that it won't be long before we see him on TV.

J: Hmm … Well, I'd take that with a pinch of salt if I were you. It could just mean he gets a bit of advertising work or something.

A: No, according to Kate, it's more than that. They talked about him getting acting parts on TV.

J: Really? Well, that'd be fantastic. I heard that it was really difficult to get that kind of work.

A: I think it is, which shows he must have really impressed them. But don't tell anyone just yet. I think he wants to keep quiet about it.

J: Don't worry. I'm not the type to spread gossip. Does the agency take a big fee?

A: It seems that they only take 10% or 15%, supposedly.

J: That sounds all right. Well, that's great news. Thanks for telling me.

🎵 2.26

F = Friend, MA = Model answer

1
F: Did you hear the good news about taxes?
MA: Good news about taxes? No, what happened?

2
F: Apparently, the government is going to reduce taxes for all workers.
MA: Really? That doesn't sound very likely. Who told you that?

3
F: Ben told me. It seems that everyone will only pay half the tax they are paying now.
MA: Half? Hmm ... Take no notice of what Ben says.

4
F: Well, maybe he's blown it a bit out of proportion. He said it will be on the news tonight.
MA: OK. Well, I'll watch the news and see.

5
F: What do you reckon is the truth of it?
MA: I reckon that they've reduced taxes by half a percent or something and Ben misunderstood.

Unit 9

🎵 2.27

P = Presenter, M = Marjorie Barakowski

P: Ronald Reagan was raised in a small village in Illinois and he graduated from Eureka College, Illinois with a degree in economics and sociology. He worked for a short time as a radio broadcaster in Iowa, and then moved to Los Angeles to follow a career as an actor in films and television. After joining the Republican Party in 1962, his skills as an orator were noticed and he was persuaded to run for Governor of California. He did a good job as Governor and this led to his nomination for Republican presidential candidate in 1980, which he won. He then went on to become the President of the United States between 1981 and 1989. He took a hard line against communism and his second term of office saw the collapse of the Soviet Union and the beginning of the end of communism in eastern Europe. He was often ridiculed for not being very clever – a second-rate actor, who could only read the lines he was given by his advisors – but he remains one of the most popular American Presidents of the past 50 years. Why? I put that question to political historian Marjorie Barakowski.

M: Ronald Reagan understood the fundamental essence of leadership: that is, that you have to be able to communicate. Reagan always gave the impression that he was listening when he was speaking to you. It was almost as if it didn't matter what his political views were. He made people feel that they mattered. He looked you in the eye, smiled at you, made you feel special. That is a fantastic quality to have.

I'd also have to say that he presided over a time of great economic growth in America. When he came to power, things weren't great for most Americans and he gave them hope. It obviously helped that the economy thrived during his presidency. But, nevertheless, Reagan's style of communication stands out as a model for all leaders. If you can connect with the ordinary person, there's very little you can do wrong.

🎵 2.29

1 I guess I was lucky to do a subject that not many other people at college did. I studied plant sciences and after my course, I got a job as a research assistant at the Institute of Botany.

2 It's not easy to be an artist and make a living from it. You are always wondering if it would be better just to get a job with a regular income.

3 I was always told that having good qualifications and the right degree opens doors, but actually it's good communication skills that help you advance in an organisation.

🎵 2.30

I = Interviewer, V = Virginia Stanton

I: What are the particular qualities that men and women bring to leadership? Does it in fact make any difference to an organisation if its leader is a man or a woman? I have with me Virginia Stanton, author of *Women who Lead*. Virginia, surely in this day and age it doesn't matter that much, does it, what gender a leader is, as long as they're a good leader?

V: Well, if you say that, you're actually ignoring the differences that a number of studies have identified between male and female leaders.

I: And what are they?

V: Well, some of them will probably surprise you. It's statistically proven that women are a) more adventurous – they're happy to take risks and b) more effective – they focus harder on getting the job done.

I: That is a little surprising, yes.

V: Less surprising perhaps is that they tend to be more sensitive and caring – that is to say, they listen better than men and try to take other people's views into account before making a decision. That's because they seem to care more about their relationships with those around them.

I: And I suppose you're going to say, then, that men are more assertive and dominant – they force their own will on others around them. That's a bit of a stereotype, isn't it?

V: Well, actually, the studies show that women, in fact, are better at insisting on a point – on things being done the way they want them. They tend to be more persuasive than men.

I: I wouldn't have guessed that, I must say.

V: Well, I think the important thing here is that whereas in the past, leaders – male leaders, that is – were more autocratic – 'just do what I tell you to do and don't answer back' – these days you need to be more inclusive and gentler in your dealings with people. It's long been recognised that women, who traditionally have been the ones to organise and manage families or groups of volunteers in charity organisations, have these qualities. More and more, these are qualities that are needed today in the world of business and politics.

🔊 2.31
effective   sensitive   assertive   persuasive   inclusive

🔊 2.33
Speaker 1
Well, I'd be interested to know a bit more about the job, because although I'm very keen on the idea of working with young people – people are always telling me that I'm very good with children – I actually don't have much direct experience of this age group.

Speaker 2
I specialise in canoeing and various other water sports, but I feel comfortable with most outdoor activities really – as long as you're not going to expect me to lead a climbing expedition up a glacier or anything. I haven't done mountaineering. But I have led groups before, so I've got organisational skills.

Speaker 3
I think I'd be very well suited to this job, actually. Although I haven't led expeditions as such, I've been working as a physical education teacher at my local secondary school for the last four years. I'm good at quite a number of sports, in fact. But when I saw your advertisement, I thought, 'This could be just the thing for me.' I'm familiar with your organisation and I really like the fact that you run these activities for kids from poor backgrounds.

🔊 2.35
I = Interviewer, MA = Model answer
1
I: So what did you study at university?
MA: I studied media, but I specialised in newspaper journalism.
2
I: And what attracted you to our newspaper?
MA: I want to follow a career in journalism and I'm very interested in local news.
3
I: How do you feel about working to very strict deadlines?
MA: I think I'm good at working under pressure. I had a lot of experience of that at university.
4
I: Have you had any experience of writing for a newspaper before?
MA: Not really, but I think I write well and I'm very keen to learn.
5
I: If you get the job, don't you think you might become bored just dealing with local news stories?
MA: No. I'm serious about wanting to become a professional journalist and this would be a perfect place to start.

Unit 10

🔊 2.36
Speaker 1
People who are in favour of teaching your children at home generally argue that the local schools don't stretch children enough, or that they don't recognise their child's individual needs. I'm sure these people mean well, but I think they're missing the point. Interaction with other children from a range of backgrounds – not just your own brothers and

sisters – is a key part of learning and you just don't get that if you're stuck in your own house all day.

Speaker 2
Parents often discipline their children for fighting or being unkind to each other, but there's new evidence to suggest that this kind of behaviour may not be a bad thing. Psychologists say that by competing in this way, children are learning valuable social skills. It's common for brothers and sisters to squabble over toys or to compete for attention. They will even continue to do this later in life – fight for their parents' approval, that is – but generally they find a way of working it out so that no one's hurt. That type of negotiation in relationships is important training for later life.

Speaker 3
Where you are in the family clearly has an influence on your behaviour more generally. We're all familiar with eldest children who are organising and bossy types and middle children who feel ignored. Being the baby of our family, I'm particularly interested in youngest child syndrome. Certainly you have to fight more for attention – that's why younger children are often the clowns of the family. Parents tend to let you get away with things that your brothers and sisters didn't. You also have the advantage of learning from your older siblings ... and their mistakes.

Speaker 4
I think far too much attention is paid to how parents should bring up children and far too little to how much other environmental factors affect them. Have you ever watched a two-year-old when another slightly older child comes into the room? They're fascinated. They watch what they do, they try to join in – much more than with an adult. What's more, the elder child will quickly take on the role of teacher or parent, explaining pictures in a book, for example, 'Look. That's a lion! Can you say "lion"?' In a lot of societies, it's quite normal in large families just to leave the children to get on with it. I think parents in the West should do that instead of intervening so much.

🔊 2.37
Everything depends on what you see as the future role of your children. In other words, what is it that you are raising them to do?

Do you want them to be good members of society? If so, you will teach them values such as obeying the law, co-operating with others and generally being good citizens.

Or do you want them to be successful individuals? If so, you will help them to be free thinkers and to be independent.

Or is it important that they are good family members? Then you will teach them to respect their elders and to follow family traditions.

🔊 2.39
/uː/: blue, fortune, lunar, rude, suit, truce
/juː/: consume, humanity, humour, menu, used, usually

🔊 2.40
Desmond Morris trained originally as a zoologist and in that capacity, he observed the behaviour of many different species of animals. However, his lifelong interest has been human rather than animal behaviour, and unlike the traditional experts in human behaviour – the psychologist, the sociologist and the anthropologist – he is not so interested in what people say, but rather in what they do. In fact, he gives little attention to human speech because he feels that human actions tell us far more about people than

anything they might say. Indeed, it is said that in human communication, as much as 90% is non-verbal.

In an interview given some years ago on BBC's Radio 4, Morris gave a fascinating example of this. The non-verbal communication that he described was called 'postural echo' and this is how he explained it. Morris and the presenter were sitting discussing Morris's work in a radio studio. They were both sitting down facing each other across a table. Both had one forearm resting on the table and the other forearm upright with their chin resting on one hand. Both were leaning forward interestedly as they talked to each other. They had adopted what Morris called postural echo: that is to say, because they had a common interest, they were imitating each other's posture. This particular posture I've just described is typical when people are showing interest in what they are hearing.

In another situation, though, such postural echo might be totally inappropriate. The example Morris gave was that of a job interview. Imagine you are being interviewed for a job and the boss who is interviewing you sits back in his chair and puts his feet up on a stool. His posture is showing that he is in a relaxed and dominant position. Your posture, on the other hand, should show that you are in a subordinate position: in other words you should be sitting upright, perhaps leaning forward a little to show interest, with your hands on your lap. If you were to echo his posture, it would send the message that you felt as relaxed as him and he is not hiring another boss – he is looking for a subordinate. At best, you would not get the job; at worst, the boss would find it deeply insulting and end the interview immediately.

🎧 **2.42**

Dowry-giving, the gift of money from one family to another on the occasion of a marriage, is still common in certain parts of the world. It symbolises different things. For example, it can be a sign of wealth and increase social status. It can have a historical and practical meaning: as a rule, in the past, brides did not go out to work, so this was her financial contribution to the marriage. It's customary for a dowry to be given by the bride's family to the groom's family, but it can work the other way around, as in Nigeria, where a small dowry is given by the groom's family.

The engagement ceremony in Nigeria marks the beginning of the wedding celebrations and is an occasion for people to celebrate and have fun before the official ceremony, and also to give gifts to the couple. It takes place on the evening or a couple of nights before the wedding itself. During the party, there's a lot of music, often played by a live band, and dancing. It used to be traditional for money to be thrown at the couple's feet while they danced, but now people usually bring regular wedding gifts. After the party, the groom's family delivers a kind of dowry to the bride's family's house in the form of a gift of traditional clothes and jewellery. It's not the last time the groom has to visit the bride's house. On the night of the wedding, after the reception party is finished, the bride goes back to her own house where she waits until she's claimed by the groom and taken to their new home.

🎧 **2.44**

F = Friend, MA = Model answer

1

F: What does the groom wear on his wedding day?

MA: It's traditional for the groom to wear a morning suit and a top hat, but these days, he can also wear an ordinary suit.

2

F: What symbolic acts are there at the ceremony?

MA: The bride arrives with her father and he then gives her hand to the groom. That symbolises the handing over of his responsibility for her to the groom.

3

F: What happens after the wedding ceremony?

MA: The bride and groom go to a reception, usually in a special car, where they have a big party with all their friends and family.

4

F: What kinds of gifts are given?

MA: Usually people give the couple things that will be useful in their new home: kitchen equipment and so on.

5

F: Is special music played at the reception?

MA: Not really. Once the bride and groom have had their first dance together, everyone usually dances to pop music.

Unit 11

🎧 **3.1**

Dr K. David Harrison believes that language diversity is just as important as bio-diversity. He's part of a *National Geographic* project called 'Enduring Voices', whose aim is to document languages which are little known and in danger of becoming extinct. It's estimated that over half the world's 7,000 languages will disappear by 2050 and so the race is on to trace and record these languages, and also to help keep them alive.

Diversity does not depend on the size of a territory or country. In Bolivia, which only has a population of twelve million, there are 37 different languages, belonging to eighteen language families. This is the same number as the whole of Europe.

Dr Harrison seeks out these language 'hotspots' – places where there is a great diversity of languages spoken and where some are in danger. Studies in the Oklahoma region of the USA succeeded in discovering 26 languages, one of which, Yuchi, had as few as seven speakers. By highlighting this fact, researchers were able to help the community to keep this dying language alive.

Why is this work important? According to Harrison, 'When we lose a language, we lose centuries of human thinking about time, seasons, sea creatures, reindeer, edible flowers, mathematics, landscapes, myths, music ... the unknown and the everyday.' Some ancient cultures managed to build large monuments by which we can remember their achievements, but all cultures express their genius through their languages and stories. We would be shocked if the Great Pyramid at Giza disappeared; we should be equally concerned when we lose a language.

These languages store knowledge which can be of huge benefit to people today. The Yupik language is spoken by the Eskimo peoples of Siberia and Alaska. A book written a few years ago by Yupik elders and scientists in which they described the changing conditions of the ice in the Arctic was able to help other scientists to understand how climate change is affecting the polar ice.

One of the original arguments for globalisation was that it could bring us all closer together. And in some ways this may be true – but that doesn't mean we all have to do the same thing – eat the same food and speak the same language. If anything, globalisation has reminded us how important differences and diversity are. He couldn't save Ubykh – a language spoken near the Black Sea – from extinction, or Kakadu – an Australian aboriginal language, but Harrison and his team aim to save as many languages as they can.

3.2

1 Examples of two languages that have become extinct this century are Munichi – M-U-N-I-C-H-I – from Peru and Wappo – W-A-P-P-O – from the San Francisco area of the USA.

2 David Harrison is a linguist at Swarthmore College (S-W-A-R-T-H-M-O-R-E) in Pennsylvania (P-E-N-N-S-Y-L-V-A-N-I-A).

3 In 2008, the Enduring Voices project found a new language in Arunchal Pradesh (A-R-U-N-C-H-A-L) in India, called Koro, K-O-R-O.

4 Chary is a word from the Siberian language 'Tofa'. Spelt C-H-A-R-Y, it means a four-year-old domesticated reindeer.

5 The longest non-scientific word in the English language is floccinaucinihilipilification, which means the habit of regarding something as unimportant. I'll spell it: F-L-O-C-C-I-N-A-U-C-I-N-I-H-I-L-I-P-I-L-I-F-I-C-A-T-I-O-N.

3.4

1 Meg is a border collie, a smart breed of dog used by farmers because they understand instructions well and they like to be helpful. Their usual job is to round up and direct sheep. You can show Meg a picture of a toy and tell her its name (like a duck or a frisbee), then ask her to go and find it in a room full of toys. Once she has found it once and learned the name, all you have to do the next time is to ask her to fetch the the duck or the frisbee from the room and she will go and find it.

2 Betty is a New Caledonian crow. These animals are pretty inventive tool makers. In the wild, they use sticks, for example, to get insects out of trees. But what they found in the lab was that these birds were able to make tools from materials that they had never used before. Experimenters placed a piece of meat in a little basket and put it in a tube. Betty looked at the problem, then found a straight piece of wire, bent it into the shape of a hook using her beak and lifted the basket from the tube.

3 Maya is a dolphin. I think most people know that dolphins have incredible imitative abilities. They can see an action performed and then repeat it when ordered to. They also seem to understand spoken directions from humans very well. So you can get two of them to leap out of the water and turn a somersault at the same time. But in fact they do these kinds of synchronised tricks in the wild anyway, because they're naturally playful creatures, but no one really understands how they communicate with each other to get the timing so perfect.

4 Kanzi is a Bonobo monkey who has been taught sign language so that he can communicate with humans. One anecdote about his intelligence is that on a walk in the woods, Kanzi indicated that he wanted marshmallows and a fire. He was given the marshmallows and some matches. He found some twigs, broke them into pieces, built a fire, lit it with the matches and then, most amazingly, toasted the marshmallows on a stick over the fire. Bonobos are known for being expressive and good communicators, but even experts who study them were surprised by this behaviour.

5 Psychobird is a western scrub-jay. These birds are known for being pretty mischevious – they play tricks all the time. They're also supposed to be the only non-mammals that plan ahead. They hide food that they're storing up for future use in stores or caches. Their large memories allow them to remember as many as 200 such hiding places. In a lab, Psychobird hid food so carefully that none of the experimenters could work out where she had put it.

3.5

S = Student, L = Lecturer

S: Hi, have you got a minute? I just wanted to ask a bit more about this course.

L: Sure, how can I help?

S: Well, first of all thanks for the interesting lecture. [L: You're welcome – glad you found it interesting …] but there's quite a lot to take in and I don't really have the same background knowledge as some of the other students.

L: Don't worry – I think a lot of people find it difficult at first. Things will become clearer.

S: Well, can you explain what the course is going to be about, because I thought it was going to be about Roman history mainly.

L: Well, it's a mixture of Greek – mainly Hellenistic – and Roman history.

S: Sorry, I didn't catch that word – Helle-something?

L: Hellenistic – Alexander the Great and so on.

S: Oh, yeah … OK. And are you saying that no previous knowledge of ancient history is needed?

L: Well, a little understanding of the geography of the Eastern Mediterranean is very helpful, and if you've heard or read some Greek myths and legends, it helps too.

S: Sorry, I'm not really with you. You mean stories like the war at Troy and so on?

L: Exactly.

S: OK, well could you give me an example of a book I could read now, outside class?

L: Um, you could have a look at some texts by Herodotus. He was a historian of the 5th century BC and his histories read more like good bedtime stories!

S: Did you say Herodotus?

L: That's right, H-E-R-O-D-O-T-U-S.

S: OK, thanks. I'll do that.

3.7

T = Teacher, MA = Model answer

1
T: So you wanted to ask me a question about the exam at the end of this course?

MA: Yes. Can you explain what the exam involves?

2
T: Yes, there's a two-hour written exam and then a short 'viva' afterwards.

MA: Sorry, what do you mean by 'viva'.

3
T: It's a short oral exam to discuss what you have written. They ask you simple questions.

MA: Could you give me an example of the questions?

4
T: Yes, they might ask you to explain your reasons for an argument. But this part only carries a small proportion of the total mark.

MA: Sorry, I'm not really with you.

5
T: What I mean is the viva or oral exam is only 15% of the total marks.

MA: Did you say 15 or 50%?

Unit 12

3.8

How does national character affect economics? Well, let's just consider people's attitude to money at its simplest level. There are basically two types of people – savers and spenders – and we all know people who fit these descriptions. Savers are prudent and careful, never wasteful. Of course they spend money too, but only when they can afford it and only if it's a wise or long-term investment. On the other side, we have the spenders, the more extravagant types. For them, life is too short to worry about saving a little money here or there.

So, can you apply such simple stereotypes on a national scale? During the 2010–2011 global debt crisis, some commentators tried to do exactly that, saying that certain countries had been irresponsible with the money that they had borrowed from banks and governments in more prudent countries. As a result, people in these countries would have to work longer hours, pay more taxes and even accept lower wages if they wanted to receive any more loans.

The question these commentators failed to ask was whether it was irresponsible of the so-called 'prudent countries' to lend the money in the first place. Because when you lend money, you take two risks: you risk perhaps losing the money, but you also risk putting the borrower in a difficult situation. In such a transaction, both parties have a similar motive – to get more money – and so both have a shared responsibility.

To portray one country as a nation of extravagant spenders and another as a nation of prudent savers is too simplistic. What drives economies in most developed or developing countries is the desire to have a better standard of living. And that goes for all of us, spenders and savers alike. For some people it will mean spending money that they don't have at the moment – taking out a loan to get a new car, for example. For others, it will mean saving money to earn interest on it. And in order for the economy to function successfully, we need both types of person, but only as long as they lend and borrow responsibly.

3.9

I think that people often get into debt because they want a lifestyle that they can't really afford.

It's a lifestyle which is sold to them constantly through advertisements, for example on TV and in magazines.

This desire to have a better lifestyle can affect some governments too. They want to improve their citizens' standard of living so that people will vote for them again.

3.11

/ʃ/: wash, abolished, sugar
/tʃ/: watch, cheap, riches
/ʒ/: pleasure, decision, usually
/dʒ/: change, carriage, wages

3.12

I = Interviewer, R = Rick Castro
I: Most of us will be familiar with the concept of barter from our notions of how primitive societies work: you have a chicken I want and I've just made a new hunting spear that you need. So let's do a deal. But is 'barter' as a system of buying and selling goods and services coming back into fashion? With me is Rick Castro of the Barter Society. Rick, is this a serious alternative to current systems of trade or just a romantic notion?
R: The first thing I'd say is that barter never went out of fashion. People have been using barter as a way of exchanging goods for a lot longer than they have been using money and it is, as you've said, a feature of almost every primitive society past and present. But ... it's also very much a feature of the modern economy. People are making bartering arrangements all the time – it's just that conventional economic statistics – GDP figures and so on – don't record it. How could they?
I: Can you give us an example of that?
R: Yes, I can, but firstly we should make an important distinction between direct barter – that's like the

example you gave of two people exchanging a chicken for a spear – and then there's what we call 'exchange barter', which is where you belong to a barter group and make more indirect exchanges ...
I: What does that mean?
R: Well, imagine I'm a yoga teacher and you're a tree surgeon. I need to have a tree cut down in my garden and I'm ready to offer you a whole year of yoga classes in return. But you don't want to do yoga. What happens then? Well, if we belong to a barter exchange group, like 'Bartercard' ...
I: 'Bartercard'? You're not serious ...
R: Perfectly serious. If I belong to a group like that, I can sell my yoga classes for 'trade credits'. These can then be spent buying the goods or services of over 75,000 other members – restaurants, sports shops, almost anything. So if you're a member, I can buy your tree surgery services with my credits.
I: Hang on, though. This is just a tax dodge, isn't it? Normally I would have to pay tax on my tree surgery bill, wouldn't I? And you should charge tax on your yoga classes.
R: Of course these exchanges are liable to tax – at least that's the law in most developed countries.
I: So what's the advantage then? I'm trying hard to see one. Why not just use money?
R: Well, because if you belong to a group like that, it gives you access to a new market – a big circle of new contacts who will potentially become regular customers and ... possibly some of them your friends too!

3.13

A = Client, B = Caterer
A: So there'll be about 60 of us. We want some food but, to be honest, nothing too fancy. I suspect a lot of people will be going home and having supper later anyway.
B: OK, so what did you have in mind? A few canapés, some sandwiches?
A: Well, I was hoping we could have something a bit more exciting than sandwiches.
B: Perhaps if we prepared some sushi, some smoked salmon, a few samosas ...?
A: Yes, that would be much more like it. Is that going to be very pricey?
B: About £10 per person.
A: Mmm ... that's quite a lot, but let's face it, it is an important occasion. You know, it's a leaving party for someone who's been working with us for 37 years, so we don't want it looking cheap.
B: I think that's a good way to look at it. If I were in your shoes, I'd like to put on an event that people would remember. By the way, the £10 also includes the waiting staff for two hours.
A: Oh, we don't need that. We can just help ourselves. Would that reduce the price a bit, then?
B: No, I'm sorry. You have to appreciate that we have to come and set it all up and take it away anyway, so we might as well serve it while we're there.
A: I see. Well, the key thing for us is that it's a nice relaxing event, so we'll go with that, I guess.
B: Great. Just let me know exact numbers when you have them.

3.15

C = Caterer, MA = Model answer
1
C: So what kind of food did you have in mind? Some sandwiches?
MA: I was hoping we could have some hot food too.
2
C: OK. We could provide a few hot pastries as well. How does that sound?

MA: Yes, that would be great.

3

C: That would be about £10 per person.

MA: That's quite a lot. Could you move a bit on that price?

4

C: Sorry. You have to appreciate it's a lot of work for us. We could do it more cheaply but the food would be much more basic.

MA: No. The key thing for us is that it's nice food.

5

C: Well, if I were in your shoes, I would go for the more expensive menu.

MA: I suppose you're right. OK then. We'll do that.

IELTS practice test

🔊 3.16

Presenter: In this test you'll hear a number of different recordings and you'll have to answer questions on what you hear. There will be time for you to read the instructions and questions and you will have a chance to check your answers. The recording will be played once only. The test is in four sections.

Now turn to section one on page 100 of your book. You will hear a student called Martin telling his friend about a careers day which is being held in the city where they are studying. First you have some time to look at questions 1 to 5. You will see that there is also an example which has been done for you.

Now we shall begin. You should answer the questions as you listen, because you will not hear the recording a second time. Listen carefully and answer questions 1 to 5.

Woman: Hi, Martin. Did you hear about the careers day that the college is holding? My tutor was just talking about it.

Martin: Yeah, apparently there's something on the notice board about it, or so my flatmate was saying.

Woman: Well, it's probably this leaflet he saw pinned up there. Look, it's got all the details.

Martin: Great. Is it being held in the college then? I heard they were going to hire space in the Town Hall.

Woman: Really? I think you must be thinking of some other event. Our college is actually sharing the day with the technical university, and they're putting the day on at their campus. It's going to be outside in the grounds if the weather's nice.

Martin: Look, it goes on all day from ten till five. I wouldn't want to hang around that long though, just the morning or the afternoon would suit me fine. I start getting bored after a couple of hours at these things.

Woman: Well, look at the programme of talks – it'll help you decide which.

Martin: Anyway, there's a website with all the talks on, so it doesn't matter if you miss some of them.

Woman: Well, the event is free to students enrolled at the college, but the website isn't: you'd have to sign up like anybody else, and there's a monthly fee. But then you do see stuff from other similar events around the country too.

Martin: Sounds good. There are some sessions on in the lunchtime too. Look. And it's not the usual talks

by old students or videos about voluntary work in other countries either. You can get tips on how to put a CV together or go to a seminar led by one of the big recruitment agencies.

Woman: Right. My careers advisor was recommending those when I met her for my one-to-one advice session the other day.

Martin: Should be good then.

Presenter: Before you listen to the rest of the conversation, you have some time to read questions 6 to 10.

Now listen and answer questions 6 to 10.

Martin: So what are the main talks on the programme, then?

Woman: Well, each faculty's put up one speaker. Our college in the morning and the technical university in the afternoon. But the speakers aren't only talking about stuff relevant to those subjects.

Martin: Sure. So let's see. It starts at ten and the Law faculty is putting up Professor Jaynes.

Woman: The famous judge?

Martin: No, you're thinking of James. This is Jaynes, J . A . Y . N . E . S. And he's talking about contracts of employment.

Woman: Oh right. Could be interesting though.

Martin: Maybe. But eleven o'clock you've got Professor Smith talking about internships – that should be more interesting. She lectures in accountancy, apparently. So which faculty's that? Economics?

Woman: Business Studies actually.

Martin: Oh yes, of course. Then Dr Wentworth is representing the Languages faculty at eleven. I heard her give a really good talk on cross-cultural misunderstandings last term – you know gestures and stuff you can get wrong – it was brilliant. But this time, she's doing technical translations.

Woman: Oh right. Yeah, she's a good speaker.

Martin: Then after lunch, there's Dr Shah from the Engineering faculty. It says here he's an expert in computer modelling, but he's going to be talking about openings in the construction industry.

Woman: Shame, I'd rather hear about the models.

Martin: Me too. Then there's Dr Bellucci from Sports Science – she's doing something on the Olympic Games which should be interesting – all the different jobs from different disciplines that are involved.

Woman: Right. And then it's our old friend Dr Fulton doing interview techniques. He's working in the Geology department at the technical university now, and they've put him up for this. Though when he was here, he was in the faculty of Geography.

Martin: Still he's a great speaker – always gets a laugh.

Woman: So what do you think ...

Presenter: Now turn to Section 2 on page 102 of your book. You will hear some information about Jodrell Bank, a famous radio telescope, which is part of the University of Manchester. First you have some time to look at questions 11 to 14.

Now listen and answer questions 11 to 14.

Man: Good evening. I'm here to tell you about the Jodrell Bank Observatory, which has been a world leader in radio astronomy since the second half of the twentieth century. The site is part of the University of Manchester and there's also an arboretum with over 2,500 rare trees. A visitor centre provides information about both the famous radio telescope and the trees.

The giant Lovell Telescope that stands on the site is an internationally renowned and awe-inspiring landmark. This is a radio telescope so visitors cannot look through it directly. The observatory buildings are also still in use for operating the telescope so are not usually open to the public. But the visitor centre provides a good view of the telescope and visitors can walk along a pathway not far from the base, where they will find plenty of notices providing information about the history of the telescope and how it works. The centre also provides opportunities to meet the scientists who work at the Observatory.

The visitor centre also provides activities for visitors of all ages. Admission prices at the centre vary according to the type of ticket and the season in which the visit is made. For example, an adult single ticket would cost £6.50 in the summer months and £5.50 at other times of year, whereas a family ticket would cost either £24 or £20. An annual ticket is available for individuals at £19.50 and for families at £60. Concessionary tickets are available at all times for children, students and retired people.

In terms of facilities available at the visitor centre, these are divided between two buildings: the Planet Pavilion, where you'll find the entrance as well as the glass-walled café with outside terrace – you get amazing views of the telescope from there. There's also a gift shop and a small exhibition space where visitors can learn about the planets. The second building is the Space Pavilion, which is the main exhibition area. Here visitors can find answers to the wonders of the universe, listen to the sound of the Big Bang and explore the universe using hands-on activities. As many returning visitors are aware, our planetarium was demolished in 2003, along with the old visitor centre. But we are looking to secure funding to restore this feature in the not-too-distant future.

Presenter: Before you hear the rest of the presentation, you have some time to look at questions 15 to 20.

Now listen and answer questions 15 to 20.

Man: Next, a bit about the history of the telescope. It's named after Sir Bernard Lovell, who was a pioneer in the study of astrophysics in the twentieth century. The site itself, which is about fifteen miles south of the other university buildings in Manchester, first came into the university's possession in 1939. It wasn't the Astrophysics department that bought it, though, but the Botany department who were looking for a place to cultivate wild plants. In 1945, Bernard Lovell was given some equipment to use in his work, including a radar. But because of electrical interference from trams passing the university buildings, it didn't work properly in central Manchester, so he asked to move it to Jodrell Bank instead. It was installed just in time to observe a meteor shower that was visible that year.

Over the next few years, Lovell installed other equipment on the site, including an aerial on a searchlight mount in 1946, and in 1947, the 218-foot Transit Telescope – at the time the largest in the world. This telescope was superseded by a larger and more up-to-date model in 1957. This was named the Mark One Telescope, later upgraded and eventually renamed the Lovell Telescope in honour of Sir Bernard. This telescope became famous in the 1960s for tracking manned and unmanned space missions, as well as providing information about astronomy itself. And the telescope remains a world leader in this field.

Further developments followed in the 1960s and 1970s, including a teaching telescope for use by undergraduates, and the creation of the arboretum in 1972. This features national collections of various rare trees and other plants as well as a scale model of the solar system.

More recent developments at the site have included the opening of a new Discovery Centre in 2011, an event which coincided with a decision to place Jodrell Bank on the UK shortlist for consideration as a site with World Heritage status. In July that year the site also hosted a rock concert called 'Live from Jodrell Bank'. These are excellent examples of how the scientists at Jodrell Bank have always worked hard to engage with the wider community and increase the impact of their science.

Presenter: Now turn to Section 3 on page 103 of your book. You will hear an interview with a medical student called Damian, who is talking about his elective, a period of work experience he did overseas as part of his degree course. First you have some time to look at questions 21 to 24.

Now listen and answer questions 21 to 24.

Woman: Hi, Damian.

Damian: Hi.

Woman: Thanks for coming to talk to college radio about your elective. Now that's a period of work experience in a hospital you do in your final year as a medical student, isn't it?

Damian: That's right. The idea is that being a doctor is about understanding the psycho-social factors involved in each patient, as well as the medical ones. You do an elective in a speciality, to explore it in greater breadth and depth, and that's especially interesting when the placement's abroad.

Woman: So is it a sort of working holiday really?

Damian: No. I wouldn't say that. But electives do also give you the opportunity to travel and have fun. How you balance these two aspects is up to you. Whilst in Belize, I learnt to scuba dive, climbed Mayan ruins and explored the jungle, not something you can say about every medical placement!

Woman:	And it's up to you to organise the whole thing, isn't it?
Damian:	That's right. Many students have problems when it comes to organising an elective. For some it's the first time they've travelled alone or the first experience of being exposed to different cultures. I was cool with all that, but it's important to choose your speciality well. I had no idea where I wanted to go because I hadn't even chosen a speciality, so that made it tough.
Woman:	Do you have to spend the whole period in one place, or can you split it up?
Damian:	You can choose. I chose to divide mine into a six-week placement abroad and a two-week placement at home in the UK. Many people would argue that a two-week placement doesn't give you enough time to fit into a team and gain relevant experience, and I'd go along with that. With the benefit of hindsight, I'd have done better with a straight four-week split.
Woman:	And where can you go for help with these decisions?
Damian:	Well, many companies will organise elective placements for you, as well as providing cover and support ... at a price! But there are lots of companies out there, and I've heard that if you're willing to hunt around, you can find some reasonably priced deals. It's always worth asking round though. If you can talk to people about companies they've used, you can check whether those companies are any good or not. That's how I found the one I went with and I've no complaints.
Presenter:	Before you hear the rest of the conversation, you have some time to look at questions 25 to 30.
	Now listen and answer questions 25 to 30.
Woman:	So Damian, tell us about your placement in Belize.
Damian:	Well, having been undecided for a long time between specialising in surgery or emergency medicine, I went for emergency, because I thought it would give me a broader experience than surgery would. My first choice of country would've been Jamaica, but they only had places for dermatology and obstetrics, so that's how Belize came up. I'd never really heard of the country before.
Woman:	And was it a company that helped you?
Damian:	Yes, they provided photos of medical and non-medical facilities in a couple of different countries in the Caribbean and Central America. In the end, it wasn't the photos of the hospital, but those of the beach that drew me to Belize – perhaps I shouldn't admit to that!
Woman:	So tell us a bit about working there.
Damian:	The health system in Belize is a mixed one of both public and private. The government subsidises a significant proportion of health care for the average Belizean, although there's a limited number of hospitals with in-patient facilities. Belize has an area of 22,000 square kilometres with only 300,000 people spread sparsely around it, and a big town is one

	with about 20,000 inhabitants. It means that a significant percentage of the population is rural based and nowhere near a free national hospital.
Woman:	Right.
Damian:	I was one of three British students placed by the company: the two others were in the south of the country and I think they had a different experience, but up in the north where I was, the biggest frustration was that despite Belize being an English-speaking country, the default language was Spanish, because a lot of the doctors working there are actually Cuban. I speak French, but not Spanish, so when consultations weren't in English, I needed the doctor to explain what had been said.
Woman:	Would you go to Belize again?
Damian:	Yes. And people do sometimes get jobs in the places they've been to on electives. But next time I wouldn't go with the idea of being a hospital doctor, I'd rather think of teaching the staff. But I think I could've made better use of my clinical experience if I'd learned basic Spanish – so that would be a priority before I went back.
Woman:	Damian. Thanks.
Presenter:	Now turn to Section 4 on page 104 of your book. You will hear a student giving a presentation about the Antiguan Racer Snake, a rare species living on a Caribbean island. First you have some time to look at questions 31 to 35.
	Now listen and answer questions 31 to 35.
Woman:	In my presentation today I want to talk about the rarest snake in the world – the Antiguan Racer Snake – an animal that has been rescued from the brink of extinction by the efforts of conservationists.
	The snake is one of the racer snake family that is found in various regions across the Americas. It's a small harmless snake that grows to around one metre, with the female being slightly longer than the male.
	Many of the racer snakes found in the Caribbean region, and especially those in the southern states of the USA, are black in colour, whereas the Antiguan racer is lighter. The male is closer in colouring to the black racers, being a dark brown, whilst the female is distinguishable by its silver-grey skin.
	The Antiguan racer is found in various habitats, including sandy beaches and rocky ridges, but has a preference for dense undergrowth, which is one of the reasons why it's relatively rarely seen.
	In terms of diet, the Antiguan racer is very choosy. Other racer snakes feed on small mammals and amphibians such as frogs, but the Antiguan sub-species tends to rely on lizards as its main source of food. Maybe this is one of the reasons why it's an endangered species, although there is little evidence that its prey has ever been in short supply.
Presenter:	Before you hear the rest of the presentation, you

have some time to look at questions 36 to 40.

Now listen and answer questions 36 to 40.

Woman: By the end of the twentieth century, it was feared that the Antiguan racer, which was once common on the large island of Antigua after which it's named, had indeed become extinct. And this was probably the case. The snake had once been common on the neighbouring island of Barbuda too, but hadn't survived the human development of these large islands. But the local inhabitants were convinced that the snakes might be surviving on one of the smaller islands off the Antiguan coast, such as Rabbit Island or Crump Island, or on Bird Island – the place where one was eventually spotted in 1995.

The tiny island was uninhabited and looked after by the Antiguan Forestry Unit, which was keen for scientists to establish how many snakes might be living there. They commissioned a six-week survey, to be carried out by one of the conservationists who had made the discovery, Mark Day, who later went on to work for the conservation body, Fauna and Flora International.

What was established by his work was that the small island, only measuring some

18,000 square metres, was supporting a racer population of around 100 individuals. The rarest snake in the world was alive and well, but seriously endangered. In 1996, a conservation project was set up to ensure its survival.

And with the current population standing at around 500 snakes, this project has been hailed a success. A captive breeding programme has been effective in increasing numbers, even though it was adversely affected by disease at first. Reintroduction to other nearby islands, and to the mainland of Antigua, has meant eradicating the rats that had decimated the snake population in the twentieth century – a programme that has worked, although the snake's habitat does remain vulnerable to hurricane damage. Now that the species is officially protected, there are unlikely to be further incursions of tourist development into its natural habitat, another cause of its earlier decline. The right kind of habitat is not found over a wide area, though, and this will eventually limit the extent of the snake population. So before I go on to ...

Answer key

Unit 7

7a (pages 96 and 97)

1
Items which are mentioned: repairing broken water pipes, reusing rainwater, turning salt water into fresh water, making artificial rainclouds

2
1 c 2 b 3 b 4 b 5 c

3
a end-user b hosepipe c water meter d water butt
e on the face of it f ecological footprint g sceptic
h every cloud has a silver lining

4
1 hadn't imposed; would be (mixed conditional)
2 had; would use (second conditional)
3 introduce; will buy (first conditional) or introduced; would buy (second conditional)
4 was; wouldn't need (second conditional)
5 weren't; would have been built (mixed conditional)
6 hadn't been; would feel (mixed conditional)
7 works; are (zero conditional)
8 had thought; would be (mixed conditional)

6
1 run out of 2 save 3 waste; conserve 4 preserve
5 protect 6 spend; consume

7b (pages 98 and 99)

1
1 oil tanker 2 oil rig 3 oil slick 4 oil refinery
5 oil field 6 oil well 7 oil barrel 8 oil pipeline

2
No, he doesn't.

3
1 c 2 a 3 b 4 a 5 c 6 b

4
1 would go 2 was able 3 hadn't started 4 have
5 was 6 ran

5
1 drove 2 had 3 would stop 4 had bought
5 not think 6 would become 7 had seen 8 didn't speak

7
The recent discovery of oil in the tar sands of Alberta has put Canada in third place in the world in oil reserves.

However, extracting this oil creates two to four times the quantity of greenhouse gases as conventional methods of extraction.

As a result, Canada has been under a lot of pressure to limit the environmental impact of its new oil industry.

7c (page 100)

1
1 forest, Cancún, no 2 giraffe, yes 3 tree, Britain, yes

2
1 F 2 T 3 T 4 N 5 N 6 F

3
1 rotting 2 classic 3 sale 4 victims 5 heroic
6 wonderful 7 small 8 rarest

4
1 classic   2 a decade   3 a victim   4 buried
5 for sale   6 rotting

5
Emotive words: back-breaking, deplore, desperate, majestic, obsessed with

6
1 rescue   2 deprived   3 giant   4 exploit   5 wonderful
6 most threatened   7 plummeting   8 over-developed

7d (page 101)

1
1 F   2 A   3 F   4 A

2
1 understand each other better
2 in rich countries to have cheaper goods and also goods out of season
3 natural economic phenomenon
4 the gap between the world's rich and poor

3
1 not, point   2 just, accept   3 be honest   4 approaching, wrong   5 Imagine   6 Let, give   7 doubt

4
Speaker 1: c and e
Speaker 2: d
Speaker 3: a and d
Speaker 4: d

5a
1 Globalisation may have helped the <u>rich</u>, but it hasn't helped the <u>poor</u>.
2 Globalisation is not something that has been <u>invented</u>; it's a <u>natural</u> phenomenon.
3 I <u>like</u> having things that I can't buy locally, but I don't actually <u>need</u> them.
4 Globalisation doesn't <u>harm</u> poor countries; it <u>helps</u> them.
5 I <u>wish</u> you were <u>right</u>, but the <u>facts</u> show the <u>opposite</u>.

6
Students' own answers.

7e (page 102)

1
1 The writer feels that people waste resources such as food, energy and clothes.
2 There will be no more resources left.

2a
1 who live in more difficult circumstances than us
2 which is near its sell-by date
3 such as flat-screen TVs, computers or mobile phones
4 with only one driver in them
5 especially items of fashion clothing

2b
Possible answers:
1 with over 70 apartments
2 such as the black poplar tree, which is not found anywhere else in the city
3 where old and young people can come and relax
4 like the old industrial estate in Meadow Leys
5 because they are ugly and in need of modernising

3
1 c   2 b   3 e   4 a   5 d

4
1 to wait   2 calling   3 do   4 to know

Wordbuilding / Learning skills / Check! (page 103)

1
1 wind instrument   2 air bridge   3 wind farm

4 wind chill   5 water leak   6 air force   7 water jug
8 air vent   9 water lily

2
sunrise and sunset

4
1 Globalisation <u>helps</u> <u>people</u> <u>in</u> <u>rich</u> <u>countries</u>.
2 They can have goods out of season.
3 But to be <u>honest</u>, I don't <u>need</u> <u>flowers</u> imported from Africa in December.

6
Across: 1 renewable   4 unique   5 ecosystem   7 salt
10 Colorado   12 save   13 well
Down: 1 reuse   2 loggers   3 extract   6 scarce   8 Aral
9 wool   11 oil

Unit 8

8a (pages 104 and 105)

1
Across: 1 hard   3 soft   7 editorial   8 news
Down: 2 article   4 feature   5 headline   6 column

2
1 cover; 1982
2 Nancy; Week

3
1 F   2 T   3 F   4 T   5 F   6 F   7 T   8 F

5
1 of manipulating reality.
2 altering the image *or* that they had altered the image.
3 doing anything wrong. *or* that they had done anything wrong.
4 modern technology for making it easy to alter images.
5 their designers (that it is OK) to alter images for covers.
6 about being given a false impression. *or* that they had been given a false impression.
7 not to trust a photo if there's anything important riding on it.

6
1 for invading   2 (for) taking   3 for manipulating
4 to alter   5 touching   6 to add   7 for making   8 to accept

7
1 capture the moment
2 open the shutter
3 record events
4 see through the lens
5 take a photo
6 take a snapshot

8
1 recommends using an analogue camera
2 encourages you to look at the preview before you take a photo; keeps you in the moment
3 that with a digital camera, you need more time to edit the images after they've been taken
4 you can make them look like the image as you saw it

8b (pages 106 and 107)

1
1 b   2 d   3 a   4 c

2
a 3   b 2   c 3   d 4   e 1   f 1

3
1 wrecked   2 donations   3 longevity   4 zimmer frame
5 brainchild   6 brighten up   7 plunged   8 speeding

4
1 it is estimated that rioters

2 It was reported that
3 It is believed that
4 It is not thought that

5
1 It is said that
2 It is understood that
3 It was known that
4 It was believed that
5 It has been estimated that
6 It is thought that
7 It had been hoped that
8 It is supposed that

6
1 It is said that for every negative, there is always a positive.
2 It is expected that Mr Biber will carry on doing what he loves.
3 In the past, it was thought that a glass of red wine a day helped/would help you to live longer.
4 It is not recommended that you eat fast food if you want to live longer.
5 It was hoped that secret gifts would brighten up someone's day.
6 It was supposed that the tree prevented/had prevented the car falling further.
7 It was considered that the man had been/was lucky to survive the accident.
8 It has been reported that the idea was very successful.

7
amusing – serious
charming – dreary
inspiring – uninspiring
quirky – ordinary
encouraging – depressing
optimistic – pessimistic

8c (page 108)

1
1 T   2 F   3 F

2
1 view   2 wonders   3 beauty   4 pipeline   5 Strictly
6 jumped   7 dilemma   8 the last word

3
1 strictly speaking   2 wonders   3 have the last word
4 balanced view   5 dilemma   6 jump the gun

4
1 b   2 b   3 a   4 a

5
1 word of mouth   2 eat my words
3 one person's word against another's
4 don't take my word for it   5 gave his word
6 From the word go   7 was lost for words
8 have the last word

8d (page 109)

1
1 take (B)   2 gets (B)   3 spread (D)   4 Take (D)
5 blown (D)   6 take (D)

2
1 Philip has been signed up by a theatrical agent.
2 Kate
3 Not to tell anyone. Patrick wants to keep quiet about it.

3
1 about; Guess   2 apparently   3 reckons   4 pinch
5 according to   6 heard   7 gossip   8 seems; supposedly

4
1 com**e**dy   2 festiv**a**l   3 **a**pparently   4 reck**o**n   5 **a**ccording
6 **di**fficult   7 ag**e**ncy   8 the**a**trical

5
Students' own answers.

8e (page 110)

1
1 attend, hold
2 make, put forward
3 make, reach
4 discuss, weigh up
5 draft, write

2
1 A meeting was held to discuss how to raise the money.
2 All the options were discussed.
3 One suggestion was to ask the local council for help.
4 Another idea was to have some fun events.
5 It was agreed that organising events would take too long.
6 No decision was reached/could be reached about funding the project.

3
1 Advantages: the incinerator will generate electricity and dispose of waste
Disadvantages: it will cause a lot of pollution
2 Everyone in the area would sign a petition. Harry would research another kind of plant.
3 To present some alternative locations.

4
1 a meeting was held to decide
2 It was suggested
3 It was agreed
4 It was thought that
5 The point was made
6 It was proposed that
7 This option would be researched and discussed

Wordbuilding / Learning skills / Check! (page 111)

1
1 worrying   2 confusing   3 refreshing   4 charming
5 inspiring   6 depressing   7 touching   8 tiring

2
1 inventive   2 persuasive   3 creative   4 competitive
5 productive   6 talkative   7 protective   8 unresponsive

3, 4 and 5
Students' own answers.

6
1a words   b sell   c fast
2a zero   b iconic   c exinct
3a mouth   b feel-good   c spread   d feature

Unit 9
9a (pages 112 and 113)

1
1 small village in Illinois
2 radio broadcaster; (an) actor
3 the Soviet Union
4 was not very clever *or* read the lines given to him
5 listen to people *or* make people feel special
6 economic growth

2
1 b   2 a   3 a   4 b   5 b   6 a

3
1 graduated   2 worked   3 follow *or* pursue   4 joining
5 did   6 become

4
1 the United Arab Emirates, the Netherlands
2 the Amazon River, the countryside, the Moon
3 the weekend, the spring
4 the police, the poor
All the other nouns take zero article.

5
1 the; the; – 2 the; – 3 the; the 4 the; – 5 the 6 the
7 –; – 8 –; – 9 the 10 the

6

1 /r/ 2 /j/ 3 /w/ 4 /j/ 5 /r/ 6 /r/ 7 /j/
8 /w/ 9 /w/

7

1 I guess I was lucky to do a subject that not many other people at college did. I studied plant sciences and after my course, I got a job as a research assistant at the Institute of Botany.
2 It's not easy to be an artist and make a living from it. You are always wondering if it would be better just to get a job with a regular income.
3 I was always told that having good qualifications and the right degree opens doors, but actually it's good communication skills that help you advance in an organisation.

8

1 background 2 experience 3 qualifications
4 qualities 5 knowledge 6 talents

9b (pages 114 and 115)

1

1 My mission is to find simple, inexpensive ways to monitor health
2 these medicines can cause liver damage
3 The small piece of paper is a low-tech tool
4 to attend university
5 I want all women to believe in themselves and know they can transform society *or* to encourage young women who attend university abroad to bring their skills back to their homelands

2
1 c 2 b 3 c 4 a 5 b 6 b

3
1 a 2 b 3 c 4 b 5 c 6 c

4
1 … which detects disease by analysing bodily fluids.
2 … who attend university abroad
3 … which show up in less than a minute
4 … costing just a penny apiece
5 … pioneered by a team at Harvard University

5
1 The piece of paper, **which** is the size of a postage stamp, could save thousands of lives. *or* The piece of paper, **which** could save thousands of lives, is the size of a postage stamp.
2 The charity 'Diagnostics for All', **which** was co-founded by Sindi, produces the tool. *or* The charity 'Diagnostics for All', **which** produces the tool, was co-founded by Sindi.
3 The tool will be used in developing countries **where** it is difficult to find clinics.
4 People take powerful drugs, **which** can cause liver damage, to combat diseases.
5 The results show up on the paper, **whose** colour changes if there is a problem.
6 Sindi went to England **when** she was a young woman.
7 Sindi, **who** was the first Saudi woman to study biotechnology at Cambridge, later went to Harvard. *or* Sindi, **who** later went to Harvard, was the first Saudi woman to study biotechnology at Cambridge.
8 Sindi has become a role model for other women **who** want to follow her example.

6
1 Sindi's low-tech tool helps people **suffering from the negative effects of the drugs.**
2 People **living far away from hospitals and clinics** will benefit from this technology.

3 The same medicines, **designed to fight disease**, can also harm people.
4 Sindi, **determined to succeed**, studied up to twenty hours a day.
5 Sindi uses her own experience to inspire other women **wishing to become scientists**.
6 A new foundation, **launched** recently by Sindi, offers help to young women **wanting to follow a career in science**.

7
1 determination 2 accomplishment 3 inspiration 4 passion

8
1 passionate 2 articulate 3 analytical 4 patient
5 independent 6 adaptable 7 daring 8 easy-going

9c (page 116)

1
1 W 2 W 3 W 4 W 5 W 6 M 7 W 8 W

2
1 T 2 T 3 F 4 F 5 F 6 T

3
1 adventur**ous** 2 effec**tive** 3 sensi**tive** 4 car**ing**
5 asser**tive** 6 persua**sive** 7 autocratic 8 inclu**sive**

4a
1 e<u>ffe</u>ctive 2 <u>sen</u>sitive 3 a<u>sser</u>tive 4 per<u>sua</u>sive
5 in<u>clu</u>sive
The stress always falls on the second syllable. The exception is 'sensitive', where it falls on the first syllable.

4b
1 pro<u>tec</u>tive 2 cre<u>a</u>tive 3 per<u>cep</u>tive 4 i<u>ma</u>ginative
5 res<u>pon</u>sive 6 im<u>pul</u>sive

5
1 j 2 a 3 c 4 h 5 b 6 e 7 f 8 g 9 d 10 i

9d (page 117)

1
1 in 2 with 3 at 4 of 5 to 6 with 7 on 8 about

2
A job to lead outdoor activities and expeditions for young people.

3
1
Applicant 1: good at working with young children
Applicant 2: canoeing, water sports and outdoor activities; good organisational skills
Applicant 3: good at a number of different sports; experienced PE teacher

2
Applicant 1: hasn't got experience working with this age group
Applicant 2: hasn't got experience of mountaineering
Applicant 3: hasn't got experience of leading expeditions

4
1 participating 2 to leave 3 travelling 4 doing
5 to work *or* on working 6 to find out *or* in finding out

6
Students' own answers.

9e (page118)

1
1 b 2 d 3 a 4 f 5 c 6 e

2
1 marketing jobs
2 Japanese and English
3 she's highly qualified

3a
1 My job involves advising a British supermarket on their market plan for Japan.
2 I was responsible for the 'Winnie the Pooh' account.
3 I translated marketing documents for various British and US companies.
4 I'm currently doing a distance learning MBA.

3b
1 Specialist website designer
2 Designing interactive website for local sports and leisure centre
3 Computer programmer, British Telecom
  Designer, patient communications website, local hospital
  Set up company in 2010
4 Buckingham Grammar School;
  Liverpool University

Wordbuilding / Learning skills / Check! (page 119)

1
The verbs which do not collocate are:
1 do   2 make   3 get   4 make   5 acquire   6 win   7 own
8 work   9 earn   10 take on

2
1 took   2 follow   3 get *or* do   4 had   5 get
6 joined *or* set up   7 got *or* gained   8 acquire *or* learn

3
1 d   2 f   3 b   4 h   5 e   6 a   7 c   8 g

4
1 felt   2 definite article   3 acquire *or* get   4 yes
5 semi-formal

5
1 a a mahout   b an explorer
2 step, leap, mankind
3 a the Atlantic Ocean   d the USA   e the Moon
4 c

Unit 10
10a (pages 120 and 121)

1
Speaker 1: e
Speaker 2: d
Speaker 3: a
Speaker 4: c

2
a 2   b 4   c 2   d 1   e 3   f 4

3
1 b   2 a   3 a   4 c   5 b   6 a

4
Possible answers:
1 take   2 think   3 teach   4 will follow *or* follow   5 will design *or* design   6 are always fighting   7 squabbling
8 argue *or* will argue   9 say   10 helps *or* will help   11 tend
12 generally follow *or* will generally follow   13 will be
14 always follow *or* will always follow   15 often get *or* will often get

5
1 She's always talking
2 He's always asking if
3 She's always spending ages
4 He's always talking
5 He's always playing
6 She's always leaving

6
1 brought   2 spoil   3 punished   4 discipline   5 disobey
6 nagging   7 rebelled   8 pestering   9 give   10 reward

7
Everything depends on what you see as the future role of your children. In other words, what is it that you are raising them to do?
Do you want them to be good members of society? If so, you will teach them values such as obeying the law, co-operating with others and generally being good citizens. Or do you want them to be successful individuals? If so, you will help them to be free thinkers and to be independent. Or is it important that they are good family members? Then you will teach them to respect their elders and to follow family traditions.

10b (pages 122 and 123)

1
c

2
1 b   2 c   3 a   4 a   5 c

3
1 used to eat   2 used to use   3 are used to eating
4 have got used to eating *or* usually eat   5 usually eat out
6 are used to seeing   7 used to eat   8 usually eat

4
1 didn't use to cook   2 used to cook   3 wanted   4 used to hang *or* would hang   5 was   6 had   7 used to cook *or* would cook   8 were used to doing *or* used to do

5a
/uː/: blue, fortune, lunar, rude, suit, truce
/juː/: consume, humanity, humour, menu, used, usually

6
1 D/S, P   2 F, F, P   3 S/F, P/D   4 P, D

10c (page 124)

1
1 F   2 F   3 T   4 F   5 F   6 T

2
1 d   2 b

3
1 rather   2 Unlike   3 little   4 such   5 At worst

5
a common good
b common interest

6
Across: 4 ground   5 sense
Down: 1 knowledge   2 mistakes   3 interest   4 good

10d (page 125)

1
1 honeymoon   2 vows   3 stag   4 veil   5 bells   6 groom
7 proposal

2
1 It's a sign of wealth and social status.
2 for the bride not working
3 the bride's family
4 the groom's family
5 They bring gifts.
6 clothes and jewellery

3
1 symbolises   2 rule   3 customary   4 marks   5 occasion
6 place   7 traditional   8 On

4
1 /z/   2 /s/   3 /z/   4 /s/   5 /s/   6 /z/   7 /s/   8 /s/
9 /z/   10 /s/   11 /z/   12 /z/

5
Students' own answers.

10e (page 126)

1
Possible answer:

Hi Annabelle

<u>Very good</u> to see you the other day. <u>Hope</u> you <u>got back</u> to Leipzig safely. I forgot to mention that <u>I'm</u> travelling to Poland next month on business to visit a supplier. <u>I've really got no idea about</u> business customs in Poland and wondered if there was anything <u>I should know especially</u>. For example, should I take some gifts with me? Will they be <u>put out</u> that I <u>don't</u> speak any Polish? I certainly <u>don't</u> want to <u>put my foot in it</u> with my hosts in any way.

I <u>don't</u> want to <u>bother</u> you, but if <u>you've got</u> a moment to write a few words of advice, <u>I'd be really</u> grateful.

<u>All the best</u>

2
Possible answers:
1 Hi 2 Good to see 3 thanks 4 helping
5 Unfortunately 6 here's 7 don't 8 big
9 be embarrassing 10 You'll 11 seem *or* are 12 That's
13 I'm sure 14 they'll 15 About 16 It's 17 Hope
18 let me know 19 when you get back 20 All the best

Wordbuilding / Learning skills / Check! (page 127)

1
1 bride and groom
2 husband and wife
3 friends and family
4 suit and tie
5 food and drink
6 singing and dancing
7 bits and pieces
8 time and trouble
9 plans and arrangements
10 pomp and ceremony
11 fun and games
12 life and soul

2
1 pomp and ceremony 2 time and trouble 3 bits and pieces 4 life and soul 5 friends and family 6 suit and tie

5
1 in 2 out 3 back 4 in 5 sense 6 ground 7 foot 8 hen

Unit 11

11a (pages 128 and 129)

1
c

2
1 b 2 c 3 c 4 a 5 c 6 a

3
1 document 2 trace; record 3 seeks out 4 express
5 store 6 save

4
1 succeeded in discovering
2 were able to help
3 managed to build
4 was able to help
5 could bring
6 couldn't save

5
Possible answers:
1 managed to find *or* was able to find
2 could speak *or* was able to speak
3 never managed to convince *or* never succeeded in convincing *or* were never able to convince
4 couldn't understand *or* wasn't able to understand

5 could express *or* was able to express
6 could remember *or* was able to remember *or* managed to remember *or* succeeded in remembering

6
1 c 2 f 3 h 4 g 5 d 6 a 7 b 8 e

7
1 pick (it) up
2 inspire *or* motivate *or* engage with
3 ignorant
4 have a basic grasp
5 engage with *or* grasp *or* pick up
6 take in *or* grasp

8a
1a Munichi b Wappo
2a Swarthmore b Pennsylvania
3a Arunchal b Koro
4 chary
5 floccinaucinihilipilification

8b
a 5 b 2a c 4 d 1b e 3b

11b (pages 130 and 131)

1
a 2 b 1 c 3

2
1 T 2 F 3 F 4 N 5 F 6 N 7 F 8 T 9 T

3
1 blank (something) out 2 ran into 3 came up (to)
4 turned out (that) 5 come across 6 get away with

4
Text 1
1 My sister and I **were just about to go** to bed … *or* **were just going to go** to bed …
2 My sister **was going to say** goodnight … *or* **was about to say** goodnight …

Text 2
3 I **would have asked** his name …
4 I **was supposed to know** …

Text 3
5 who **was going to give** evidence in court … *or* **was supposed to give** evidence in court … *or* **was about to give evidence** in court …
6 her neighbour **wouldn't get away with** it … *or* **wasn't going to get away with** it …

5
1 was going to write *or* would have written
2 was just about to book; would be full
3 would speak
4 would have lasted *or* was supposed to last; were about to finish *or* were going to finish
5 was going to take *or* would have taken *or* was supposed to take
6 was just about to ask *or* was just going to ask

6a
1 I was <u>going</u> to <u>email</u> him, but I decided it would better to speak face to face.
2 He was <u>supposed</u> to get here <u>early</u>, but he's already ten minutes late.
3 I <u>would</u> have come by <u>train</u>, but there's a strike on at the moment.
4 She said she would be <u>pleased</u> if I talked to him, but she seemed really angry.
5 I was <u>about</u> to <u>buy</u> a flat, but Katie said I could rent hers for six months while she was away.
6 Liz was <u>going</u> to be in charge of the project, but now she's just acting as an advisor.

6b
1 I was going to email him, but I decided it would better to speak <u>face to face.</u>
2 He was supposed to get here early, but he's already <u>ten minutes late.</u>
3 I would have come by train, but there's a <u>strike</u> on at the moment.
4 She said she would be pleased if I talked to him, but she seemed <u>really angry.</u>
5 I was about to buy a flat, but Katie said I could <u>rent hers</u> for six months while she was away.
6 Liz was going to be in charge of the project, but now she's just acting as an <u>advisor.</u>

7
1 c   2 d   3 a   4 e   5 b

11c (page 132)

1
1 border collie   2 crow   3 dolphin   4 Bonobo monkey
5 scrub-jay

2
a 3   b 4   c 1   d 5   e 2

3
a 2   b 3   c 5   d 1   e 4

4
1 smart   2 inventive   3 playful   4 expressive
5 mischievous

5
1 walk   2 late   3 mistakes   4 tricks   5 lesson   6 live
7 way   8 heart

11d (page 133)

1
1 mean   2 speak   3 explain   4 'm   5 saying   6 give
7 take   8 catch *or* hear

2
1 Greek and Roman history
2 He doesn't have as much background knowledge as the other students.
3 Reading some history *or* a book by Herodotus.

3
1 what the course is going to be about
2 no previous knowledge of ancient history is needed
3 stories like the war at Troy and so on
4 a book I could read now, outside class
5 Herodotus

4
1 me   5 me   6 me
The other sentences don't need an indirect personal object.

6
Students' own answers.

11e (page 134)

1
1 c   2 e   3 d   4 b   5 a
The writer's application for a course has been rejected even though he/she applied before the deadline.

2
1 While we sympathise with your situation, it is too late to do anything about it now.
2 Although you sent your form in before the deadline, we had already received too many applications.
3 You say in your letter that we have no right to do this, but in actual fact, the college has the right to close the application process early.

4 We don't 'make up the rules as we go along' as you suggest. On the contrary, we are very careful to follow the rules.
5 Whereas most colleges would keep your application fee, we are refunding it to you.

3
Model answer:

Dear Sir/Madam

I am writing to inform you that I will be unable to attend the accountancy course (B102) this term owing to a misunderstanding.

When I enrolled for the course, I had assumed it was an evening class. In actual fact it turns out to be on Tuesdays between 10 a.m. and 12.30 p.m. I have asked my employer if it would be possible to release me for this period each Tuesday. Although they would like to do this, they say that the timing makes it impossible.

While I realise that this is probably my fault for not reading the timetable carefully enough, I hope you will be sympathetic. I hope to enrol on a future course, but for the moment I would be grateful if you could refund the course fees I have paid.

I look forward to hearing from you.

Yours faithfully

Mark Riley

Wordbuilding / Learning skills / Check! (page 135)

1
1 e *or* d   2 a   3 d *or* e   4 c   5 b   6 f

2, 3, 4 and 5
Students' own answers.

6
Across: 1 engage   5 selective   7 tip   8 external   10 catch
Down: 2 grasp   3 succeed   4 botanist   6 ignorant
8 error   9 late

Unit 12

12a (pages 136 and 137)

1
1 savers and spenders
2 No, these stereotypes are too simplistic.

2
1 b   2 a   3 c   4 a   5 b   6 c

3
fund – finance
prudent – careful
transaction – deal
wages – salaries
wasteful – extravagant

4
1 hard up   2 afford   3 reasonable; cheap   4 pricey
5 earnings   6 well off   7 loaded

R	H	P	I	M	O	I	N
E	A	R	N	I	N	G	S
A	R	I	C	C	F	O	T
S	D	C	H	E	A	P	O
O	U	E	S	O	F	U	L
N	P	Y	B	A	F	L	E
A	W	E	L	L	O	F	F
B	I	L	E	F	R	A	T
L	O	A	D	E	D	E	S
E	S	T	O	N	R	I	A

5
1 just *or* also
2 as well *or* too; only
3 even *or* also
4 also
5 only

6
1 Some people believe that if you go through life ONLY saving money, you will never have any fun. *or* Some people believe that if you ONLY go through life saving money, you will never have any fun.
2 Some people carry on spending money EVEN when they can't afford to.
3 You can guard against bad times by putting aside JUST a small amount of money each week.
4 If ONLY a few people save money, the banks won't have any to lend.
5 I'm not the only person who has debts. Other people ALSO have them. *or* Other people have them ALSO.
6 Attitude to money is partly a cultural thing, but it has something to do with your upbringing AS WELL.
7 Some people are careful with money in hard times and in good times TOO.
8 Borrowers admit that EVEN they sometimes borrow money irresponsibly. *or* EVEN borrowers admit that they sometimes borrow money irresponsibly.

7
1 payments   2 spending   3 investment   4 loan   5 grant
6 borrowing   7 debts   8 earnings

8
I think that people often get into debt because they want a lifestyle that they can't really afford.

It's a lifestyle which is sold to them constantly through advertisements, for example on TV and in magazines.

This desire to have a better lifestyle can affect some governments too. They want to improve their citizens' standard of living so that people will vote for them again.

12b (pages 138 and 139)

1
a

2
1 F   2 T   3 N   4 T   5 N   6 T   7 N   8 T

3
1 track   2 striking   3 sufficient   4 competent
5 of choice   6 infirm   7 blacksmith   8 trade

4
1 have people work
2 get their work done
3 get your labourers to work
4 had 10,000 slaves a year sent
5 got the slaves to work
6 had their slaves work
7 got them to learn
8 had cheap cotton shipped

5a
/ʃ/: abolished, sugar
/tʃ/: cheap, riches
/ʒ/: decision, usually
/dʒ/: carriage, wages

6
1 fit   2 put   3 decorate   4 assemble   5 fixed   6 tiled
7 plaster   8 hang

7
1 b   2 f   3 a   4 d   5 c   6 e

12c (page 140)

1
b

2
1 c   2 b   3 b   4 c   5 a

3
1 hard up   2 hard-headed   3 hard bargain
4 hard feelings   5 hard done by

4
| | |
1a is running hard   3a hardly know
1b is hardly running   4a thought hard
2a hardly works *or* is hardly   4b hardly thought
   working   5a hardly tried
2b works hard *or* is working hard   5b tried hard

12d (page 141)

1
1 d   2 b   3 f   4 a   5 c   6 e

2
1 a leaving party for a colleague
2 a reduction in the price

3
1 honest   2 mind   3 hoping   4 would   5 face   6 shoes
7 appreciate   8 key

4
1 Can I just <u>explain</u> our <u>position</u>?
2 To tell you the <u>truth</u>, …
3 If you look at it from <u>our side</u>, …
4 That's going to be a <u>bit</u> of a <u>sticking point</u>.
5 To be <u>perfectly honest</u>, …
6 What you have to <u>bear</u> in <u>mind</u> is …

5
1 I'm afraid that would be difficult for me.
2 Would you move a bit on the price?
3 Would you be willing to negotiate?
4 I would need to have some kind of guarantee.
5 When would you need to know?
6 I wouldn't want to put you to any trouble.

6
Students' own answers.

12e (page 142)

1
The report is about the catering for the Annual General Meeting.

2
1
• How much food do we need to provide?
• Cost?
• Any special dietary needs?
2
• Hot food: about £10 per person
• Cold food: about £7 per person
3
I propose that we go with Angel Foods. They seemed to understand better what we want, and I think they will do it all for a better price.

3
Summary
I visited our caterer to discuss the arrangements for our office party on 12th December.

Food
• Sandwiches: £6 per person
• Sandwiches and cold canapés: £8 per person
• Sandwiches and hot canapés: £10 per person

Drinks
• The caterer can provide drinks or we can buy our own.
• Charge: £1 per person.

Recommendation
I propose we go for the mixture of sandwiches and cold canapés, and provide our own drinks.

Wordbuilding / Learning skills / Check! (page 143)

1
1 the rich 2 the unemployed 3 the poor 4 the homeless
5 the elderly 6 the famous 7 the blind 8 the deaf
9 the illiterate 10 the sick

2
1 P 2 N 3 N 4 N 5 X 6 P 7 X 8 X 9 N 10 N

3 and 4
Students' own answers.

5
1 relative 2 investing 3 cleaner 4 hunter 5 end
6 spending
Word: RICHES

IELTS practice test

Listening
1 C outside in the grounds
2 B just the morning or the afternoon would suit me fine
3 A you'd have to sign up like anyone else – and there's a monthly fee
4 A tips on how to put a CV together
5 D a seminar led by one of the big recruitment agencies
6 JAYNES J.A.Y.N.E.S
7 Business Studies M: Which faculty's that? Economics? F: Business Studies actually
8 technical translations This time she's doing technical translations
9 construction industry He's going to be talking about openings in the construction industry
10 Geology He's working in the Geology department
11 C provides opportunities to meet the scientists who work at the Observatory
12 B an adult single ticket would cost £6.50 in the summer months and £5.50 at other times of year, whereas a family ticket would cost either £24.00 or £20.00.
13 C/D explore the universe using hands-on activities
14 D/C the glass-walled café with outside terrace
15 Botany it wasn't the Astrophysics department that bought it though, but the Botany department.
16 meteor shower installed just in time to observe a meteor shower
17 1947 in 1947 the 218-foot Transit Telescope
18 Mark 1/One/I This was named the Mark One Telescope
19 solar system a scale model of the solar system
20 World Heritage to place Jodrell Bank on the UK shortlist for consideration as a site with World Heritage status
21 A how you balance these two aspects is up to you
22 C I hadn't even chosen a speciality – so that made it tough.
23 B I'd have done better with a straight four-week split.
24 A talk to people ... That's how I found the one I went with
25 emergency I went for emergency
26 beach photos ... of the beach that drew me to Belize

27 300,000 with 300,000 people
28 (the) North up north where I was
29 Cuban a lot of the doctors working there are actually Cuban
30 teaching (the staff) I'd rather think of teaching the staff
31 One/1 metre/meter that grows to around one metre
32 Dark brown the male ... is a dark brown
33 Silver(-)grey/grey the female is distinguishable by its silver-grey skin
34 (Dense) undergrowth has a preference for dense undergrowth
35 Lizard(s) tends to rely on lizards as its main source of food
36 Bird Bird island, the place where one was eventually spotted
37 (six-week) survey They commissioned a six-week survey
38 100 supporting a racer population of around 100 individuals
39 B/C The right kind of habitat is not found over a wide area
40 C/B although the snake's habitat does remain vulnerable to hurricane damage

Reading
1 TRUE start by identifying the appropriate granting body to contact
2 TRUE check ... the deadline for the submission of applications
3 FALSE Your proposal should be written out in the format stipulated
4 FALSE It's a good idea to propose only those objectives that you feel confident of achieving within the grant period
5 NOT GIVEN (there is no mention of whether this is advisable or not)
6 TRUE cover what is already known about the problem in the scientific literature
7 FALSE In addition, many forms now have a section ... required to describe how the research is likely to contribute to economic development
8 NOT GIVEN (there is no mention of whether they do this or not)
9 TRUE state clearly that you're aware of the limitations of your approach
10 FALSE describe briefly any particular strengths of your laboratory
11 iii like to see a concise description of the results of any work you have already carried out
12 v your application should include latitude, longitude, elevation, vegetation ...
13 vii Describe how you plan to find people to take part in experiments
14 ii laboratory procedures ... a brief description of the various analytical techniques that you will carry out
15 vi how it will be entered on a computerised database and what software will be used
16 viii the partners with whom you intend to work
17 C evidence for at least 15 separate occasions when it acted as a home
18 B predate other known instances of plant matting by approximately 50,000 years
19 A a tree whose foliage contains chemicals that kill biting insects. Dr Wadley thus thinks ... mattresses on which the inhabitants slept
20 A a range of hitherto unknown artefacts ... pictograms
21 C a range of hitherto unknown artefacts ... arrows
22 D a range of hitherto unknown artefacts ... needles

23 (a/the) tree(s)   They probably settled in trees at night
24 climbing   they still retained features useful for climbing, such as curved fingers and long arms
25 chimpanzees   just as chimpanzees do today
26 fire   once hominids learned how to control fire they discovered they could sleep on the ground
27 grass   Neanderthals were also building grass beds
28 cellulose   *Macrotermes* species live on cellulose
29 gardens   by cultivating gardens for fungi
30 (digestible) nutrients   which can turn it into digestible nutrients
31 heat   heat from the fungi's metabolism and the termites' bodies
32 (central) chimney   causes stagnant air ... to rise up a central chimney

33 base   air is sucked in at the base
34 humidity   their temperature and humidity closely controlled
35 TRUE   This simple ... idea spawned at least one artificial imitation
36 TRUE   rules out the kind of buoyant outward flow ... showed little evidence of steady, convective air circulation
37 NOT GIVEN   (there is no mention of their methodology)
38 TRUE   the mound functions as a giant lung
39 FALSE   Turner thinks there's something to be gleaned from the termites' approach.
40 FALSE   idea among the biologists that architects could learn much from us. I think the opposite is also true

Photos:
The publisher would like to thank the following sources for permission to reproduce their copyright protected photos:

Cover: Paul Cheung/My Shot/National Geographic Image Collection
Inside: 6 tr Image Source/Alamy, 6 cl Barcroft Media/Getty Images, 6 cr Patrick Aventurier/Getty Images, 6 bl Tim Laman/National Geographic Image Collection, 6 br Michael Nichols/National Geographic Image Collection, 6 r Aurora Photos/Alamy, 7 l Insadco Photography/Alamy, 8 tl Shivji Joshi/Shivji Joshi, 8 tl Shivji Joshi/Shivji Joshi, 8 tc Dario Mitidieri/Hulton Archive/Getty Images, 8 tr Shutterstock/Shutterstock, 8 bl David Doubilet/National Geographic Image Collection, 8 bl Nigel Swinn/National Geographic My Shot/National Geographic Image Collection, 8 bc George Steinmetz/National Geographic Image Collection, 8 br Jodi Cobb/National Geographic Image Collection, 8 cbr Robert Harding Travel/Photolibrary Group, 8 ctl Emanuele Picchirallo/National Geographic My Shot/National Geographic Image Collection, 8 ctc George Steinmetz/National Geographic Image Collection, 8 ctr Hemis/Alamy, 9 David Doubilet/National Geographic Image Collection, 10 Pacific Stock/Photolibrary Group, 11 Gerd Ludwig/National Geographic Image Collection, 12/13 Panoramic Images/National Geographic Image Collection, 15 Minden/Frank Lane Picture Agency, 16 Shutterstock/Shutterstock, 20 Tim Laman/National Geographic Image Collection, 20 Justin Guariglia/National Geographic Image Collection, 21 Reuters/Stringer China/Reuters Media, 22 Steve McCurry/National Geographic Image Collection, 22 Steve McCurry/National Geographic Image Collection, 24 Image Source/Alamy, 25 Corbis Cusp/Alamy, 27 Cate Gillon News/Getty Images, 30 Aurora Photos/Alamy, 32 Wong Maye-E/Associated Press/Press Association Images, 33 Robert Harding Travel/Photolibrary Group, 34 NASA, 36/37 Wes C. Skiles/National Geographic Image Collection, 37 Kira Salak, 37 Stephon Alexander/Diana Rogers, 37 Wes C. Skiles/National Geographic Image Collection, 39 Kenneth Garrett/National Geographic Image Collection, 39 Kenneth Garrett/National Geographic Image Collection, 40 ShelterBox, 41 Shutterstock/Shutterstock, 42 Christie's Images/Alamy, 44 Bjoern Bertheau/Synthesis International, 45 Nigel Swinn/National Geographic My Shot/National Geographic Image Collection, 46 Asiaselects/Alamy, 48 Minden/Frank Lane Picture Agency, 51 Stefano Massai/National Geographic My Shot/National Geographic Image Collection, 52 James L. Stanfield/National Geographic Image Collection, 53 Shutterstock/Shutterstock, 54 Barcroft Media/Getty Images, 56 Krista Rossow/National Geographic Image Collection, 57 George Steinmetz/National Geographic Image Collection, 58 Renee Fadiman, 60 Maggie Steber/National Geographic Image Collection, 63 Vincent J. Musi/National Geographic Image Collection, 64 Shutterstock/Shutterstock, 66 Michael Nichols/National Geographic Image Collection, 68 Shutterstock/Shutterstock, 69 Jodi Cobb/National Geographic Image Collection, 70 Luka Tambaca/National Geographic Image Collection, 72 Maria Stenzel/National Geographic Image Collection, 73 Joel Sartore/National Geographic Image Collection, 75 Justin Guariglia/National Geographic Image Collection, 76 CTK/Alamy, 78 Mattias Klum/National Geographic Image Collection, 78 Sam Abell/National Geographic Image Collection, 80 Justin Guariglia/National Geographic Image Collection, 81 Motoring Picture Library/Alamy, 84 Motoring Picture Library/Alamy, 96 Greatstock Photographic Library/Alamy, 98 tl Ian Tragen/Shutterstock, 98 tr michal kodym/Alamy, 98 bl Eky Studio/Shutterstock, 98 br nesjerry/Shutterstock, 98 cbl Scott Darsney/Getty Images, 98 cbr Shutterstock, 98 ctl Shutterstock, 98 ctr Tomas Sereda/Fotolia, 99 Christopher Kolaczan/Shutterstock, 100 woraput/iStockphoto, 100 riekephotos/Shutterstock, 100 VeSilvio/Fotolia, 101 Andrew Woodley/Alamy, 104 Gordon Gahan/National Geographic Image Collection, 106 Joyce Dale/National Geographic Image Collection, 108 Paul Nicklen/National Geographic Image Collection, 109 Anton Gvozdikov/Shutterstock, 110 Thierry Planche/Fotolia, 112 Alliance Images/Alamy, 114 courtesy of Hayat Sindi, 116 KeystoneUSA-ZUMA/Rex Features, 118 elkor/Getty Images, 119 Robert Harding Travel/Photolibrary/Getty Images, 119 Wes C. Skiles/National Geographic Image Collection, 120 Rossario/Shutterstock, 123 Steve Raymer/National Geographic Image Collection, 125 Kerstin Geier/Gallo Images/Corbis UK Ltd, 128 Chris Rainier/Chris Rainier, 130 FirePhoto/Alamy, 132 Shutterstock, 132 Shutterstock, 132 Shutterstock, 132 Shutterstock, 132 Shutterstock, 132 Shutterstock, 136 Sam72/Shutterstock, 138 New York Historical Society, 140 Maurice Joseph/Alamy, 141 Shutterstock, 143 Justin Guariglia/National Geographic Image Collection

Illustrations by Celia Hart pp28 b, 28 c, 28 t; Kevin Hopgood Illustration p124; National Geographic Image Collection p6